A NOTE FR

Dear Reader,

The book you are holding provides a new metaphysic for our time. In this time of confusion and cruelty, grief, anger, and imminent death, it provides meaning where there is none. A next stone to jump to.

Some of the drawings are rough. We know that, but the executives at Will Spring insisted we get this word out now and let the drawings catch up.

The book you are holding is the first edition of what will become an important (beloved and reviled) book of our time, but only if you do your part. We're a small operation here at Johnny Appleseed, and we depend on light-hearted people like you to help this seed find fertile soil.

This is a philosophy book, and it's a pretty heavy read. It is not for everybody, but I know you know that one young person- with a head of dreams and a heartache bursting with anger and love- that it will be perfect for. Give it to them as a gift.

Even if they never read it, the book will plant the seed of an enduring memory of your precious love.

And if you are the reader this book has longed for, share and argue it with friends. The book must navigate its way through treacherous waters to find its people, and to do that, we need your help. Digitally and in person, perhaps, you will choose to appleseed?

Who knows what magic flows through us? What I do know is that most magic I've seen operates through the hard work and creative collaboration of human individuals. And that means you.

There is a Uranian quality to the author's work. And once the book finds its readers, in a flash, you will light up the skies with all new revelations. Even if painful, a diagnosis and explanation of the world that makes sense of my experience will feel like a salve and medicine and sticking point in this time of meaninglessness, societal breakdown, and loss. It is empowering- and necessary- to have solid ground beneath our feet, to understand what the hell is going on. We do not have that now, but we will, and thoughts presented here will help us get there.

We are grateful for your part, your time, your friendship, your perspective. That you might feel our love for you across the ages, I pray.

In gratitude, humility, honesty, courage, playfulness, solidarity, and love, I am

Johnny Appleseed
Chief Executive Officer, Johnny Appleseed Publishing
March 23, 2023

birth of christ

birth of christ
a relativistic metaphysic

Timothy J. Turecek

Johnny Appleseed Publications
Ithaca, NY

Copyright © 2023 by Timothy J. Turecek

beyond christ: a relativistic metaphysic

All rights reserved. No part of this publication may be reproduced, distributed or transmitted in any form or by any means, including photocopying, recording, or other electronic or mechanical methods, without the prior written permission of the publisher, except in the case of brief quotations embodied in critical reviews and certain other noncommercial uses permitted by copyright law.

Although the author and publisher have made every effort to ensure that the information in this book was correct at press time, the author and publisher do not assume and hereby disclaim any liability to any party for any loss, damage, or disruption caused by errors or omissions, whether such errors or omissions result from negligence, accident, or any other cause.

Adherence to all applicable laws and regulations, including international, federal, state and local governing professional licensing, business practices, advertising, and all other aspects of doing business in the US, Canada or any other jurisdiction is the sole responsibility of the reader and consumer.

Neither the author nor the publisher assumes any responsibility or liability whatsoever on behalf of the consumer or reader of this material. Any perceived slight of any individual or organization is purely unintentional.

The resources in this book are provided for informational purposes only and should not be used to replace the specialized training and professional judgment of a health care or mental health care professional.

Neither the author nor the publisher can be held responsible for the use of the information provided within this book. Please always consult a trained professional before making any decision regarding treatment of yourself or others.

IISBN: 979-8-89109-395-9 - paperback

ISBN: 979-8-89109-396-6 - ebook

ISBN: 979-8-89109-403-1 - hardcover

birth *of* christ
a relativistic metaphysic

"It's a lie, but you nonetheless act as if it is the truth." –S. Zizek

SIMULTANEITY AND EVOLUTION 1
Linear Explanations 1
Simultaneity 3
Reason in Myth 4
Reason in Science 13

THE BEGINNING 19
Terrible Birth 19
People Draw a Circle 21

FIRST LIGHT-THE DEED 25
First Murder 25
First Reversal 28
Freud's Half Truth 30
Myth and Reason 32
Circle, Center, Cross, and Motion 43

FIRST LIGHT- THE MISTAKE 51
Garden of Eden 51

    Who is God? 58

    Birth of God 62

    The Cross. 67

WORLD AS WILL AND REPRESENTATION 69

    Emotions and Reason 69

    Ambivalence 73

    Adequate and Inadequate Ideas 74

    The Wellspring. 76

    The World as Will 79

    Centripetal and Centrifugal Motion 87

    The Impossible Representation 92

    "Not Objects" 93

    Circle and the Cross. 94

HIS STORY 97

    Birth of Reason 97

    The Garden of Eden and Western Society Today 101

    Old Testament Murders 105

    Job. 109

    God as Representation. .111

    Either/Or. 114

    Murder of Isaac 116

    Band of Brothers 117

THE GESTURE 123

God's First Gesture of Love 123

Both/And 125

Murder of God 127

On the Cross. 129

The Seed 129

IN GOD'S IMAGE 131

The Divorce. 131

The Myth of Science 132

The Fundamental Error 136

When the Circle Becomes a Prison 139

Where Evil Comes From 142

Fundamentalism 153

Disembodied and Dismembered Gods. 157

Tiamat. 160

Devil Worship. 164

Twin Terrors 169

MARRIAGE 173

The Irrationality of Reason. 173

Three becomes Four. 178

An Honest Mistake 181

Kant and Eve. 183

Copernican Revolution 184

Freud's Hypothesis. 187

Turning Inward 189

The Exceptional Cruelty of Freud 192

Relativity 206

Time 210

Contemporaneous Myth 213

Simultaneity 217

THE SACRED HOOP 221

The Idea of Christ 221

Replace the Circle 222

The Collective Circle 224

Mother Earth 226

A Dialectical Perspective 229

Each a Cell in the Human Body .251

A Mirror to the World 254

Movement of Totem 263

Four Murders 270

The Meaning of Relativity 284

Human Bubbles 288

My Pathology 292

THE SHADOW 295

The Crucible and the Alchemist .295

The Whirlpool 297

Myth of Self, Truth of Other 299

Search for the Center 308

Ancestors 313

The Beauty of the Individual 318

Traversing the Bubble 324

Ancestor Tree 326

Birth of christ 327

Three becomes Four 329

The Next Stone 331

THE BIRTH 341

The Crucible 341

Second Coming 344

The Tree 348

SIMULTANEITY AND EVOLUTION

Linear Explanations

Writing is a difficult practice reflective of life. Through it, we seek to reduce down something infinite to something finite without losing thereby its crucial essence. When successful, writing- and life- become art- whereby the finite opens a window unto the infinite and provides a lens through which to view, and to understand, and to begin to grasp the essence in ways that did not exist before.

We humans live our lives linearly. Though it is a circle we traverse from birth through growth to decline and death, we are bound in our journey by time and move only in one direction. You cannot change the past and you cannot tell the future. The story that we tell with our life and actions has, like every story, a beginning, a middle, and an end. But underneath it all, underneath the stream of our consciousness and the story of our life, lays an infinite something that eludes our time and reason. To be fully human means to inform our lives with themes, insights, and directions that will capture a glimpse of this infinite- for ourselves as well as others- in the story that we tell.

Writing, like life, provides a linear thread of explanation for a human experience that is multi-layered, self-contradictory, and simultaneous. It is difficult to say, sometimes, what should come first, and where there is cause and what is the effect. When we are objective in our thinking, writing, and living, we are not continually harangued by so many anomalies and contradictions. Objectivity keeps on task and along the straight and narrow path. It sticks to the facts and makes decisions based on data.

In my world, this objectivity that science declares as its highest virtue is, instead, its greatest vice. Together, we are moving beyond science to a next stage in knowing that lies deeper than mere objectivity, linear thinking, and facts.

What is tricky in this transition is that, in overcoming science, objectivity, and facts, we do not wish, must never allow ourselves, to abandon them completely. Our goal- I in my writing and all of us in our lives- must be to do honor to science and art, both, to objectivity and to inspiration, to facts and to our insights, emotions, intuitions, imagination, experiences, and ideas. Mine is a philosophy of both/and, both science and art, and not an either/or. The highest creative expression of humans- and what I seek- is the unification of science and art in a new and beautiful truth about the world.

The challenge to a writer becomes particularly acute when the writer aspires to philosophy- that is, to use words and reason to describe those elements of human experience that lie beyond the circle of words and reason. We seek to understand and explain mysteries and miracles, and so cannot dispense with story- a higher incarnation of reason than science, it turns out, if applied with rigor and with consciousness, with objectivity, perhaps, but also with something more.

My goal is to, through this book, expand consciousness in ways that will begin to bring us closer to the elusive truths- the mysteries and miracles- that, though we sometimes try, human beings ignore at our peril.

There is something behind, underneath, beyond this book. It peeks out from the margins to scare me and inspire. An intuition of something more, something else- beyond this consciousness- is only beginning to emerge for me, and writing is the vehicle by which I am making an approach. Along the way, then, I will say and think some things that are stupid and wrong. I am sorry for these red herrings and must leave it to my readers to distinguish the wheat from the chafe. I am still infected with the old ways of thinking in ways that I, myself, cannot see or understand. My writing is an alchemical process by which I melt away base elements in my thoughts and life. Reducing the truth down by linear explanation is, for me, a necessary crucible through which, I suppose, I, myself, seek to cheat death and transcend finitude.

Simultaneity

The levels of consciousness I describe here illustrate human beings' contradictory relationship to time. We expand our consciousness through growth and evolution and learning- through time, but when we grow into a new stage in the evolution of our consciousness, the old ways of understanding do not die. They go underground- where they continue to function and form the core of who we are, how we see, and the actions that we take.

We learned with Copernicus that human beings are not the center of the universe. We all understand that now. We get it. Our collective consciousness has been transformed and informed by that knowledge. Despite all that, we still feel, think, and act like we are the center of the universe. We can't help ourselves, and, the truth is, at a certain level of human experience, we are the center of the universe.

It is best that we recognize the fact that earlier forms of knowledge continue to operate in our lives and in our societies. We need to name and point to these dark and buried forces from our past, as it is by thus bringing these primitive understandings to the light of day, and not suppressing our knowledge of and motivation from them, that we are able to more fully operate at deeper levels of consciousness.

Both history and the present seem to indicate that, once attained, higher levels of consciousness- i.e. reason- may be abandoned in favor of prehistoric responses. Human beings seem to "fall back" to primordial levels of consciousness under times of stress or when breakdowns and/or schisms seem to threaten the highest levels of consciousness once achieved. It is worth noting, too, that certain individuals' emotional development gets stuck at earlier levels of consciousness as a result of trauma(s), deprivation(s), and, mostly, indoctrinations under the guise of education.

We begin by articulating how we made sense of our experience through earlier incarnations of our consciousness.

Reason in Myth

Consciousness is established through creation of a distance between a perceiver and perceived. A crack of light is carved out from the blackness; an eye is opened (someday we'll name it "I"), and that eye creates, simultaneously, a self and world. Consciousness is built on a series of contradictions- inside/outside, I/other, body/mind- impossible dualities- that this eye applies to life.

SIMULTANEITY AND EVOLUTION

In the earliest days of consciousness, the separation is only just begun. Our first experience of this separation comes in the form of feelings (largely undifferentiated at first) that, because they control us far more than we control them, lend a pervasive experience of dread, terror, and vulnerability to this newly emerging consciousness and world. It will take millennia before we can speak of "reason," proper, but, in the meantime, we will use these earliest expressions of our reason- our emotions- to shape explanations and rituals- that will simultaneously connect us to and protect us from the indifferent force of darkness. Through myth and ritual, we establish a beginning foothold in the chaos of this world. Through this first, mythological epoch in human consciousness, certain patterns are established whereby we may gain greater mastery and control over the dangers of a world we find ourselves simultaneously embedded in and separated from.

Upon the establishment of certain fundamental structures (the circle, the center, and the cross) a dialectic can commence by which the sensory flood becomes filtered and slowed through the dualistic structures of our consciousness. We can stop the motion for a second. Take a snapshot and collect these snapshots to begin to tell a story, to create order, and tame the world. Once "a sticking point" is established in the midst of chaos, through our myth and ritual (the first expressions of our reason), our world and self can begin to grow.

The story of this emerging consciousness is told in the Haudenosaunee creation myth where our Creator, Grandmother walks our Mother in circles around a single clump of dirt until that clump will grow and that Mother will give birth. Through our stories and ritual, we participate in this birth and become simultaneous with our Mother in the creation of our self and world. Through story, we find a center for the movement; through ritual, we establish a pattern, peace and order to the chaos. And, too, we can begin to use this base of operations to affect change and mastery over the external world.

These two, inner and outer, converge in our bodies and in our experience. This point of "I" forms the center of both consciousness and universe. Without I, there would be no consciousness and so no world. The eye ("I"), then, becomes the necessary window onto the universe, and, furthermore, that "I" is necessarily housed in my body (this "little clump of earth") without which there is no I, no world, no consciousness, no thing. Our self, too, then, has both an external and internal aspect. We have an inner existence that is necessarily contained in an external existence, a mind inside a body.

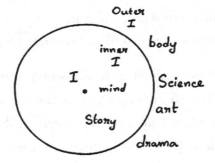

These two discriminations- 1) between I and other and 2) between mind and body in myself- are constitutive of human consciousness and experience.

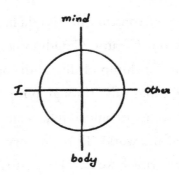

SIMULTANEITY AND EVOLUTION

In the earliest days of human consciousness, we are necessarily self-centered and do not notice yet that in addition to this eye, there are other eyes as well. That moment when we do at last realize the existence of others beside ourselves is the same moment we first become aware of our self. The moment we discover others is the moment the eye becomes an "I;" it is the moment when a consciousness of consciousness is first concieved. So it is that through the first few orbits of our consciousness, our first attempts to filter the madness through our "reason," that our self and others emerge to complete the structure of our consciousness. A centrifugal motion, a motion analogous to the spin cycle on the washer,

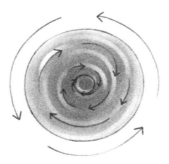

sorts out self from others, and a world is born.

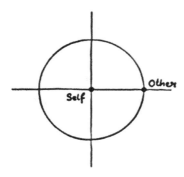

Interestingly, though, our awareness of the others still passes necessarily and exclusively through that single point of "I." As Kant will eventually teach, "all our knowledge begins with experience" and all experience is filtered through an "I." It will be millennia before we become fully aware of all these aspects of our consciousness, their interdependencies and implications. Such awareness we are building still- me, as I write, and you, as you read, but these aspects and structures to our consciousness have been operational in our construction of a self and world since that first moment of mystery and miracle when an eye opened out of nowhere.

This invention or discovery of I and other will lead us next to a series of mutual constructions. We collaborate on our descriptions and in our analyses and, together, build agreements about the world. Through science, and its applications (technology), we gain an ever greater mastery over, and definition of, the external conditions of our existence. Through art, and its applications (story), we gain an ever greater mastery over, and definition of, the internal aspects of our self.

Through story, we dive, like little muskrat, to the bottom of the ocean, to the core of our existence, and find our meaning, sense and "truth," a little clump of earth upon which we build. Through story we find a sticking point, the center, and so create an antidote to the horror and the chaos, the trauma and desertion, inherent in the separation that is consciousness. We seek through story and through ritual to heal the rift of self and world, I and other, inner/outer, mind and body. We seek a restoration of our place in the universe, peace, balance, truth, connection.

SIMULTANEITY AND EVOLUTION

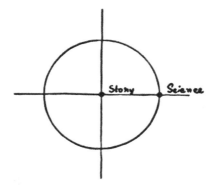

While myth focuses on the (re)establishment of emotional security and sense, science and technologies focus- even in these earliest days of consciousness- on the establishment of physical security, food and warmth. Science, from its very beginnings, focuses its attention on the material, the external aspects, the "world" of objects. So it is that our earliest mythological explanations will coincide with the first crucial inventions that provide human beings with some permanence and security- pottery, language, agriculture, and the domestication of animals.

Through myth, we filter our emotions and sensations. By naming them, we begin to differentiate them. We slow things down and bring order to our experience. It is by means of story and ritual and social agreements about the world that our emotions will form a bridge to reason, will form a bridge to others, and will form a bridge to the world we have found our self separated from. It will take millennia for humans' capacity for reason to fully emerge from this swirl of emotions that must have been our earliest consciousness, but from our earliest days, we know to look to the skies for guidance.

The history of consciousness is one of progressive differentiation and separation, and our early emotional consciousness, expressed through ritual and myth, is one in which that separation is still significantly incomplete. We remain embedded in the world of "objects" and others in ways that science would seek eventually to overcome.

By learning to tame our emotions, through shared myth and ritual, we bring sense and order to our experience. As either a cause or an effect of this greater internal mastery, we begin to tame the external world as well. By taming fire and domesticating animals, by the inventions of pottery and farming, we create a far greater security and mastery that will allow us to, dialectically, improve our explanations of the world as well.

New challenges would arise, of course- natural disasters, disease, predatory men, but, once made, this advance to domestication and farming would be difficult to reverse, and every generation afterwards could be expected to benefit from this new "floor" to human security. So, too, would our first explanations serve as the foundation for new and more comprehensive stories. From the earliest days, we would apply our science and technologies to the external and material world as we would apply our imagination and stories to the internal and ideal world.

It should be pointed out that just as every story is incomplete and, well, wrong, so too, would every technological advance carry within it certain unintended and, almost always, negative implications for human attitudes and development as well. In this case, for example, we learned from our success with animals that not only animals but other human beings, as well, could be domesticated- women, children, conquered and/or "inferior" races, for example, and so we set in motion a Master-Slave dynamic that has continued to inform Western civilization down through the present day.

SIMULTANEITY AND EVOLUTION

Through science and technology we sought- and attained- ever greater physical security and mastery just as through story and ritual we sought and attained ever greater emotional security and mastery. Each will serve as both cause and effect of the other that will result in our ever greater mastery of both our self and the world, and with each advance, human life became more predictable, certain, and secure. The imminent threat of pain, suffering, and death could be reduced for some, at least, of their people. And at each stage in our development, individuals and groups who enjoyed this greater security in the moment had "space" to further increase their distance and reflection and knowledge to pursue fundamental questions about humans' place in the universe and the meaning of life.

Thus it was that, over time, people joined together to construct agreements about the world and "truth." By the dialectics of consciousness, we will eventually build a shared reality of both a collective unconscious and an "objective" truth.

The answers we devise to life's most fundamental questions have not been luxuries in this process but, rather, have been the driving force behind our continually evolving ability to anticipate the future, to generate new ideas, and to adapt and capitalize on the changes and the shortcomings of the present day. The only problem- that persists and screams to us in the present day- is that, unfortunately, these collective "truths" remain fictions, and the opposites remain irreconcilable. During most eras, these facts do not slow the progress of our creations, but there are certain periods- and ours is such a one- when the truths we build our world upon are so transparently wrong and injurious to life that we are paralyzed. The old and original terror, desperation, and chaos returns as we know that we must change the world- we must restore order and truth- but do not know how.

Human progress has not been linear but cyclical. There are universal patterns that repeat themselves throughout history and consciousness that we can draw upon and learn from as we seek to understand what is happening in our present day. There is also a progression through predictable stages in development that become a part of a still larger, universal pattern that we must come to understand as well.

In both respects, we have much to learn from the mythological stage in human consciousness and the process by which our current scientific age grew out of it. In both (mythological and scientific) stages, it is the application of human thought and reason that separates humans from the world, allowing us to "stand back" and make sense of the world through a description/story through which we reconcile the opposites.

Mythological explanations seek to reconcile the opposites (A/A', mind/body, I/other) through a restoration of unity through relation. Gods are the vehicle by which we seek this restoration and, in relation to them, we are the supplicant and the dependent partner. We seek to influence the gods who control the world and nature through ritual, faith, sacrifice, and obedience. For the most part, this union is sought through a restorative relationship, and it is a fundamental "rule" of consciousness that to have a relationship must, necessarily, require some degree of distance.

But there is a certain temptation, too, at every stage in the development of our consciousness to collapse that difference that makes relationship, a self, and world possible. There is, ever present, a certain "death instinct" in humans' consciousness that calls to us- to obliterate the difference, forget the separation, let go of consciousness and return, in relief and ecstasy…orgiastic ecstasy, to the original darkness. This impulse to regress, to give up, to let go, to fall back to a stage of lesser discrimination and greater immanence- even to complete surrender-remains an ever present and haunting possibility to both human individuals and whole civilizations throughout our history. In times of stress and failure, times of breakdown in our truths, this temptation to move backwards- to "simpler times," to more infantile relationships and responsibilities- will naturally be greater.

The gravitational pull of such release and liberation from the burdens of human consciousness become particularly compelling- irresistible, addicting- in times such as our own, when the truth that once sustained us is dead and rotting to the core. It is tempting to accept that all "truth is relative" and that life is meaningless. The proof is all around us. And so we party and forget, live to fuck and eat, watch football, drink, and gamble or we "give ourselves to Christ" in an apocalyptic wet dream and fantasy that only we and the people that we love will be plucked from the inevitable blackness and chosen to be forever saved.

We must resist this fantasy- a temptation from the Devil, but we cannot do it on our own. We must identify the next stone that we can jump to- a next incarnation of the truth. And though that truth must incorporate the wisdom of our myth, the wisdom of emotions, it must not consist of a mere regression to these earlier "truths." We must spin the dialectic, and though it must now pass through to science and to reason, we must not stop our progress there. Only myth and science, together, will show us the way.

Reason in Science

As we will find to be the case with every stage of human consciousness, the mythological consciousness contains within itself the seed of its own destruction. In its attempt to reconcile the opposites through story and relationship with god(s) (not forgetting and regression), the mythological consciousness has the effect of increasing humans' definition and, thus, separation. It advances the dialectic of consciousness towards more comprehensive understandings of the truth. As our stories become more complex and more refined, our consciousness is building, our technologies are improving, and we are learning how to learn.

Growth in human consciousness is both incremental and revolutionary. The mythological understanding (and, so, too, the scientific understanding that will follow) answers the fundamental questions- it reconciles the irreconcilables- and so establishes the fundamental structures of the universe and defines our fundamental relationships- to self, to others, to the planet, and to gods. Within this world, permutations and refinements will develop over many generations. Incremental, not revolutionary, changes will be ongoing.

Eventually and inevitably, however, these incremental changes will undermine the fundamental assumptions, the foundational answers of this world and explanation. The necessary self-destruction in any effective world view (effective in that it "takes hold" and so successfully advances consciousness) lies in the fact that it attempts to reconcile a contradiction. It can never be all right.

Human consciousness is shaped by contradiction. Our recognition of this single and insurmountable fact will not keep us from, once again, generating a new explanation and definition of the world (though we admit our story is a fiction). And, too, our recognition of the fundamental irreconcilability at the core of human consciousness will not save our own explanation of the world from ultimate failure and rejection. We will tell a story, too, based on contradiction and that will someday be overcome by ones who suffer the failures in our view and, building on these failures, generate a story that sees further and more clearly- that will make new sense of the world again in our time of greatest need.

Which brings us, now, to science. Science offered a solution- a resolution- to the problems that arose in our mythological explanation of the world. Science grew out of myth, had its seed in myth and the mythological advance of reason. Without the distance created by mythological consciousness, without the transitional sciences of alchemy and astrology, there could be no science, and so, too, now, without science there could be no…what is it we will call what we are moving to? Relativity? Alchemy and astrology?

Through our mythology, we sought to reconnect with what was lost through an experience of simultaneity and the collapse of distance. What science achieved in its transition from mythology was a revaluation of values. What mythological consciousness saw as a problem to be overcome- human separation from nature- science saw as the highest virtue. Through science, objectivity, and reason, human beings sought to make sense of, and to gain mastery over, the world by accentuating that separation and bringing it to completion. The Christian God served as our model in this quest, this story, the scientific solution. If we could become "like God" and, through application of our reason and our faith, transcend the limits of nature (our mortal bodies) that continued to inhere in us, we might, then, become, at last, free and whole.

Mythology gave to reason an important but secondary role. Most fundamental to mythological understandings was the connection(s) that we felt to others, the planet, and the gods. In myth, reason is still in the process of being born. Emotional connections remain primary; reason we used to explain the relationships that sustained this connection and made that connection possible. Reason, then, is the handmaiden of the emotions in the mythological stage. The separation that reason drives us towards, and fully (?) realizes, in the scientific, objective "Age of Reason" can be seen in its state of becoming through myth.

For science, the emotions (and the subjectivity and "inner life" they were symptomatic of) became the problem- the thing getting in the way of our understanding of the truth. For science, truth was redefined as the purely objective, the "factual," and so, science used reason to widen the gap and to divorce ourselves from the personal experience of emotions that, under a mythological consciousness, had kept us in a state of dependency and vulnerability.

The evolution of our mythology (the incremental changes that had taken place over multiple generations and, even, civilizations) had, at last, in the Judeo-Christian text, provided us a model for this separation- that is, the model of God. So it was that in their moments of greatest blasphemy and hubris, the early founders of the scientific world- men like Copernicus, Kepler, Galileo, Newton, Bacon, and Descartes- were imitating God.

Though they were seen by many as the enemies of God and the Church, these early scientists actually saw themselves as most fully Christian. They saw that, while their scientific observations and analyses served to undermine the prevalent version of Christianity, they were doing God's work after all. The old, mythological descriptions of the Church were patently wrong and, so, unworthy of God. From their perspective, scientists were correcting humans' errors about the Word and example of God. Through their science, they would establish the one, the true, the objective path to Christian understanding.

So it will be always in times of revolutionary change. The bringers of the new truth will be seen as blasphemers and heretics. The medicine they bring will be mistaken for a poison, particularly by those powerful few who refuse to admit that we are even sick (political, church, and business "leaders" who profit in the short term from the old truth, turned lie). What happens during such a revolutionary period- what happened in the previous transition from mythology to science, and what is happening today- is a revaluation of values that have the effect of turning truth upon its head.

When such a revaluation, or flipping of the poles, occurs in human consciousness, what is most fundamental and true in the old way of seeing is still preserved. In fact, it would be accurate to say, that which is most fundamental and true is rescued from the fallacies, mistakes, exaggerations, and lies that were the world of old. It is a birth, and the revaluation of values that comes with a new world explanation feels like the first breath of life after long and painful suffocation.

The frightening time is before the birth. The frightening time is now. The danger lies not in the birth, but rather, in the threat of strangulation by an old world view that refuses to die. The danger lies in the apocalyptic wet dream, the siren call to blackness, rest and relief that disguises itself in a myth of eternal salvation. Our job is to be a midwife for the new truth- a feminine profession giving birth, as it turns out this time, to a vision for the future that is both feminine and masculine, both emotional and rational, both story and reason.

Today's birth, in particular, seems especially fraught with difficulty and danger. The old world view that must give way has, by its own fundamental principles, been consistently hostile to life and threatened by a reconciliation to the blackness. Ruthless, unfeeling, distant, disconnected, and, yes, irrational- the old world view lingers on far past its time: raping, rabid, desperate, destructive, and insane.

THE BEGINNING

As traumatic as the first moment of birth must be to a human infant, the first moments of consciousness must be even more terrible and frightening. Now there is "someone" there to perceive the trauma and the terror, and it is only natural, of course, that that newborn consciousness would grasp at something to bring it order and stability just as the newborn infant gulps in air to bring it life.

Terrible Birth

A terrible and marvelous awakening gave rise, once upon a time, to our mythical understanding. Before that, there was no consciousness of separation; there was no consciousness at all. Physical pain, perhaps, hunger, coldness, but not dread. Dread was something new. It involved a sense of time, a sense of I, of not-I. It was a revelation and a terror.
Somehow in this time before even myth, the mind detached itself from the human body, and some "one" was suddenly there. There was, for the first time, an experiencer, and so, a "world." By a miracle and a mystery, there was somehow born an "I". A birth of God, perhaps. But once this "I" was opened, we could not close it. Can the infant crawl back into the womb?

birth of christ

"Not ready yet" and terrified, consciousness was born nonetheless, and the break, the birth, was irreversible. Immediately, in this first moment, human beings must have searched "the world" for some comfort, for some meaning, for some return to the "paradise" they had lost, though they did not know it was paradise until now.

It was in this moment of estrangement, fear, and desperation that human beings created myth. Or, no. Let's be accurate. It would be in moments later, ages hence, when sitting by the fire, comfortably fed, people would consult the stars, who told stories of the ancestors' terror "once upon a time," and these ancestors would be them. Through story, primitive at first, the first humans found a passage back to the heart of the universe from which they came. To assuage their fear and desperation, human beings made meaning. Out of darkness, they made light.

And with time, they learned to play with, and began to master, the new powers they had gained through this original and fateful break. Though much was lost, more was gained; and over millennia they would use these myths not only to reestablish a lost union, but, also, to influence the gods. It was by this tendency that people sowed seeds of the next break- with their mythological consciousness- and the next birth, terrible and marvelous, too- of human reason: science and technology, history and law.

The path of human development is revolutionary. Growth in human understanding does not come through steady increments like stalactites and stalagmites grow. Rather, growth comes through cataclysmic annihilations of previous understandings. In shock and horror, we find, our eyes are opened.

Scientists and teachers, journalists and politicians, moms and dads, and we pretend that human history continues along in a steady stream of progress. No one wants to believe this is a cataclysmic age. We are scared- as humans always have been- at such moments in our history.

"We are all going to die!" The dread breaks out in dreams, anxieties, and in the myths we tell ourselves.

And, yes, it's true. We are being born anew, and "it" has not always been this way.

People Draw a Circle

For consciousness- and for the world that consciousness creates- to exist, human beings must draw a circle. This circle defines their self and provides a necessary vantage point from which they are able to define the world around them. The circle is an abstraction and a fiction necessary to distinguish us from all that is not I, necessary for the generation of all concepts and ideas- including the most basic concepts of space, time, self, and others, and God.

The circle is a psychological construct imposed on nature by the structure of the human mind. It is the lens through which the world comes into being and that brings sense and order and an illusion, at least, of permanence, to our understanding of nature.

Without the security of the circle- without the security of the known and permanent- people would not be able to survive. We can see the phenomenon in the lives of those around us and in our own as well. A great deal of human energy is spent to shore up this circle- the security, the permanence, the dependability and predictability and rationality of the world around us. We use money, we use knowledge, our family, the good job, philosophy, religion, a home, a hundred things to convince ourselves of the viability and truth of the circle that we draw- that we use to bring meaning to the world.

Most fundamentally, a people's metaphysic establishes this ground of permanence, reliability, and truth. It is from our metaphysic- even, and especially, where it has not been made fully conscious- that people gain the confidence in their understanding and creation of the world. The problem is that the circle is a fiction, and at times of transition in human consciousness it becomes necessary to acknowledge this fact. In times of transition- in times such as our own- the metaphysic is failing. The circle has been broken. The world does not make sense.

Even, and especially, when the evidence of brokenness is all around them, people don't want to hear it. They can't stand to hear it. They want to pretend that the truth is still intact, because they intuitively know that without the truth- without a truth- human beings cannot survive. And the world will be at an end. Human beings hate people like me who point out this failure of their truth, particularly when the evidence of failure is so transparent and undeniable.

Except, I provide a next stone to jump to. I draw another circle- an explanation that is more comprehensive and complete, deeper and more true that will make new sense again of all the dissonant evidence around us, and that will thereby provide greater security for those embraced by it on into the future.

We have been in labor with this truth for quite some time already; the birthing process can feel exhausting, like it will never end. But truth is coming. Push.

Human consciousness has grown in leaps and bounds, through a series of reversals, and we are living through- participating in- one such major reversal now. When we are done, what is most essential from previous stages of understanding will be retained and resuscitated, but, make no mistake, the world and truth will be turned upon its head. And once the flip is made, there will be no turning back- and who would want to? As meaning, purpose, understanding, and truth will, at last, be restored.

The world will make sense again, and though there is great and difficult work ahead- cleaning up the mess, to save our planet and our children's souls, we will have found the new foundation upon which our work will build, and, also, a community of like-minded others, and, too, perhaps- for some, at least- a new pathway to and possibility of the infinite- what human beings have longed for since the birth of time.

Masculine and feminine are not an either/or. That way- the way we have been taking- is leading us to death, but we can make it better. We human beings, creatures of mystery and miracle, creatures most like God, can reverse course, make peace, be born to a new incarnation of the truth. Masculine and feminine are both/and. Eve is not an enemy. God misunderstood, and, in the name of God, we misunderstood as well. It is time now to get it right.

FIRST LIGHT – THE DEED

By applying tools of reason to the mythological evidence from humans' early consciousness, Sigmund Freud reconstructed events from the prehistory of human beings. He takes us back to a time before time to tell a story of how consciousness, and the world, and human beings, and gods were born. "In the beginning was the deed."

First Murder

We started out as animals, of course, and are animals still, but something happened in humans' history- a miracle and a mystery- that distinguished us from our animal brethren and created a world. "God" said "Let there be Light," and there was Light.
Surely, there must have been light before us and so, too, there will be light after we are gone, and yet we cannot know for sure- and never will, as our knowledge is limited to the small circle of our individual and collective experiences. All we can know with some certainty is that that light was born at some point in and for us, and that is when time and the world began.

Freud draws upon newly available evidence from a wide range of mythologies from a variety of cultures, but, for him, everything gets filtered through the lens of his own- Jewish- culture and mythology. Thus, while he propounds a universal application of his story to the birth of all human consciousness, this story must be particularly resonant and reflective of the Judeo-Christian origins and world view.

Freud traces back patterns he finds in other stories from Jewish history (especially Abraham and Moses) to decipher a story of the beginning that would make sense of later developments. As such, I believe that Freud offers us an exceptionally clear vision into the taproot- in violence and reversal- of Western, Judeo-Christian, white civilization. It may be supposed that some trauma is inherent in the awakening of any consciousness, but that the particular violence of Freud's recollection may be specific to white civilization.

If this first birth establishes the pattern for later epochs in our history (as Freud hypothesizes), there must have been some trauma- some death- some emotionally excruciating break with the previous circle of understanding- for a new stage to break through and be born.

In <u>Totem and Taboo</u>, Freud does not speak in terms of the birth of consciousness. That is my addition to his analysis. Freud seeks to explain the origin and function of gods, specifically, the totemistic religions and their accompanying prohibitions, and, by extension, the evolution of the Judeo-Christian God. By my own analysis, I find that where there is a god(s), there is consciousness and vice versa. This association of god(s) with consciousness has everything to do with the projections of self I will address in answer to the question of "Who is God?" Such association of God and consciousness is a part of the story that I tell, and I will leave it to the reader to persist in or abandon such association in the tales that they create.

FIRST LIGHT—THE DEED

God was born by murder, according to Sigmund Freud. Before time and light of consciousness, we lived in animal societies similar to those of certain primates observed by our biologists. These societies, Freud argues, were dominated by an alpha male who kept all the females to himself. The sons and weaker males were denied an opportunity to fornicate until, fueled by frustration and desire, they banded together to act. The "sons" joined together to kill the "father" and so changed their world forever. This deed was enacted in the prehistory of all human beings, according to Freud, and traces of its memory are everywhere in the mythologies of the most diverse civilizations.

In the moment of execution, the consciousness of the brothers took a shift. They "woke up" to their collective madness. Anger turned to revulsion as they realized with horror what they had done.

In ages hence, the shame and memory of this event would be suppressed and hidden but could not be erased. Remembrance of the deed would become taboo and strategies devised to expurgate their collective guilt. The trauma of participation in such a deed may have been enough to shock these brothers into an awareness that would require adjustment and an explanation.

The shock and horror of their participation in the father's murder may have been enough to give birth to light and consciousness. A first separation between self and world, between self and others, between mind and body, between past and present, between life and death may have been enacted in this moment of His death. What took place on this first and fateful eve may have been spark enough to ignite our human consciousness.

If this story is true, it lends credence to the claims of our patriarchal tradition that it is men, not women, who are responsible for the first birth of light. It is a violent act of men, born of biological desire, that gives birth to human consciousness, and, though suppressed, such act becomes a core part of our collective memory that gets reenacted again and again throughout our history. The complicity and exclusivity of the group are no small part of the seed experience. It is a collective crime, and the collective Lie and cover-up that follows will be the glue that really binds the group.

First Reversal

What follows from this fateful day are the beginnings of civilization and of myth. Human beings- the brothers and their women- would need to devise a means of governing themselves now that the ruling father was gone. It makes sense that this moment would mark the beginning of the Neolithic period in human history when the domestication of animals and the introduction of agriculture would take root for the first time.

Without being too cute about it, I think it makes sense that women would take over governance from the brothers after their commitment of the deed. Women would, I expect, be more competent, more committed and reliable, in the development of collective government than this collection of horny, impulsive, irresponsible and violent men.

And so would begin that long period in human history through which humans gained an ever greater degree of mastery and stability through the invention of pottery, language, social order, agriculture, music, art, and explanatory myth. And so, too, though the first deed was committed by the men, it makes sense that women would take the lead in each of these first and crucial adaptations to our new reality- the primordial manifestations of humans' science, reason, technology, and art.

FIRST LIGHT—THE DEED

What happened in this first moment of the deed, however, will set the pattern for all future leaps forward in our Western consciousness. A murder will serve as precedent for a new birth of knowledge. A trauma, shock, and horror will force us from unconscious complacency in a previous version of the truth. We will find ourselves exposed and naked, vulnerable and guilty, confused, disoriented, lost, and wrong. All that we assumed as real is, in a flash of lightening, revealed to us as false, and there is no returning to the womb.

Faced with this primordial flash of light and consciousness, the brothers would commit the first in a series of reversals that would enable them "to make things right" and so restore the equilibrium necessary for human beings to survive. They would transform the "father" they had killed into a god they would worship. Lacking, as they did, a fully developed capacity for abstraction, our first brothers latched on to some thing- the totem or idol- some object or animal upon which they might project an ambivalent mix of fidelity and guilt.

They devised an explanation of the world that would highlight their devotion to, and their dependence on, this one that they had killed- in the "person" of an idol, and, later, in the "person" of an infinite (Judeo-Christian) God. It is by this deed that the concept of death first awakens in us, and thus it is that we are forced to acknowledge for the first time the limits to our lives, to our knowledge, to our experience, and to our powers. Ironically, it is just this first awareness of death and limitations that opens the window on the possibility of the infinite. It awakens the possibility of consciousness of self.

The seed for the idea of God was planted in the deed, but a long period of latency and/or gestation would be necessary before the language and concepts necessary for the articulation of this infinite aspect of consciousness would sprout. God goes underground, is buried, like the seed He is, as human beings attempt, through the first half of the mythological epoch to reunite with the Mother, Earth, Being from whom they find themselves estranged. The brothers' identification with the father that they killed will return to human consciousness later in the epoch. Through murder, though, we have begun to walk the road to understanding and the infinite.

Freud's Half Truth

That is the story Freud tells; there is enough truth in it, in my judgement, that I am willing to "suspend disbelief" and, so, accept Freud's account of this first murder and first origin of consciousness. What makes Freud's origin story compelling is that he extrapolates this first experience of trauma and awakening from the events and patterns of behavior that follow (in the Jews' own account of their history, the Torah). Freud's explanation "makes sense" in light of the repetitions that follow.

But, as with all mythologies, though Freud's story may contain elements of truth, it can never comprehend "the whole truth." There are horizons to Freud's story, limits to his "truth," and understanding the consequences of these limits will prove crucial to understanding our own experience and developing our own truths.

Freud spends a lot of time in Totem and Taboo (where he unpacks this story of first light) to explain how this first murder leads to a sublimation of the murdered Father into the shape of totem poles and animals. The totems, Freud reasons, are transitional "rough drafts" of the one, true God made necessary by man's limited and still developing reason. At this early stage in the evolution of consciousness, men must still tie their reasoning to the concrete manifestations of their more primitive sensory understanding. Over generations and millennia, the

Jews achieve (what Freud, as man and Jew, is so, so proud of) the final uncoupling of reason from these merely physical manifestations in man's awakening to birth the one, true, universal, eternal and infinite God- Yahweh, the ideal sublimation of their murdered Father.

Freud goes on and on trying to establish this connection between the first murder and totems, because, I suspect, he is trying to convince himself; his argument does not hold up, he intuits, but he does not know how to fix it.

It does not occur to Freud to credit women with what seems to Freud a merely transitional period in the development of man's reason. Only man is capable of this kind of creation (the creation of gods, ideas) in Freud's limited understanding, and, like the pattern of murders Freud traces throughout history, this limit, too, will recreate itself again and again and even now in the white, Western patriarchy that follows.

Viewed through the lens of matriarchy, these totems and totem animals make way more sense both as an end in themselves and as an effective means to reconnect with the world we feel ourselves estranged from. I do agree with Freud that the aim of the totem, animal guides, the matriarchal religions, is to reestablish a lost bond with the rhythms of life and creation and that the Jewish Yahweh stands as an exact reversal and repudiation of this original impulse of women. The restoration and healing of a wound that totemistic religions value most becomes, under Judaism, their greatest shortcoming and vice, thereby setting the pattern for all future instantiations of the patriarchal vision.

What humans find and create through these matriarchal stories and nations (what I am calling the first half of the mythological epoch), is a shared participation with others in a world guided by gods, animals, spirits that revolves around a single, common center. The I has yet to distinguish itself in this early matriarchal period, though the "we" is an ever-present and defining feature of life in this world. Ages hence, the great educational philosopher, Lev Vygotsky, will describe how "the 'we' gives birth to I," in accordance with this, our human history- a truth that seems self-evident to us now, though Freud and John Dewey, blinded by assumptions of the patriarchy, failed to see it.

Perhaps it was the "I" that was awakened in Freud's mythological first moment- a first awareness of my self as separate, alone- and wrong, a shocking experience replicated in the horror we each have felt at certain moments in life when our "true," unwelcome and unacknowledged self stands exposed before the other. It may be fair to extrapolate how and why women took control and a step back from this horror introduced by men to make use of this flash of lightning/truth to build a first civilization(s) based on We, a (now) conscious manifestation of our species.

But even in this time of matriarchy, this time of prosperity and peace, we may find our band of brothers- bored, disgruntled, and out of power still- in private meetings on the outskirts, nursing songs of grievance and revenge.

Myth and Reason

Consciousness creates an abstraction. It "draws a circle," and so makes a distinction, within the psyche of the individual that does not exist in and for the other animals. This circle creates a psyche, a "person"- an inside- and a world- an outside. It makes us stand out from the world and sets in motion time and space, self and concepts- all things that do not exist for animals but only for we humans. So it is that life confronts human beings with a question and a challenge of overcoming opposites that does not exist, as far as we know, for any other creature. A miracle and a mystery.

FIRST LIGHT – THE DEED

People tell a story- to themselves and one another- to reconcile these opposites and so to bring sense and order to a confusing, hostile, and scary world. It would appear in the beginning that the light by which we come to know the world comes through and from us. Now, it may be that, as in the birth of the individual human, the light was there all along, and all that has changed is that an eye/an I has opened to perceive it. As consciousness is experienced, however, both in the case of the individual and in the case of the whole race, the light and world begins with us and us alone. We see through the I/eye that is opened but only much later do we become aware of the I/eye, itself. In the beginning, all we know as real are the reflections back from the light of our own consciousness, which we do not yet recognize as reflections.

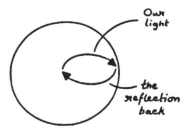

We imbue the world with life through the projection of our light. There is not as yet any consciousness of I, though ironically, this unconscious I is the source of all the world there is. And so, in the beginning, distinctions between self and world are not clear. The circle by which we create a world is drawn, though we do not yet see that circle clearly. It is the lens and window through which the world is born.

Some day we may come to view this light that comes pouring in through us to create a world as an awesome, God-like power that could, and does, inspire hubris in men- and women, too- but in the early days of consciousness there is no such consciousness of self. In that first moment of human consciousness, in fact, that light is most often experienced as a break, a fall, a shock, a horror, and a loss. And our separation from the world to which we once belonged must be perceived as a problem to be solved, an unsettling ambiguity and emptiness, a longing and dis-ease.

It is understandable, then, that human beings' first impulse was to seek, through their stories and their rituals, a restoration of that lost wholeness, what Mercea Eliade called the Myth of Eternal Return. Then as now, human beings sought mastery and control, some degree of power, through their stories and their inventions. They have tried by their stories to gain for themselves- and for the ones they love- a degree of certainty and security, stability and "truth."

And it is understandable, too, then, that throughout the first half of the mythological epoch in human consciousness the focus of our stories is on a reunion with the forces and rhythms of nature reflected in and by our consciousness. These "forces" are the "what is," what Kant calls the noumena, what Sartre calls "being-in-itself." They are "the world" before consciousness, often personified as gods in our myth. We are separated from this "being" at the moment our mind and abstraction is born.

For obvious reasons, pre-Judeo-Christian myth is unconsciously self-centered. We naturally assume we are the center of the universe. And like all universal truths, this one is replicated in the experience of the individual. Just as children see the world as if it revolves around them (and so, their world does) so, too, do all people put themselves at the world's center. That is why some form of the totem pole is a universal and primordial invention of all consciousness. It fixes the point of reference necessary for all future growth in consciousness. It stands at the navel, at the birthplace, of the world, at the center of our consciousness and circle, connecting us to sky and underworld, space and time, land and others.

In the early days of human consciousness, it is common for us to populate the universe with a multiplicity of gods. Early light manifests itself through the many objects, the material incarnations, and all participate in the divinity of this early light. And so the multiplicity of gods reflects the diversity of the external world our light shines upon. We take its central elements- things like sun and moon, earth and sky, plants and animals, snow and rain, stars and lakes, men and women, old folks and the children- and we personify these through a pantheon of gods. These early gods are never far away (except perhaps the sky god) but always near us, always present, listening and watching, like eyes waiting in the darkness. And we must make peace, form relations with these gods to keep them from devouring us, to help us to survive.

From the earliest days of human consciousness, the whole world is imbued with a psychic aspect- with a spirit and a will that may turn hostile or be friendly, depending on our actions, depending on our relations. It is only later- much later- that we will generate the new myth of "objects"- mere things without the power of will and life and consciousness- but in these early days, the stars breathe and rocks live. We rest in the embrace of this web of life; vulnerable, dependent, awed, we find ourselves standing at its center. Great care is taken, then, to establish and maintain right relation with the lives and souls around us. Ceremonies, rituals, beliefs are formed and practiced and refined in an attempt to, best as we are able, reestablish lost connection, maintain right relations, build security, keep peace.

It should not surprise us that the various clusters of human beings scattered across the planet would develop languages and symbols, stories and prayers that would resonate with one another and replicate many of the same and common themes. They all, after all, had very similar materials to work with and pressures on their lives. All saw night and day, the circle of the seasons, the moon and stars and sun. All sought water and needed food, met animals and plants and learned to use them to meet their needs. They all dealt with the mysteries of birth and death, of men and women, shit and sex. Humans are a social animal and so all must, perforce, develop rules and structures for social interaction. There were old people and young. And there was this strangely mysterious question of their own mind and the light- what it was, where it came from, and whether it was a blessing or a curse.

Add to the similarities in the external worlds a similarity in the structures of their mind or consciousness, and we can begin to understand how it is that so many commonalities developed in these stories of first explanation that Carl Jung could later (and rightly) postulate a Collective Unconscious that is the inheritance of every human consciousness from her or his ancient ancestors of these earliest days. In fact, I will argue that there is a necessary and universal structure to the human consciousness as surely as there is a universal structure to the human body, and, like the human body, the structure of human consciousness is subject to an infinite number of variations, but the fundamental form and structure remains consistent in all.

Like the human body, the variations in our human consciousness is partially set at birth but also profoundly influenced by our experience in the world. The human mind contains masculine and feminine aspects and in equal measure. This difference- that our bodies tend towards a single gender but our mind is both- accounts for much of the confusion and struggle we humans experience in reconciling our body to our mind. It also represents an area of greatest promise that, along the patriarchal, Judeo-Christian path our civilization has so far followed, has remained largely unexplored, misunderstood, and perverted. We can and will correct (you are correcting) course on this point, though we must leave that discussion for another time and to someone who knows what they are talking about.

But this original longing we find in our early myths- this longing to return from whence we came, to the time before time, before the break and light, has not gone away in our experience as humans. The fact that part of us, at least, still longs for this return will serve as the first, but not the last, indication that, as we advance through the different layers of human consciousness, we never leave these earliest layers behind. We do not shirk off our earlier ways of knowing like a snake sloughs off its skins. Rather, they remain in us like the rings of growth inside a tree. We expand upon these first representations of the world and truth. They do not die in us; they remain as the living core of our beliefs.

It is debatable whether our longing for this "paradise lost" is greater in these first people or in us, but, it is clear, the force and desire for return is great in all human beings and is balanced only by an equal force and desire to venture further out. One of the complexities and contradictions of this circle that we draw, one of the mysteries and miracles of consciousness, is that it never moves in only one direction. From its earliest days, consciousness spins in simultaneous and opposing centrifugal and centripetal motions- inward, toward the center and the psyche, and outward, into matter and the world.

And so it is that all people engage in two simultaneous, and what could appear as contradictory, movements of mind. While we are busy, through our stories, searching for the center and the meaning by which we will rediscover the truth and wholeness we have lost, we are, at the same time, making observations, collecting feedback from the world outside ourselves, and so adjusting our behaviors and our explanations to better navigate and succeed in this world. Even from the earliest days of human consciousness, human beings are busily applying their science and reason- their powers of observation, experiment, and analysis- to manipulate the external world so as to gain mastery over the material conditions upon which they depend. So it is that the first stage of mythological explanations corresponds with the Neolithic period of development that saw the introduction of domesticated animals and farming.

One difference between preconscious awareness and consciousness, that is, a difference between animals and humans, is that animals adapt to their environment whereas humans adapt their environment to themselves. That difference, for me, at least, defines science and technology and the uniquely human capacity for reason. This movement of humans' reason causes consciousness to expand outward and so to acquire new learning and more comprehensive understandings of "what is" at the same time that their stories move their consciousness inward in search of root causes, beginnings, meaning, and truth.

The stimuli acquired through the application of humans' science is fuel for this internal process focused on the generation of story and concerned with the big picture questions unique to human beings: Who am I? Where did I come from? What is my right relation to others and the world? Where are we going and where have we been? And what lies beyond my understanding?

To satisfy this inward, centripetal movement in our consciousness, to bring meaning to our existence, the first human beings- and every human after them- generate explanatory stories- myths- that become part of a collective understanding by which people learn to understand and govern their role and relationships to others and the world. These stories come to revolve around and be represented by a totem pole or other symbol by which human beings mark out a center for their understanding and definition, a center or navel of the world. No consciousness is possible- there is no human being- without this psychic center and, wrapped around that center, some story of explanation. It is how we are built.

And so it is that there is both a center and a circle as necessary to human consciousness, and while it may be true that in the earliest days of human consciousness emphasis is on the projection of internal mental and emotional states onto the world beyond our bodies, and though at first we would populate the world with our own internal perceptions, it would not be long before we would begin to receive feedback from the world around us and, through the acknowledgement and analysis of this evidence from without, give birth to science, reason and technology as well as myth.

In a later epoch- "the age of reason"- we will get to, humans would learn to be "more objective" and so would learn to balance the original omnipotence of our thinking with the evidence derived from the world outside, but the development of consciousness is dialectical. It grows by movement between extremes, and so a day would come- the present day- when this movement towards objectivity would go too far as well and that balance would be restored through yet another revolution- a new reversal- in the history of consciousness.

In later times- including our own- human beings would look down their nose and scoff at this early stage of mythological consciousness. We modern men (you women, too, now!) are called to be rational and mature. The emotionality, the dependence, the vulnerability of these earlier mythological strategies are considered embarrassing, infantile, womanish, childish, self-centered, irrational and so are to be purged from our repertoire of understanding. Dreams, where these stories stubbornly resurface on a nightly basis, are to be ignored, dismissed as nonsense, a jumble of confusion and disturbed logic.

This attitude is all part of the reversal that was necessary for the abstract law, reason, science, technology and Christianity of the patriarchal system to triumph over the mythological cults that came before. And, today, it is just this reversal that we, in our turn, will be reversing, but not- as those who misunderstand "relativity" in these earliest days of its incarnation- by going backwards. To go backwards- to seek return to our lost paradise- to return to an earlier and mythological "truth" and explanation, would shrink our consciousness. It would be a retreat, a defeat, a failure, and a mistake, but, let us be clear- just such a movement backwards is, today, offered up to human beings in a multitude of forms, and these forms are incredibly attractive, even addictive and irresistible, though impossible.

The failure of our reason and science to satisfy human beings' visceral need for union and for meaning and for peace and for truth has led us to look elsewhere, and just like any creature- even cells- faced with hardship, one tendency is to shrink inside ourselves, to return to earlier forms of knowing, to flee, in pain and desperation, back into the womb. That describes the attraction of drunkenness and football, opiates and evangelical Christianity. We see no way out but backwards, but that limit in our thinking is just a function of our trap by the explanations of reason, a trap that this book will help us to break free from.

Our job is to resist this temptation to retreat to an earlier, and failed, strategy for fulfillment. We must resist the temptation to abandon our arid reason and, instead, see that reason through to get to the other side of reason- where myth and reason are rejoined. Our job must be to turn our reason inward- with Freud, Jung, Einstein, Kant, Mary Daly, Henri Bergson and the others- and thereby resuscitate, sublimate, and transform this ancient mythological wisdom that our patriarchy has tried- and continues to try with ever increasing hysteria- to bury and destroy. Mythological consciousness, along with the emotional wellsprings that feed it- and us- with such overwhelming power- mythological consciousness must live again, not in its ancient forms, but in new forms. New wine skins, perhaps, for old wine fermenting inside of me, inside of you.

For here is a part of the mistake that the patriarchy, based on reason, has made; here is a part of the truth of myth that we rational and mature ones have forgotten- we never really leave our earlier forms of understanding behind- nor should we want to. We are shaped by our memories, nourished by our bodies' memories- as individuals and as a human race. This fact is one we should celebrate; this source of knowledge is one we must mine in order to move forward with wisdom, and love, and emotional understanding- that is just as important, but no more important- then our reason.

It is only through a purposeful dialectic of the two- myth and reason, story and science, body and mind, the centripetal and centrifugal movements in consciousness- that we will reach the next oasis of human understanding. And I don't need to tell you how desperately we need that water. In our present desert of alienation, objectification, bureaucracy, brutality, inhumanity, technology, and data, we all need to rediscover the lost wellspring of life, of visceral connection, of truth. The way to this wellspring is through myth- personal and collective, both of which are universal.

We just forgot, or never knew, but now, at last, we can remember. The structure of human consciousness is like a tree. At the center, at the core is our myth. Reason represents later rings of growth, rings of achievements that we are rightfully proud of, but the vitality of our consciousness cannot depend upon one- science and reason- to the exclusion of the other- myth and the emotions. Consciousness is not an either/or as we have been thinking of it. Our vital consciousness depends on both.

As the age of reason spirals towards its end, the outer circle of our consciousness described by reason grows rigid. The circle becomes a prison. Just like the egg that once nurtured and protected the chick to help it grow, so, now, our science and our reason- is suffocating and will kill us if we do not break through the limits it has set.

Like a tree whose outer rings have lost vitality and cease to grow, our lifeblood is choked off at the core, in the insane delusion that only one- either reason or myth, either the centrifugal or the centripetal motion, only the outer rings or the core- can survive, when in truth, of course, each must depend upon the other. What was once our most significant and recent advance in human consciousness- reason- has now grown rigid, unforgiving, and, so, deadly. We must break that shell, consciousness reborn. It is an awesome and traumatic time we live in- to see an old truth die that new truth may be born.

We are fortunate at least that, as is the way with consciousness, our science provides us with the solution to the problem that it, itself, creates. By turning reason inward we discover the remedy necessary to correct our insane obsession with material growth.

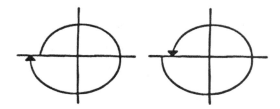

Circle, Center, Cross, and Motion

To understand the evolution of consciousness through its various stages we must be cognizant of both necessary aspects to consciousness- the seer and the seen. In the first stage of the mythological epoch- from Deed until the birth of God- human beings have drawn a circle that distinguishes them from the surrounding world, but they remain enmeshed and embedded in that world. The seer at this stage has earned the ability to be conscious of a world but has not built the perspective necessary to be conscious of themselves.

Consciousness at this point consists of the preliminary discrimination and simultaneous birth of One and Two, but there is not yet a Three. With the birth of God, the location of the seer shifts- the seer gains distance, elevation, transcendence, perspective. We see through the eyes of God, and that is why, as the Garden of Eden quite accurately describes, we become simultaneously conscious of our self (Adam), the other (Eve), God, and time. We do not really know our selves, or know that we are a self, until we gain distance on ourselves through the invention of the Divine, disembodied, external, abstract perspective.

By the same token, though we have felt the force of their actions and their presence, we have never really come to know an other until we take a step back- outside the circle of our own perception and see them "for what they are."

Before God, in what I am calling the first half of the mythological consciousness, is a shared participation with others in a world centered around a totem we hold in common. The individual, I, remains largely (though not completely) embedded in the group in much the same way that we humans, in general, remain enmeshed (though not completely) in the surrounding world. To the same degree that the (individual) I is emerging so are our god(s) emerging as a distinct but embedded vantage point from which we may define ourselves.

The Three (God), Freud would argue, is conceived of and gestating but not yet fully born. Prior to this birth of Three, there is a dialogue that takes place between One and Two, but it is not a conscious dialogue. Though it takes place beneath the surface of consciousness, a process of definition and reflection takes place in our interactions with an other(s) that gives birth to a world. Through the unconscious dialogue of One and Two, of I and Other, we successfully create a shared ("objective") representation and world upon which each individual can- and must- build. Social and individual, objective and subjective aspects, inhere in all constellations of our human consciousness.

This world of ideas, of concepts, and of "objects" is generated, then, through the "underground," unconscious dialogue between I and other. Together with the other(s), we author the disembodied, abstract, elevated perspective of God, through which we will learn, for the first time about finitude- the finitude of ourselves and the finitude of others- because only through the eyes of God can we become defined. We become some thing. We exist in a way that we did not exist before- we exist in consciousness as we, ourselves, become defined objects in the world.

Great benefits accrue to human beings from this invented perspective of God, but there is a great price to pay- a great sacrifice- for this knowledge as well. We have been building towards this moment of realization- the invention of the Three- progressively, incrementally, and over thousands of years. Our identification of the center of our consciousness and world was a crucial and inevitable consequence of the first miracle- the drawing of the circle. Marking that center with the totem gave us a point of contrast with the border of awareness, the periphery of the circle- where our body meets the world.

The creation of the totem also establishes, for the first time, a center to the world and consciousness that lies outside our self. The totem is a collective construction, and this external center will generate a tension with our original self-center that will have both an unsettling and a generative effect. The subsequent dialectic and dissonance of our individual and social aspects will cause a consciousness and world to grow. Consciousness is a social construction, and, along the mythological path, the body's totem is displaced by the collective totem that serves to ground the community as a whole.

One of the crucial shifts in consciousness accomplished by the totem is the shift from self-centered physical responses to a social, emotional consciousness, one we construct through intercourse and dialogue with the others. With the invention of the totem, the center of the world moves from inside the individual (point of light) to a world outside our bodies, a world we share with others.

It may be argued that this first stage in the development of our mythological consciousness marks our rebirth into a new body that extends beyond the limits of our own. This new body is the social body, the community, and the responses of this body come, not merely through physical sensations but through the emotions that connect us each to others. The first birth of "reason," then, the first birth of consciousness expresses itself through the emotions, a capacity that begins to distinguish us from the animals and begins to (re)connect us to the world and others. The shock of the deed shifts the center to the individual. The totem marks a reconciliation to the original union.

The totem is the community's representation of the center. It marks the naval of this social body. The invention of this social body and the totem also sets a pattern for the development of consciousness whereby the defined, agreed upon, assumed center of the world periodically shifts. Through future shifts in the world's center, our consciousness will grow in leaps and bounds.

Each shift will either reverse or replicate this primordial shift of center from the inside to the outside, from the individual to the social body. This continuing dialectic from one side of a duality to another and then back and back again will be the engine of growth in our consciousness from which I and we emerge. In this first flip, the center shifts from (unconscious) "I" to we, from a dark, internal center to one that is externalized and shared through its manifestation in an agreed upon material object- the carrier of our mutual meaning- the totem. A first representation, Schopenhauer would say.

FIRST LIGHT—THE DEED

It is almost as if, in the development of our consciousness, "someone" (miracle and mystery) keeps moving the center of the world on us, and our lives become a long search, by individuals and whole societies, for the true center of the universe. At the center, we intuitively know from these earliest stages, we will find meaning, security, and peace. The social invention of the totem will serve as a precursor for future shifts- the invention of God, the invention of Christ, the birth of Self, and, someday soon, the birth of christ as well.

The seed for God was planted long ago, in the moment of the Deed, and so was awaiting realization/birth as first consciousnesses worked together to overcome the dissonances, to gain greater control over the external universe, and, too, to gain mastery over the swirl of emotions they felt subjected to inside. The mutual definition of a center, and the construction of the totem helped to still that swirl of emotions and to fix consciousness in space and time, but as our consciousness continued to grow, the totem could not hold forever. We would have to move on to the next incarnation, chase the next flip of center, rediscover and redefine the source of consciousness, world, and truth.

In Freud's Judeo-Christian story, the totem leads eventually to God. The invention of God will complete the structure of human consciousness with the marking of the cross. The cross, in combination with the circle, gives us the instrument we need to "take measure" of the world and self, what Herman Melville calls "the chronometer" or "internal compass."

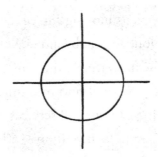

Together, circle and cross introduce the concept of finitude, of definition. Without the cross, the world is experienced as a swirl of motion beyond our human control, but with the invention of the cross, we gain capacity to stop that motion- even temporarily, to fix our knowledge, to define our self and others and the world and objects. The cross gives human beings the power to break the world into pieces that are finite, small, and manageable. Every thing is no longer imbued with the whole. We are not imbued with the whole, and so we can begin to think of our self with a degree of separation, of independence, even self-will, self-mastery and freedom.

We are like the infant who, having established for themselves some divisions between darkness and light, between I and the other, between my will and desires and the external world, begins to manipulate that world, to experiment, and explore and so, too, begin the course towards mastery of their universe. The child is still a very dependent creature, there can be no doubt, as we, ourselves, remain dependent upon a petulant and angry (Old Testament) God. But we see the potential at least for greater mastery and freedom, and we experience ourselves as possible agents of change. Like Martin Luther.

The cross in our schema symbolizes the creation of a third dimension in the consciousness of humans. No longer limited to a two-dimensional consciousness in which we are enmeshed without mastery or control, we begin to exert our new found powers and accept the limitations under which these powers are granted. The cross is the abstraction of the totem.

From totem to cross represents a shift of center once again- from its material representation in an external world back into the internal world of psyche where the cross belongs, where the cross came from in the first place. Our invention of God is really just the reflection and consequence of this shift, indicative of the invention or discovery of a psyche, of a mind, of a person, of an I.

Thus, the invention of God (by the Jews) reflects a shift by which the Jews take the totem back into themselves (and out of the external sphere). Thus, their prohibition of idols and the mark the men make on their penises. God is no longer worshipped as at the center, but, rather, in the sky, and men aspire to Him.

In retrospect, it may seem quite remarkable to us that Jews and Christians did not recognize what an asshole their God is. They persistently claimed for Him to be a God of Love when every single indication, every piece of evidence pointed to just the opposite. But consciousness at this stage in our development was not in the business of examining God. God was the seer. We used God. We needed God, and He was there for us. We used His eyes, His distance, His elevation, His infinitude to define and understand and master ourselves. We were too indebted to God to question Him further. God had given a gift that we were so busy exploiting, there was no reason, no motivation, and no capacity to question the seer, God.

As we look back on Him now, well, we have plenty of reason to question God, to be angry at God, to abandon God. God led us into this mess; God has failed us. In our perspective today, the seer has shifted away from God. We have established a new vantage point from which we may constellate a more accurate understanding of self, the world, others, and God.

Some people still cling to God, still cling to the illusion that despite all appearances to the contrary, God is not an asshole. God is a God of love. These are frightened people; they lack the ability to imagine a different world, a world without God, and some can be scary people, when, in their hysterical insistence on a truth they know is not true, they will kill you if you try to take it from them- try to kill their God.

Some folks are so wedded to their representation of God that it keeps them from the experience of God. To know God, we must go beyond representations, beyond images, beyond idols. We must learn to know each other as subjects and not objects- the I and Thou of Martin Buber. What some folks fail to understand, fail to accept, is that the circle and the cross creates a dynamic- again, accurately illustrated in the story of the Garden and our exile.

They would make of the structure of our consciousness a fixed and objective truth- the one, absolute, eternal truth- just like their image of God. But we are beyond that stage now. It is not the Cross that we should worship but, rather, what the cross allows us to do in life. The Cross is an instrument, a tool. We use it to find the center of our heart. We need to let our consciousness spin.

FIRST LIGHT– THE MISTAKE

In the beginning, God made a mistake.

Garden of Eden

The Garden of Eden tells the story of the birth of human consciousness. Before consciousness, before life, before "the fall" and birth of humans, there is only the static, nascent structure of consciousness. There is a circle unbroken, but intersected by the four rivers, the four spokes on the cross of consciousness. There is "God," though where God comes from we cannot say. In the midst of the Garden stands Adam, the creation of God. Unaware as he is of himself or of the world, Adam is only potentially human. Not yet a man, he does not even exist yet, and his existence prior to Eve and consciousness can only be told in story and in retrospect- after consciousness is born.

Before time and the story begins, Adam and Eden carry within themselves the seed of human consciousness that, in order to become activated, living, real require impregnation by an animating force that is, at once, foreign to, and part of, itself. Until Eve breathes life into the structure (a first moment we will get to), we have only the potential for consciousness, the necessary pre-conditions, the universal structure but without existence, awareness, movement, and life.

It is notable that Adam cannot become fully human- i.e. conscious- through a relationship to God alone. It will take Eve- and the counterpoint of another human- to open Adam's eyes, to make him conscious of himself and the world around him, to make him human. It is the introduction of the Other (Eve) that sets the world in motion, the introduction of duality (masculine and feminine) that gives way to the dialectic and doubt that makes us human- i.e. "like Gods." "She" comes to him in his sleep- from darkness- as a dream, and "she" comes from his own body- his breast- and, so, is a piece of his self that is outside himself. God knows that Eve and Adam have eaten from the Tree of Knowledge when they hide themselves, because they have knowledge of their nakedness, their bodies, and, so, are ashamed.

We see depicted, then, in the Garden of Eden all the elements- and contradictions-necessary to the structure and creation of human consciousness- the circle and the cross, I and other, the body and the mind. In this way, the Garden of Eden provides a perfect illustration of the earliest moments, and preconditions, of human consciousness.

Alongside these insights into the structures and origin of human consciousness, the Garden of Eden also provides us with important clues into the limitations, values, and perspective of the civilization that would eventually grow from this seed. To begin to understand these messages embedded in the Garden of Eden, we will need to look critically into the point of view of its author/protagonist- God. We are to believe that God alone created everything that is good- Eden, the plants and trees, animals, and Adam. And it is God who graciously provided the helpmate to Adam who would become the source of all the problems and all life.

FIRST LIGHT – THE MISTAKE

There is no mention in God's account of His creation what help He may have received from, say, the Mother, the earth, the darkness, matter. God has no partner in creation. As He tells the story, God depends upon Himself alone. Though Matter is silent in this account, and God speaks only of Himself, there is evidence of forces over which God has no control, forces He does not acknowledge, and, maybe, does not comprehend Himself.

Who put the serpent in the Garden? And if it was God, what happened there to make the serpent betray his Creator by goading Eve to revolution? How did the serpent know about the Tree of Knowledge? And what were the Trees of Knowledge and Life doing there in the first place? Was it God who placed them there, and why? To tempt Adam, to taunt His favored creature? To what end? Or was it perhaps someone or something else that was responsible? Did God really have a choice?

If we cannot credit another being than God, we must assume, at least, that there are certain rules and limits that constrain even acts of God. But, if this is so, what Super God creates these rules that so constrain our God? And, we must ask, where does the consciousness of God come from? In Adam, the birth of consciousness required the presence of an other- as a counterpoint and contrast to his own self-centered knowing, and if that is true for Adam, does it not make rational sense to expect a similar corollary as necessary to consciousness in God?

These questions will seem terrible, "inappropriate," and frightening to most believing Christians. "He is God," they will say and have said for centuries. God's will exceeds man's rational understanding, and, so, they seek to dismiss humans' reason and stop the questioning there. "He is a God of Love" (goddamn it), despite all evidence to the contrary. "We humans cannot be expected to understand His ways." Our job is to have "faith;" and faith exceeds our reason. We cannot presume to judge God based on (our limited understanding of) His actions. Such questioning leads to doubt, and for a certain (and widely predominant) brand of Christianity, doubt is the enemy of, the destroyer of, our faith. The work of Satan. Or the serpent. Or of our wife, the Mother, Earth and blackness.

To me, these are "Christians" of little faith. To me, this brand of Christianity is based, if not on lies, than, at least, on willful ignorance. A faith that cannot withstand the full exercise of our human powers- including our human reason- is no faith at all. It is impotent and unworthy of respect- a sham. It provides no answers, provides no meaning, provides no Salvation. We are better off with no faith at all and our honest, at least, despair.

A faith that is strong, healthy, true, and useful will withstand all doubts and questions. If God is great as Christians contend, He will withstand all assaults human beings can muster, and our faith in Him will grow stronger the more critically we look and the more thoroughly we doubt His powers. Either He is God or He isn't, and I, for one ("fallen," upstart human that I am) am bound to challenge Him to prove it, to show me He is God worthy of my faith.

Though they will hysterically deny it, I think most Christians intuit from the very beginning of the Christian story, that in His dealings, particularly, with the serpent and with Eve, this God is petulant and self-centered. He is a mean-spirited bully who, if He were as powerful as He claims, would tyrannically exclude all others from participation in both the Knowledge and Eternal Life that He so jealously safeguards for Himself alone.

I think God is lonely. He is sad and insecure.

He's done it to Himself, of course, with His bad behavior, but I do believe God would act differently if He could find the way. As humans, we have a responsibility to teach Him. Ultimately, we will have to forgive God "His trespasses against us." We are called to embrace and love this God, not because He is, Himself, a loving God, but, rather, just because He is so incapable of love. Something in Him created us, though, or had some hand, at least, in our creation, and for this we owe our Father something. God is not all bad any more than He can be all good.

We must be human towards this God, because it is the right, the humane and "christian" thing to do. But I am getting ahead of myself. To forgive and love this God, we must both understand the mistakes/the sins that He commits and own the sins/mistakes we make in His image.

God did not create the world alone. Though He thinks He did, God is wrong in this. If God was all powerful as He claims, He would have never placed the Tree of Knowledge and Tree of Life in our way. He would not have tempted us to become like Him. Or, alternatively, God intended all along for us to eat from the forbidden Tree(s), that God might have companionship and/or a consciousness He could bounce off of His own to thus become self-aware and "real."

Eve gets knowledge from the Earth- the tree, the snake, and God knows that she and Adam have eaten from "the Forbidden Tree" when they become aware of their own nakedness- their bodies- that aspect of "His" creations that He cannot control and so, it would seem, cannot really claim to own. The "fall" from the Heaven that is the Garden of Eden is, in fact, the beginning realization of humans' true place and origin between God and Mother, Heaven and Earth, mind and body, infinitude and death.

birth of christ

God claims to cast them from the Garden of Eden, but they have done this to themselves. Their "fall from grace" is an inevitable consequence of the first couple's true origin from the dialectic of God and Mother Earth. God is not lying in His claim to sole proprietorship (not even to Himself). He is just too immature in His own consciousness to understand that everything that happens in the world does not come from Him. But even this, His immaturity and His "innocence," cannot excuse the disrespect He shows our Mother.

This disrespect will repeat itself continuously throughout the histories of Christian societies that follow. True believers will mistake God's immaturity and ignorant self-absorption for a virtue and so will perpetuate an infantile understanding of the Christian faith in relation to the planet, Earth, matter, and women down through the present day.

We may take our psychological analysis of Eden further and speculate whether God in this story does not represent our own infantile understanding of the world that once assumed that all the world is our creation. The story of the Garden is not only the moment of our first birth as consciousness but also our first awareness of the other. It is our first understanding that we are not God, or "like God"- that we are not the sole creator of the universe.

We become simultaneously conscious of our self as body (and so, as finite creature) and conscious of an other- that aspect of our self that lies outside our self. It is only in this moment that we become a human, in this moment that we become self-aware; in this moment of psychological conception, the seed of human consciousness is animated, activated, born. And, though the circle of our animal unconscious and eternity has been broken, a new circle of self-awareness and identity is born within us.

We have definition, have drawn a line around ourselves- within ourselves, and so no longer need the protections of God's wall and garden within which we remain indistinguishable to ourselves and indistinguishable from the world and others. Paradoxically, with the self-definition we achieve with the help of others (Eve), we gain, for the first time, an awareness of the infinite. That is, we become "like God." The price we pay for this awareness of the infinite, though- what we could not have known before it- is our experience of finitude, our awareness of pain, suffering, and death.

In the story, we are told that God bars our way to life eternal- to the Tree of Life, and thus insures that we do not become truly, fully Gods. But the way to eternal life is barred, not by God, but by the nature of consciousness itself. Human beings will continue to seek eternal life in a multitude of forms, but it is a quixotic and impossible quest- a dream. As human, as consciousness, definition and finitude is requisite to conceiving and perceiving the infinite, our self, or anything at all. The standard Christian fantasy of Heaven is, in some respect, a longing for a return to the original Eden, but this time with the knowledge and consciousness of our self.

If human beings go to Heaven upon their death, there will be no way for them to know it, because there will be no one there who knows. There may be eternity and peace, but no way to experience it. Here is something the serpent failed to tell us, and, probably, did not understand themselves. We are cast out into pain, suffering, and death, and these are the necessary conditions for our consciousness of the infinite. These are the price we pay for sacrificing the paradise of pre-consciousness, the paradise we only recognize as paradise after it is lost. As long as we were in It, we could not, did not know this paradise, and the moment that we knew it, we could no longer be just in It. Paradise is a dream, a memory, a fiction that human beings continually seek to recreate in their experience, though to do so would destroy it. And thus it will be, as well, with Heaven and our death.

How like this birth of consciousness is, then, to our body's birth from our mother's womb. And perhaps this Garden of Eden that, God is convinced, is paradise may, in fact, have become a prison, and a shell too small (for Eve, at least, if not for Adam) from which she, or they, desperately sought release. Surely, we must eventually have struggled to be free from God's tyranny of bliss, suffocating and inhuman, and so Eve and serpent released us from this womb of ignorance and non-existence, but to be born into what, we could not know. Once across that threshold, though, there could be no turning back. Surely there are times we humans feel regret and nostalgia for a past that wasn't- a longing to return, to death, nirvana, non-existence, peace. As for me, I choose to fall with Eve.

Who is God?

God is the first projection of our own infantile self.

This fact by no means negates the importance of God, nor does it imply that God somehow does not exist. Part of the transition away from the old, dead and dying, materialist vision of the rationalists is to understand that all that is real is not rational, is not material, is not "objectively" the case.

Carl Jung, and Kant and Freud before him, taught us, for the first time, to turn our I back upon itself and so to see there a necessary, though hitherto invisible, psychic aspect to all reality. Because we see with and through this essential, subjective aspect of consciousness, we do not, at first, recognize that such a thing exists. Just as the eye cannot see the eye, except through some reflection, so, too, the I cannot see the I, though it constitutes the world. God becomes the first reflection of the I, and, with the help of God, we begin the journey to self-knowledge.

Thus it is that God's mistake is our mistake, magnified, replicated, and reflected, from the earliest days of our humanity and consciousness. As small children, and like God, we make the mistake of believing that we are, ourselves, the sole creators of the universe. Though others become visible and must be accounted for in our all-powerful creation, it does not occur to us in these earliest days of consciousness to question what role they may have had in the origins of the world. For every child, like God, the world begins with me and through me alone. Before God, before I, there was nothing, there was darkness, there was not even "not," because there was nothing to compare it to.

From a certain perspective (from within the story), this first story is absolutely true; viewed from without, the story is self-evidently delusional and absurd. So it is for every myth. So it will be, too, for human reason. And so it will be with every story human beings tell- now, then, and in the future. God is a first story we tell about the infinite aspects of our self and the world we live in/create. God is the first expression of the uniquely human aspiration to transcend all limits and so to become, like our fantasy projection, all knowing, ever present, and eternal. God is the first embodiment of a finite being's aspiration to the infinite.

Where this aspiration comes from is the miracle and a mystery at the core of all human history and consciousness. To be human, it turns out, is kind of a cosmic set up. The origin and nature of consciousness remains an impossible riddle that, though irresolvable, humans cannot stop trying to resolve.

Beginning with this first projection/fiction/explanation/story by which humans seek to reconcile the irreconcilable- beginning with God- we will excavate the evolution of human projections- and our definitions of our self- down to the present day. We will trace that development through two primary epochs in human understanding- the mythological and the rational- and will attempt to articulate a next epoch in human understanding and truth that is only now being born in each and all of us.

Consciousness has evolved through a series of "reversals" each of which has had the effect of turning our understanding of the world and our place in that world upon its head. You and I are living through- are, indeed, the very embodiment of- one such epoch reversal, as I will explain. That's why things seem so crazy, desperate, and confused. It is because human consciousness- you and I- are enduring the spasms of death and birth. Not every generation goes through this kind of convulsion; we are particularly cursed and blessed.

I will speak consistently of the fictions, stories, myths, explanations that human beings tell to bring meaning to their experience and the world. These are the circles people draw. I will simultaneously maintain the absolute truth and falsehood of each of these stories/explanations, and I will expect readers capable of joining me in this absurdity and contradiction.

Reason and science, as you will see, are to be afforded the same respect as every other human story, but no more. The delusion that science and reason are fundamentally different from, and superior to, the mythological explanations that preceded them is the cause of pathology in our technological age. There can be no doubt that, in certain respects, science is an advance upon earlier mythological explanations, but if we do not teach humility to our science, if we do not recognize the boundaries and limits and falsehood of our scientific explanations and reason, we will most certainly strangle all life from the planet and the soul.

Thank consciousness, in the waning days of the scientific epoch, science, itself, has provided the necessary bridges to escape the strangulating limits of scientific understanding. These come in the form of relativity (and the person of Einstein) and psychoanalysis (and the persons of Freud and Jung). And, most important of all, the individual who made Einstein and Freud possible, the man who turned reason upon itself and so provided us with the pathway to our salvation, is Immanuel Kant, the Copernicus of consciousness.

Ages hence, critics may make fun of my adoration of individuals, understanding as they do how consciousness develops through the cumulative efforts of the many. What I see is that as human beings, we can only access the truth, we can only access the infinite, we can only realize the divine, as individual and imperfect creatures stuck inside this fragile vessel/body that must shortly die.

It is the story of the individual, and their incomparable journey from finitude to more, that is the source of all beauty, truth, meaning, and the divine. To each story belongs both absolute truth and falsehood. And so it is that I proudly love Kant, Schopenhauer, Spinoza, Mary Shelley, Mary Daly, John Brown, Malcolm X, Brittany Spears and Tina Turner, as some of you may someday love me. Let professors scoff at our humanity; we know where truth and beauty lie and that God lives at the point of intersect between you and me.

Birth of God

An essential shift and reversal takes place in our relationship to the light and darkness between the early mythological era- the era of totem poles and totem animals- and later Judeo-Christian myth. Freud makes much of the overriding ambivalence early humans feel towards their objects of worship. In these early days of our emotional development, love and hatred, fear and devotion are mixed up and indistinguishable from one another. Early humans would either vacillate between, or experience simultaneously, these conflicting emotions towards the totem animals they used as incarnations of their gods.

In Freud's mythology, this ambivalence goes back to that very first moment of consciousness- the birth of our human reason, emotion, distance, and relation- when, having killed the oppressive father, the brothers must have experienced the simultaneous intoxication from their new found power and revulsion at their bloody violence and debasement. This ambivalent mix of love and hatred, fear and revelation persists, says Freud, in modern humans' own emotional reactions to the world, and it is just this uncontrollable power of ambivalence that makes the emotions so threatening to our modern man.

It is just the overwhelmingness of our emotions- the power they exercise over us and the helplessness we feel in the face of them- that makes it necessary for human consciousness to try and devise some strategy to defeat, overcome, or, at very least, suppress these emotions so as to gain greater control, mastery, predictability, and power over the world, ourselves and others.

The Judeo-Christian God is one- and the most powerful- invention of the early mythological consciousness to control this ambivalence and so reduce our vulnerability to forces- both within us and from the world beyond- that are beyond our control. It is perhaps ironic but fitting that to thus gain control over these emotions that rule us, we must relocate the center of power and authority outside our selves. By establishing a locus of control outside our human bodies, we continue the work of projection begun through the totem and totem animals and, more than that, we evacuate our consciousness from the source of these disturbing and overwhelming ambivalences- our own human bodies.

The invention of this God-creator marks an incredible, even miraculous shift in the location of consciousness that human beings will learn to replicate at later stages in our continuing development. This capacity to shift our understanding- to radically reverse how we see the world- will become the engine of progress that drives our unfolding human consciousness. For a most simplistic, and so understandable, illustration of the shift we are talking about, think of those "gestalt" drawings that, viewed one way, looks like an old woman, but viewed differently, becomes a young woman. Here:

And this "first" shift of responsibility for the creation of the world from ourselves (though we remain "unconscious" of this force in ourselves) to an external authority- God- remains the most profound shift, because it is the reversal that really gets the ball of consciousness moving.

Before God, we have a lens through which we see the world:

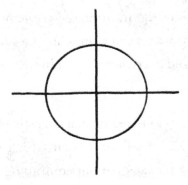

The lens comes from inside our own consciousness. It creates a distance from the immediate "what is" and results from the horror/revulsion/shock/trauma of some first experience- whether it is Freud's murder or not. The lens creates the inner, psychic aspect of consciousness necessary to create a world. The lens distinguishes human beings from other animals and makes "experience" possible.

Before God, though, there is no consciousness of the lens. There is no consciousness of consciousness. We see and "experience" through the lens but are not yet aware that there is a lens. We accept our experience as all there is, and we have no sense of time, of mastery, of self. To gain that awareness- both in our individual experience as infants and in our universal experience as human beings- requires a discourse with the others (that we do not, at first, recognize as existing) that we begin, in the universal consciousness, through totemistic rituals and stories and practices.

At some point in this process, however, something breaks through our consciousness and we wake up to the fact that there is some other than our self, that there is some point of reference outside of ourselves, outside of our own bodies, and it is at this moment that human consciousness is really born. It is at this moment- in our first recognition of an other outside ourselves- that consciousness comes to life and that time and experience and a self are truly born.

Until such moment, we have "existed," like Adam before Eve, in potential only, in utero. Conceived but not "real"ized. Strangely, almost, we exist in idea (the ideas of others?) but not in "reality," at least not our own.

The Garden of Eden is such a powerful and enduring story because, for all its faults and limitations, it pictures perfectly this first birth of consciousness, from the egg, the lens, the Garden, of potential into real life and body and time. The Garden of Eden is us- the picture of our own birth of consciousness. God is also us- or the image/representation of who we are before we are born. God is the marker by which we identify this mysterious source of our own beginning, and, too, Adam and Eve, are us as well- the two aspects of our consciousness necessary for it to come to life. In consciousness (in the psychic aspect of our self) all human beings are both masculine and feminine- both Adam and Eve, and without the spur of the feminine- without the will to live, to be conscious (and so like God), there would be no self, no world, no thing.

The reduction of Eve to the unworthy perpetrator of original sin against our God and Law lays the cornerstone beneath a long, persistent, self-annihilating denigration of women and the feminine that we will get to shortly, but in this first and miraculous birth of God, Adam, Eve, and consciousness, we are all One- the creators of all the world there is.

Birth of God, Too

It will take years of pressure (from emotional repression and shame), long gestation in darkness, and fertile ground for the seed that was planted on that fatal eve to bear new fruit. That is what the Jewish God, Yahweh, is- the final fruit of the brothers' murder and weakness, resentment, shame, and lies.

Gradually through our "conversation" with the totem animal and in relation to the totem/center, we have begun to glimpse a something/someone else- the generator of these projections and our stories, the one responsible for world and consciousness and light. The One. That Being who corresponds more fully with the center. That human One of which some remnant of memory remains, though buried, lost in darkness and forgetting. The One we killed? Or is it, rather, the One who was born that day? The One we cannot bear to embrace nor admit just yet, the murderer and source of shame, the human agent. I.

Not yet. Too soon. We bury I and give birth, instead, to the most profound projection yet. The projection of the abstract and infinite idea/identity, the generator of light and world, whom we call (who calls Himself) God. We shine our light upon the screen of the world long enough until, at last, we find reflected back the very image of our self, and we call that image God.

Ironically (but consistent with how consciousness works) we can only begin to gain a sense of our self, of I (and, too, of other) once the Universal, all powerful, all knowing and eternal God is projected out from us. We need this external God to teach us about our self- to serve as a further reflection we can learn from. And so it is that, with the help of God, we come to have some sense of our self- some knowledge that there is a self, and so begin to observe and adjust how that self interacts with the world.

According to my own argument it seems that in order to move from the totemistic, materialistic, polytheistic gods to the abstract, monotheistic God should require some murder, as, I have argued and will argue, such murders seem a necessary corollary to fundamental reversals in our consciousness.

In the deed, the seed was planted for the single, all-powerful and eternal God in heaven, but this idea was not ripe yet. It needed time- in the underground of the psyche- to percolate, to gestate, to grow until the seed that was conceived on the night of the deed finally comes to birth in the idea of the monotheistic God. We will see this pattern of murder, gestation underground, and then birth repeat itself at later stages in the evolution of our consciousness as well.

With the birth of God we mark the beginning of one such stage. From this second, Judeo-Christian stage in the mythological epoch will grow the age of science, reason, and technology. We will proceed then to consider how this next development takes place.

The Cross

God introduces the cross that makes discrimination of I and other, of black and white, inside and outside, and so, consciousness of our self, possible.

With the cross we create an arm's length that provides us vision of the circle we have drawn. It might be natural for us to call that seer, the one who holds the elements of our consciousness at arm's length, "I," and eventually we will make this shift, but in this early stage of our developing consciousness, we are still "in it" and not ready yet to think of ourselves as the creator of a world. We assign a creature, or, more accurately, an idea, "God" to explain the seer that must, it seems, exceed our human powers and limitations.

In God, we represent this "I" to ourselves in a way analogous to the way we use the totem that comes before. The difference- and the crucial advance of Judaism- is that this new representation is completely immaterial, abstract, unified, and infinite. We will check ourselves in this mirror that is God, adjust our behaviors, learn from our (and His) mistakes, and grow through this second half of the mythological epoch.

WORLD AS WILL AND REPRESENTATION

Emotions and Reason

First humans experienced an initial separation, and so creation, of mind from body as a result of emotional trauma(s) that had the effect of shocking them into consciousness. Despite their initial discrimination, though, body and mind would remain closely enmeshed for millennia. The birth of God and reason, in the second half of the mythological epoch, marks the beginning of a new strategy to complete the separation of mind from body in order to achieve increased mastery, liberation, and even infinitude.

In the first, mythological stage of human consciousness, reason is only beginning to develop. In retrospect, we might think of this mythological era as the gestation period of reason. The seed is planted in the Deed but does not come to fruition until the moment of God's birth. In the interim, there is a consciousness that was not there before, that is different from the "consciousness" of animals, that goes beyond our merely physical responses to the environment, but that does not yet participate in the degree of abstraction we humans have come to take for granted and built our educational system around.

The first consciousness of humans is an emotional awareness. There is some sense of one's self as separate from others and the world. There is a sense of agency and a beginning understanding that "I" influence and am influenced by the world around me. There is a beginning sense of "I," and simultaneous with this "I" awareness is an awareness of others and so, too, a beginning sense of "we." But none of these discriminations are clear and distinct in the early days of consciousness. Black and white distinctions are evolving but not complete.

The experience of these earlier humans, then, was significantly different than our own. Whereas we tend to perceive ourselves as some separate consciousness perceiving the world and others, earlier humans' experience was one of feeling embedded in a reality that they influenced and were influenced by without thereby being separate from. The body of these early humans would extend beyond the limits of their own physical body to include parts of others and parts of the world around them. And in the same way, their mind was not something they "owned" or "claimed" as intrinsically their own. Rather, they would perceive that they were a part of, that they participated in, a greater mind, a mind that exceeded the restrictive limits of an ill-defined "I" and that was, rather, shared with others and the world.

Theirs was what we might refer to now as a "pantheistic" universe. It was a web of relationships, a network of cells that each individual was dependent upon and contributed to. Emotion was central to this stage of our consciousness. It was through our emotions that we became aware of this network of relationships we called our "world," and it was through our emotions that we maintained our connections to (and so continuing existence in) this web of life. These emotions made us aware but also made us vulnerable. Through them, we maintained our (umbilical) connection to the world and others but also began to intuit our own contingency, dispensability, finitude, and imminent death.

The contradictions that I call constitutive of human consciousness (A / A', inside/outside, body/mind, I and other) are nascent in this early consciousness. They are present but not yet clearly drawn by consciousness. They are operational but emerging. And so, the kind of black and white distinctions we build our reason on are in the process of being built, and our sense of I and other, body/mind, inside/outside, subject/object are mixed up with each other, as depicted in the symbol of yin yang. Swirling together in a dance and dialogue, the distinct elements are at once being separated out and intimately intertwined in the centrifuge of human consciousness.

One thing that distinguishes the emotional consciousness from reason is in the emotions' tendency to continually switch allegiances between the yin and yang of consciousness. In white people's reason, we lock in our allegiance to the light as against the darkness. Doing so provides us with a degree of (an illusion of) permanence and security, but in doing so, we also lose touch with half of our true self. The emotions have no such allegiance and are capable of flipping and flopping or of participating in both contradictory points of view simultaneously. Such uncontrollable unreliability will threaten a person who insists on reason, but it is just this capacity of our emotions that makes them so valuable and important to our mental health and intelligence.

As consciousness continues to develop, we retain our emotional awareness but also grow beyond it to develop additional capacities as well. The vehicle for this growth, for the progressive separation of the elements of consciousness in the mythological epoch, were the stories people told to themselves and one another about the origins of the world and consciousness. Through story, people continually refined strategies to both maintain connections and differentiate themselves from the world and others. People explored, experimented, and manipulated this pantheistic network of emotions to accomplish their first scientific and technological adaptations of the world to meet their needs. Through these stories and manipulations of the world, human beings gained, over millennia, an ever-increasing clarity about both the distinctions and connections upon which their world and consciousness depends.

The language of this era in our consciousness was a language that we still have with us (because we also have this early stage in consciousness active within us), and that is the language of "symbols." Symbols are different than words or concepts in the same way that the emotions are different than reason. In words and concepts we have so thoroughly separated our idea from its object that an idea is embodied, at best, by indifferent scribbles on a page. In symbolic language, meaning depends upon the specific "object" or category of objects used to carry that meaning.

Symbols achieve a level of abstraction that allows finite objects to "represent" meanings that extend beyond themselves and connect those meanings with the wider world, but just as the "I" remains embedded in a wider whole, so, too, do the meanings of our symbols. And so, in this earliest stage of human consciousness, ideas and concepts are emerging. Like "I," ideas are operational but not thoroughly defined. Like consciousness, itself, our ideas are emerging but irremediably wedded to finite incarnations in the material world. Through the centrifuge of consciousness, and the dialectical tension of opposites (A/A', inside/outside, body/mind, I/other), discriminations become separated out from one another and ideas become separated out from objects creating thereby a new discrimination between subject and object that will prove intrinsic to human reason.

Ambivalence

Emotions are not as clear cut as reason. If we consider even our own experience of emotions, we will find that our feelings are often "mixed up." Often, we feel first one way and then another about a person or situation. We vacillate between feelings or we experience a simultaneous mix of contradictory feelings. This ambivalence comes in part because of the lack of separation that inheres in any emotional situation. Feeling an emotion(s) towards someone or something implies a connection. Where we have no connection to a person, thing or event, we are indifferent. We feel nothing. We do not care one way or another. Caring indicates connection, an emotional attachment indicates that our identity is tied up with the source of that emotion in some important way.

We experience more frequent and substantial reversals in our emotions than in our reason. It is almost as if we do not know which side to take, as if our identity is tied up in both sides of the equation, and nothing is as black and white as reason would like us to believe. Black becomes white and white turns to black in an emotional consciousness and so leads to the kind of fickleness that gets disparaged (as a characteristic of women, especially) in our white, Christian culture. There is also a simultaneity to an emotional awareness that can be completely unsettling to a man who demands reason. "I don't know what to think" is an accurate description of our emotional awareness.

This lack of black and white distinctions in our emotional awareness can have unsettling and frustrating effects, but it also can have certain advantages, a certain wisdom and truth that we have lost appreciation for in our demand for the facts and the objective truth of reason. Data. If we can begin to understand that our reason, our perspective, and our absolutism are definitions we impose on a situation that do not necessarily inhere (or inhere alone) in the facts, we may be able to make more tolerable and humane decisions in our interactions with other people and the planet.

Adequate and Inadequate Ideas

The best criticism of the emotions and the decisions made from emotion as opposed to reason comes from the Dutch philosopher, Benedicto Spinoza. When we act as merely emotional beings, Spinoza argues, we are less thoroughly human. Our emotions bind us to our merely animal natures in Spinoza's view, and as long as we act from these interests alone, we remain in bondage to our "inadequate ideas." When we act merely from our emotions, our actions are determined by forces external to ourselves. Human beings are capable of controlling their actions through their exercise of reason, but when we act from emotions alone, our actions are not free, we lack self-determination and freedom. We fail to fulfill our full and true human potential.

Before the birth of reason, we are not clearly defined individuals and are not agents of our actions. We are "moved by our emotions" whereas, in reason, we can be more thoroughly the source of our selves. Though our emotions may give us an illusion of agency, we are, in fact, subjected to influences beyond our control and our awareness.

In one way, the person capable of only an emotional awareness is much more self-centered. They see things only from their particular perspective in space and time. They do not see these limitations in their perspective and it does not occur to them that there might be any other way of seeing possible nor that there are limitations to their own perspective that they do not see. They are, to use Sartre's terms, merely "in itself" and not "for itself." They are working under the delusion that their own particular representation of the facts is the universal, the one and only possible, representation of the facts. It does not occur to them to "think out of the box" or that they are in a box, so busy are they thinking with that box.

There is a universality to the emotions just as there is with reason, the difference is where we locate our self, whether we are able to distinguish the universal and the particular or not. To illustrate, it works best to think of our consciousness as a bubble. A person operating from a merely emotional awareness views the world from inside that bubble and assumes that the bubble is all there is. This person assumes that "they have no choice" (and so, they don't), that they feel as they feel, it can't be helped, and that their feelings are the whole truth and nothing but the truth.

The fact that other people and/or the world do not conform to this one and only truth is a source of confusion and frustration for the merely emotional consciousness. They do not understand why others fail to cooperate. There must be something wrong with these other people or the world that they do not conform to the one and only truth, and so, the merely emotional consciousness is apt to spend their energies in railing against these others or the world, to force the world and others into conformity with their will.

A person capable of reason is able to step, at least partially, outside of their own bubble of awareness. Even if they are still compelled by the force and "truth" of their emotions, they can at least understand that their emotions may not represent the one and only truth. The advantage of this perspective outside of ourselves- outside of our own bubble, is the gift of God. A person can at least understand that some other perspective is possible and/or that another person, coming as they do from another point in space and time, coming from another body, might see things differently and/or have self-interests that conflict with my own. The ability to distance one's self from one's own emotions to step out of our original bubble of perception is the gift of God and Eve together.

A rational consciousness includes an awareness of the finitude of my own perspective, an awareness of my own limits. A rational consciousness understands that there may be differences between my interests and the interests of others and that, therefore, other people may disagree with me. The rational consciousness understands that my interests, while participating in the universal, may be particular to me. One who claims to be "rational," who believes they are "rational," is not always so.

As long as we mistake our particular interests for universals, as long as we are trapped in a merely emotional consciousness, our desires are apt to be continually frustrated and we will find ourselves in a continuous conflict with the world and others- a conflict that is beyond our powers to control. Thus it is that our emotions make us vulnerable- i.e. subject to forces beyond our individual control, i.e unfree.

The Wellspring

The evolution of human consciousness would be impossible, of course, without the physical foundation of our living bodies and the animal world. Life, itself, is a miracle and a mystery, even without this separation of body and mind that creates a world and consciousness. It remains, to my mind, the greatest mystery of all, whether this separation, whether this light of consciousness, is somehow necessary for life to begin at all; this question will need to be approached by future generations and (for now) physicists. It is too far out for me. I can approach, within the limits of my reason, the question of how consciousness is generated from merely animal life. In this arena, Arthur Schopenhauer has done the heavy lifting through his discrimination between Will and Representation. Will is the driving force, according to Schopenhauer's analysis, that makes all that follows possible. The Will to Live is as impersonal a force as gravity; it creates the movement necessary to fuel the dialectic of opposites that will give rise to human consciousness. Without the Will to Live, without our animal, physical nature, there would be no consciousness and no world. These structures of consciousness we articulate would be nothing but a dead and never-born abstraction, like God and Adam in their Garden without Eve, if we did not, first and foremost, live.

It is this wellspring of our consciousness, found at the heart and center of our world, that Western rationalism has neglected and forgotten, has poisoned and is aiming (irrationally) to consume and destroy.

In terms of symbolism, we have attempted through our Judeo-Christian religion and our scientific objectivism to plug that wellspring of life, the bubbling up of lifeblood from the darkness and bowels of our earth (what Christians mistook for Hell), with the totem and the cross. Through the totem, and then the cross, we have achieved a level of abstraction, the disembodied transcendence of ideas, that allows us a tremendous mastery over the material aspects of the world.

Abstract concepts have allowed us an expansion of consciousness, the invention of God, and a perception of the infinite that could not have been possible as long as our awareness was wedded to life and matter. This divorce of reason from material representations- symbols- was necessary for us to reach the possibility of self-awareness and enlightenment that we outliers are unpacking in the present day.

The Christian symbol, itself, illustrates this division from life that is critical for the Western consciousness. Christianity moves us from a world shaped like this:

to a world where men's ideas have been uprooted and reaching, hopelessly, towards God.

We must make a return to our original (and truer) understanding, but, when we return, we will have changed. The consciousness we've accrued does not go away.

We have gone too far; our reason is so disconnected from life that our totem is an oil rig. Oil rigs suck the lifeblood from our planet to spew into our atmosphere. We are doing to our planet what we did to our "father" so many years ago, what we did to our totem animal, what we did to our Jesus Christ. We are "worshipping" her and killing her with our ambivalent materialism. In our crazy allegiance to yang, we choose to kill the yin.

We must turn back to the wellspring. And if the totem has fallen (it has), we must embrace that death as birth. We restore the wellspring in place of Law with which, over the epoch of reason, white men held back the flood. Our salvation lies in the wellspring, no longer in the cross. From the depths of (Christian) Hell. Like their God, they just misunderstood.

The World as Will

Before there is myth, before there is consciousness as we define it- as the space, time, awareness created through the dialectical tension of body with mind, before there is a world as we know it, there is first a nascent consciousness we share with the other animals. Body and mind are one in this earliest form of awareness- a consciousness that is un-self-reflective and unconscious of itself but nonetheless responsive to stimuli from without and from within. Like subsequent layers of our consciousness, this original, bodily, animal awareness never dies in us. And while we go on to develop more differentiated explanations of the world, our self, and others, our animal awareness continues to drive our actions, decisions, and perspectives on the world.

We may acknowledge- become conscious of- "own" our body and its motives, or we can deny, suppress and try to ignore the knowledge of our body and its voices from the blackness. Choosing this second course, as the scientific, patriarchal, objective, white, professional Mind over Matter world view has tried to do, alienates us from our bodies, but can never release us from this animal aspect of our self.

The final divorce from, transcendence of, the body that Mind over Matter dreams of, will never come- not even in death, as the myth of Heaven pretends. And the more that we persist in our pursuit of this impossible dream, we force ourselves further and further into a schizoid division of our self, further and further into a self-destructive madness through which we consume the body upon which we depend.

In our alienation from the blackness- our own unconscious self- and our exclusive identification with the light (of reason, objectivity, the mind), we inevitably turn the blackness into "evil," "sin," the necessary negative to our wholly positive and ideal self. The hubris of man is to, like his God, detach himself from his own animal aspect, blackness. And yet the blackness clings to him. Cannot shake it off as the denied, though undeniable, aspect of himself.

There will be others who will describe and understand this animal layer of "consciousness" far better than I. I feel still early in the process of reclaiming my own body and my blackness. I still feel out of touch and alienated, though I am in the process, at least, of making my way back, of excavating and owning my own animal awareness- sex, hunger, and fear, love.

One who may have understood and described this fundamental animal awareness well is Arthur Schopenhauer in his explication of all life as the manifestation of an undifferentiated force of Will. All living beings, and even, mechanical and chemical reactions beneath the level of life, are, according to Schopenhauer, nothing but the multiple manifestations of Will- the sole purpose of which is to sustain and perpetuate itself.

The Will is an elemental force that, though it works through the vehicle of individual creatures, demonstrates a consistent and complete disregard for individuals. Such explanation would account for the experience we have all endured of being overwhelmed by our passions. We experience the force of Will most directly through our addictions and lust. We cannot stop ourselves. Reason is powerless, self-control impossible as we act in deliberately self-destructive ways under the influence of Will. The Will is "nothing personal." It is our animal aspect that is common to us all. It is indifferent and impersonal, as we ourselves are in this stage of consciousness.

Western, patriarchal civilization represents a single, sustained, and collaborative effort to tame and control- to domesticate- this force of Will through the application of reason. It is an effort born of desperation and helplessness, an effort bound to failure- the evidence of which we see all around us and feel inside us. Nature is more powerful than reason, and any transcendence of these forces- whether in individuals or in society as a whole- must always be temporary and incomplete, and if taken to extremes may, I fear, result in the attempted self-destruction of the Will, of life, of our bodies, our planet, our own animal self that we cannot bring ourselves to live with.

I am most often hard on pure reason and the false truth it has perpetuated- and deservedly so, too, given the destruction and continuing promise of destruction that it has wrought. But we may view more compassionately and more understandingly this particular falsehood of human consciousness if we consider what pure reason grew in response to.

Consciousness rose out of the animal blackness like a suddenly appearing island that human consciousness attached itself to, gasping, desperate, vulnerable, and terrified. Out of nothing, something solid had appeared. Humanity raised its head and began gasping for air like a drowning man, like a newborn. And we held on, held on for dear life,

birth of christ

in desperation, to this glimmer of some thing- consciousness- that had suddenly appeared.

Human beings would expand their consciousness through myth. By the power of the stories they would tell they secured a larger world and greater independence from the blackness, insecurity and death that everywhere surrounded them- particularly in the night. Through this first exercise of human reason, they expanded the circle of light, still always vulnerable to and dependent upon forces far greater than and mysterious to themselves.

The birth of science, like the domestication of animals and farming from which it derives, provides a degree- and promise- of permanence and mastery unknown to myth. Inspired by the powers of imagination, rational men picture a world where their mastery will be complete and their security permanent, where they will be "like God." In the world collectively constructed by white men, "like God" means freedom from dependence upon, and vulnerability to, the whims of nature. Protection from the indifferent serpent of the earth and blackness, night and storms, starvation, sickness, death. Mastery and dominion here on earth.

Like his God, man is confident in his role as sole Creator. "We can have it all" and forever, the dream of white civilization, reason. Who can fault earlier generations for these aspirations for the permanence, security, and meaning that we still seek today? They were mistaken and their solution flawed, this we know today, and others are just finding out (clinging as they are, to the only island of truth they have ever known, clinging as they are, to the only island of truth they can imagine as possible), but who can fault their aspiration?

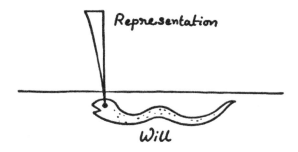

Differentiated consciousness offers humans an antidote- an island of sanity and being- in response to the undifferentiated current of blackness, animal consciousness that Schopenhauer describes as "Will." This solution of human reason, Schopenhauer describes, in the fit of humor, reason, insight, wisdom that was his life, as "the World as Representation." Out of the undifferentiated and purposeless (except to be self-sustaining) force of Will arises a uniquely human ability to form ideas, concepts, structures, edifices, things, whole worlds- to form what Schopenhauer calls Representations- that is, fictions about the world. Stories. Explanations. Objects. Agreements about what the world is.

The world created by consciousness is a bubble with the Will at our dark center, the core, our body and Representations as the images the Will projects on to the screen created by the inside wall of the bubble. Human consciousness is nothing more than a projector (the seer) and a screen (the seen), and it is the dialectic between the two that creates the history of consciousness, the world, and I. I is a bubble, and it will only be very late in the development of our consciousness that we begin to see this fact, begin to see the limits of the I, seeing, for the first time, the limiting wall of our perception and, in so seeing, creating a new vantage point for our consciousness that transcends the limits of the I.

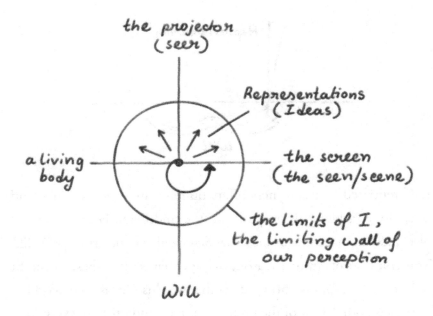

Complicating our simple image, and complicating the dialectic that actually takes place in the development of our consciousness is the fact that there is always a social aspect to our consciousness. We are never merely an I in isolation. The I is defined by the others and the we, so we are part of a larger bubble, too, transcendent of the limits of our own perception and inclusive of perspectives different than our own. Our bubble interacts with, pushes up against or reflects back and forth between, other bubbles separate from our own, but similar in structure and function. These bubbles (of the others) project representations upon us as well. And so, at the rim of our bubble of perception, our own self-images meet up with the images imposed on us by others. The dialectic and disagreements of the two, and our attempts to reconcile them, account for the greatest part of drama in our lives.

Out of this compounded dialectic of will with representations (in our own mind) and me (my self-definition) and you (how we are defined by others) grows another duality that will both make our problems deeper and more complex and, too, offer potential pathways for liberation. With the development of this next layer of dualities- in the contrast between subject and object, we have only very recently begun to comprehend the limits of our consciousness.

Symbolically and historically, that moment when our space travelers looked back to where they had been and projected to us the image of our planet- and its horizon, its limits, its smallness, even, our consciousness was changed forever. That this new image appeared at just the same moment as mind expanding drugs (the hallucinogens) were making first appearance in Western culture was not an accident but, rather, another mystery and miracle of consciousness that thus insured there would be birth in this moment of our death. This awareness of our consciousness as a bubble, this awareness of the limits of our consciousness makes possible, at long last, a release from that bubble and its limits that we could never imagine and still cannot imagine, really, until we take that leap irreversible by letting go our old dead truth, by releasing ourselves from the limiting shell of our own reason.

All the world, according to Schopenhauer, is the accumulation of human-made constructions- Maya. Illusion. Untruths that we agree to treat as truths, as if they were the whole world, as if there was a world and we could understand, agree upon what that world is. This layer of human construction, Schopenhauer explains, we lay over the truth of the World as Will- the blind instinct for self-preservation that transcends all its individual incarnations but remains unconscious of itself.

And so, in Schopenhauer's pessimistic but realistic vision, we have a truth, an immanent impulse towards self-preservation that cannot know itself overlaid with untruth, a transcendent explanation of the world that is merely fiction- what he calls "representations." Schopenhauer's solution is to resign one's self and abandon both foolhardy and false quests, to release one's self into pure consciousness and nirvana. To let go of our attachments to the Will to Live and to the false explanations (maya) of the world both and so release ourselves to an undifferentiated nothingness, pure light, it would seem, (though I am not sure why or how) as opposed to the pure blackness from which we rose.

While I greatly admire Schopenhauer's integrity, intellectual honesty, and courage, my own solution will seek a reconciliation with the dialectics of his contemporary and nemesis, Hegel, who argued for a synthesis of the opposites that said, in contrast to the neither/nor of Schopenhauer (neither Will nor Representation) that both/and (both Will (life) and Representation (reason, story)) could provide the most complete and truest version of the truth.

I would propose a different solution- not the pessimistic resignation of Schopenhauer, but the synthetic reconciliation and acceptance of the two. A solution based on an awareness that is both/and.

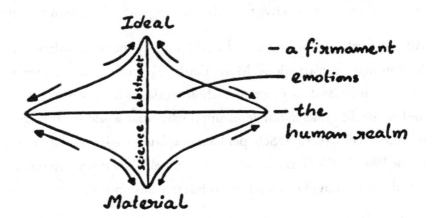

Centripetal and Centrifugal Motion

It is our interactions with the others that give rise to emotions. Early on in our development, these emotions are all mixed together, but with time, it is hoped, and with the birth of reason, we can begin to sort them out. It is through this original exercise of our emotions ("the swirl" of emotions), though, that we are able to rise above our merely animal consciousness in the first place. It is the community, the "we" that pulls us forward (through the education of our children), even in its errors.

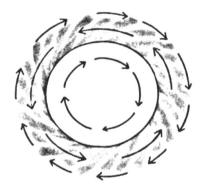

Resistance and Support create a swirl in the individual

The swirl of subjectivity responsible for depth in the individual

It is the forces external to ourselves, the influence of movements from others and from we- partly through resistance and partly through support- that creates the momentum necessary for our consciousness to grow. Ideally, these social forces will form a nest of stimulation and protection that nurtures strong individuals. It is equally essential for the human animal, if she or he is expected to become fully conscious, to have a certain level of physical, animal security, particularly early in their life. We need love, food, shelter, and limits to form "a solid foundation." Our life, our consciousness begins as animal, and the stronger our foundation, the further we will be able to grow. Thank the others, I was gifted with firm physical and emotional foundations upon which to build my reason.

At its worst, and often, the social forces can be used to oppress the individual- it can slow the individual's momentum, make her smaller, less secure, less able. In a dysfunctional family and society, the individual is not nurtured, but stunted.

The social forces overwhelm the burgeoning movement from the individual; the individual is treated like an enemy. I am treated like an object. That is the unfortunate direction our current "civilization" is moving (towards death and an annihilation of the individual). Our world is suffocating the movement of the subject, the internal momentum of the individual, that we seek here to restore.

People tell a story- to themselves and one another- to bring sense and order to a confusing, hostile, scary world. Then as now, human beings sought mastery and control, some degree of power and stability, through their stories and their science. In the early days (and even now as well), the stories people tell include prayer and supplications to higher powers we cannot see but must imagine to be out there- beyond our understanding. They include elements of ritual, repetition, mantra, and tradition that establish a degree of predictability and routine by which we human beings seek to preserve those experiments, interventions, and practices that have contributed to our success and security. Also intrinsic to this developing consciousness, though, is a certain dynamic element through which our stories and our science, our explanations and our observations, engage in a perpetual dialogue through which each informs the other. So it is that from the earliest days of human consciousness we have sought both to fix the truth, to establish some permanence and reliability to our understanding and, too, to continuously question and explore new possibilities so that we are perpetually refining our understanding.

We project our story out upon the world and the world provides feedback that confirms or contradicts the truth we have been telling. The structure of human consciousness is set from the first moments of its birth; patterns of internal discourse are established very early on and are intrinsic to the structure consciousness takes. These patterns, then, are continually replicated and perpetually building upon themselves throughout the evolution of our consciousness and continuing on through the present day.

People draw a circle in their minds, and upon this construct, our consciousness is built. Consciousness is fluid, it is in motion, it changes through its interaction with the two worlds that appear with the drawing of the circle- that is, 1) the world around us and 2) the world within us. From the very beginning, and continuing on through today, our consciousness moves in two opposite and, one may say, contradictory directions. There are, from the beginning, centripetal and centrifugal movements to our consciousness.

The movement inward generates our stories about the world; its aim is to bring order, meaning, purpose, sense, fixity, stability, permanence, security to our experience, and very early on, consciousness establishes, through its centripetal motion, a center point to the circle and the world created by the circle. This spot is marked by every culture as the naval, birthplace, centerpoint of the world by a totem pole or some symbol that serves the equivalent purpose- of fixing a point in space around which we might grow. We will find that this demand for fixity and permanence will be an essential and universal aspect to all human consciousness, and it may be conjectured that it is just this demand, this abstraction, that the circle of consciousness calls out and distinguishes from the world. We might make sense of this demand for fixity as the masculine principle in our consciousness (with fluidity and change as representative of the feminine), but, as we will see consciousness evolve, the flips and the flops of the masculine and the feminine will become dizzying at times.

This point of fixity creates a whirlpool of activity within the circle of our consciousness, but simultaneous with this inward motion, an outward movement is generated as well that moves in contrast/opposition to the movement within creating, thereby, balance, but also a tension, a "life," an experience, a world that did not exist before. An aperture is created at the center of these movements. The firmament which the light comes through.

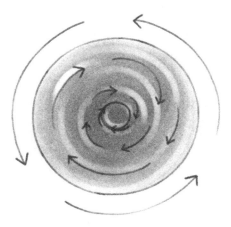

Viewed from the side, we see that it is a whirlpool forming.

An aperture is created

The outward or centrifugal movement takes place between the outer edge of our consciousness and the world of space and others that appears outside of us, beyond the limits of our body. This relation between what we call "I" and not-I remains, from the beginning to today, unresolved and ambivalent. We seek union with the other and the world but also feel alienation and disdain. We love and hate, are curious and wish to hide, but human consciousness does venture forth (ultimately, we do not have a choice; we are not allowed back inside the womb). And so, in our "conversation" with the world, we use exploration, observation, experimentation, and analysis to try to bridge the gap between the outside and the inside, the not-I and the I, and so, too, to make sense, bring order, gain mastery, earn stability. We also use love and emotion to connect. This encounter with the "outside" world represents the beginning of our science whereas the internal world is the birthplace of imagination. As we know, and will see more clearly, the two go hand and hand, yin and yang-like in the continuous development of consciousness.

The Impossible Representation

Human beings are unlike any other creature. God is unlike any other representation, because He is the representation of that essential aspect that distinguishes human beings from all other creatures. God is our representation of the seer- the one who knows but is not known. He is representative of our consciousness, our awareness of our self, the world, and others. God is the One impossible representation, because He knows no limits and cannot be defined. Any definition placed on Him (the fact that we refer to Him as a "Him" is one) must come from us- as a projection of our own limitations, our own definitions- and is not attributable to God.

It appears from our analysis of history that God is the first representation, even though He is the hardest and most impossible. It may be argued that every subsequent representation derives from Him, which is half the truth. Every possible representation derives from the discourse between God, the seer, and the scene.

God defines the limit of our own perceptions. He represents that which lies beyond our representations. In the early days of God's incarnation, He reflects back an intuition of the infinite that we feel inside ourselves, and, through this discourse with God, our consciousness grows. We learn to integrate these infinite aspects more and more thoroughly in our selves, and we learn of the finite aspects of our representation, God, as well. Through this discourse, we become more like God and God becomes more like us.

The reflection back:

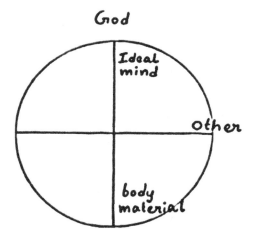

It is by looking through the eyes of God that we come to understand that we are a bubble of perception.

"Not Objects"

The circle and the cross create an internal realm, a necessary half of the world, that our own materialistic age has forgotten at our peril. There is a psychic half to all consciousness, defined by I and God and the structure of our consciousness. This half is formed through humans' miraculous power of representation, of abstraction, of separating a mental vantage point from our fixity in this body. We do not ever leave that body behind, but we can transcend it, we can go further than its limits even though we can never escape those limits.

The "not objects," the subjects, the human individuals created by this miracle are being neglected, denied, destroyed in our society's fetishistic loyalty to the objective, factual, material world.

Inside these "not objects" lies the wellspring of truth, connection, marriage between our bodies and our minds, between our will and our representations, between our Mother and the sky. The "not objects," you and I, are all that really matters. We are the site of consciousness and life, infinite and finite, and we are being destroyed by a dead and dying corporate machine that consumes human beings as fuel.

Circle and the Cross

I have struggled to make clear so far that this light, this infinite aspect that makes possible a world, comes through us — we human beings, at first, though we are not at first conscious of ourselves as the agents of this infinite aspect. The light breaks through us to reveal a surrounding world that we are left, through our science and our stories, to explain, but we humans, I am arguing, are the crucial element in the creation of a world. We draw the circle, we formulate the abstraction that creates the distance necessary for awareness to be born. Like stars. In the earliest days of consciousness, though, (by which I mean for millennia) we are not conscious of our consciousnesses. We have no consciousnesses of a light that creates a world.

The Birth of God, as described in the Judeo-Christian book of Genesis, marks a crucial and transformative moment in the history of consciousness second only to the first breakthrough of light, distance, and awareness in the moment of the deed. The single, all-powerful, all-knowing, and ever-present God of Genesis- provides the first representation of the infinite aspect of consciousness and the world.

God is an unfathomable construct, necessarily, because to be a representation implies and requires definition, limits, boundaries, and finitude, and God is a representation of the opposite. He is consciousness's representation of that which exceeds all representation, the first and crucial, enigmatic and impossible, representation of the infinite. He is God, and, as God, He represents the human aspiration for the infinite. But what a defining aspiration it is! And how this invention, how this first representation, changes everything! All we know from this point forward will be in the light of the One and infinite God. The Seer shifts his position and a new world of consciousness is born.

In trying to represent the first incarnation of human consciousness, I have pictured the light that creates a world as emanating from us and illuminating the multiplicity of "objects" out of which we construct meaning and a world. In the birth of God, the source of this light that creates a world shifts away from us. By thus placing the infinite aspect of consciousness outside ourselves, we are able to look at and see it for the first time.

In one way, this shift will be an act of ultimate humility and honesty, for though there be an infinite aspect to the world and consciousness, we must acknowledge, of course, that we are not it. We are little balls of matter, and as consciousness continues to unfold after the birth of God, there will be plenty of opportunities for this humility of man and humiliation of women to grow. In contrast, though, the invention of God will also ironically provide opportunities for hubris and the inflation of man's genius. We are little balls of matter capable of conceiving and perhaps becoming God.

In projecting the infinite aspect of consciousness onto God, we are able, for the first time, to see- to become conscious of- our self as well. The light of God shines on us and defines who we are and that we are. God, the infinite, reveals to us our finite self. We become "some body" with His help. This fact is clearly depicted in the Garden of Eden story where, with God, we come to knowledge of our self and other as well. The "curse" or cost of knowing God is the simultaneous, or immediate, experience of our own finitude and death. There is a God, and we are something else. And so begins the next round of supplications, similar to those we made earlier to our totem animals, to try and please our God, to approach Him, imitate Him, find favor in His eyes, to be the Chosen.

What follows from Genesis is the history of a people's quest to align themselves with this one true God and so to participate in the infinite aspect of life and human consciousness. The Old Testament traces humans' evolution from the mythological consciousness found in the Garden of Eden and before into a more "rational" understanding and explanation of our self, the world, others and the relations between the three. The story is an ugly one, and, if taken at face value, unbelievable and untrue. Viewed as a record of our developing consciousness, however, this testament to our journey towards enlightenment, reason, and law is illuminating and true. The story will include a series of murders that will bring us, simultaneously, nearer to God and further than we have ever been. These murders and their consequences will come to both define the particular trajectory of our civilization and the faith/story upon which it is based and will feed the dialectical unfolding of our consciousness down through the present day.

HIS STORY

Birth of Reason

1. The birth of God marks a crucial shift in strategy from myth to reason. With God's help, we commit ourselves to an embrace of that distance that separates us from "the world." Though we are pulled continuously by the gravity of old solutions, with the help of God, we will resist the temptation to collapse the distance and our consciousness and so return to darkness. Rather, we will dream of, and will work for, a re-solution to be found only at the end of a long journey in the light of God.

There came a time, once upon a time, in the lives of our Band of Brothers when they could not stand to be denied access to the females for a moment longer. Whether there was planning or the act was a spontaneous one, a tension had been building, a resentment, an emotion pent up until it had to express itself in action. And when it did, something changed in the lives and mind and experience of these brothers that they could not have anticipated. Perhaps, had they known the terror and separation they would face, they would not have acted, but they learn the consequences of their actions too late to go back. There is no crawling back into the womb.

birth of christ

And so it would be, too, for their descendants so many millennia hence when their mythological reunions were failing them and it became necessary that we try something new. For some, at least, the ambivalence and inherent vulnerability of our emotional reactions to our alienation/consciousness must have become unbearable and unsatisfactory to the point where something else had to be tried. Through our experience of rituals, worship, and sacrifice, we must have accumulated evidence of their failure, ineffectiveness, and untruth. We would have made modifications along the way, of course, tweaked our performances in an attempt to make them more effective, but such tweaks must have called the universality of their magic into still greater doubt. And there must have been, then as in any period in the history of our humanity, certain doubters, outliers, whackos who called into question our accepted practices. This handful of discontents would be ignored, of course (as they always are), then exiled, then stoned to death, but through it all, the seeds of doubt they had planted would eat away at our faith and confidence in our rituals. The doubt would spread gradually at first and then in leaps and bounds until it became overwhelming, and our rituals must have become more and more empty, more and more desperate, less and less satisfying, less and less true.

At this point in our development, some alternative solution was necessary. Some new truth was formulating itself in the unconscious minds of people until, miracle and mystery, God was born. In a flash, we saw the world, ourselves, and others in a whole new light. A new and better truth was born- a truth that promised liberation from the tyranny and vulnerability of human bodies and emotion. We realized through a miraculous reversal of consciousness that what we had previously seen as the problem to be resolved (our psychic separation from the world) was, in fact, the solution to our suffering, meaningless, vulnerability, and, perhaps even, death.

The birth of God is, in fact, the birth of reason- a new and promising solution to the contradictions that humans, through mythological explanations, had tried so hard and unsuccessfully to resolve. Reason- and the projection of the infinite God- turns these mythological solutions on their head and establishes a new strategy for liberation that continues to inform our thinking and quest for freedom down through the present day. The strategy of reason, the infinite God (and Judaism, Christianity, science, and technology that will grow from them) is to embrace and accentuate our distance from the world- to exaggerate it as far as possible until- in the end- the infinite aspect of consciousness may at last be liberated from the prison of the world, body, emotions.

2. In <u>Moses and Monotheism</u>, Sigmund Freud makes much of the transition in consciousness marked by the Old Testament mythology of God and his Chosen people. For Freud, the Bible marks the beginning of "the Word," the birth of humans' capacity for abstraction freed from material representations and images. Thus the reason for the consistent and virulent prohibition in the Old Testament against worshipping idols. A prohibition that will eventually be taken to an extreme in the Moslem prohibition against images of God or humans in Islamic art. The monotheistic God fights to replace the multiplicity of gods represented in the early totemic, mythological explanations. The birth of Yahweh begins the long tyranny of the Sun God against the many gods of night. The transition is not easy and is not without violence.

The projection of a distant and infinite God into the world corresponds with an awakening awareness of a remote and infinite aspect in our self. The projection of this infinite and all-knowing aspect marks a transition point to a growing consciousness of our self. It also marks the beginning of the scientific and rational "truth" which is a reversal of the previous mythological strategy.

Mythology prior to the monotheistic God sought reunion with the external world we were separated from with the birth of consciousness. The Jewish God represents a fundamental shift in strategy that will find fulfillment in the physics of Newton, the method of Bacon, the biology of Darwin, and the economics of Adam Smith. We find ourselves surrounded by, swallowed up in, the material incarnations of this vision/strategy/explanation that first gained birth in the Jewish Old Testament and the Garden of Eden. Like Jonah in the whale, we are in the Belly of the Beast.

The monotheistic, Jewish God embodies a new strategy for consciousness whereby the distance between mind and body is accentuated rather than closed. It is the opposite of previous myth which sought, through totemistic rituals to bridge the gap, to heal the rift between mind and body. This strategy seeks, instead, to create as wide a distance as possible. In so doing, it represents a shift in values towards freedom, transcendence, discipline, reason, and men.

To make this shift in consciousness possible, Freud argues in <u>Moses and Monotheism</u>, requires a second murder- a repetition- this time of the bringer of the Word, Moses. While I appreciate Freud's argument about the bringer of the truth, here, as always, women are beneath Freud's consideration. Without the kind of trauma and sublimation that comes through murder, Freud argues, such a dramatic shift in consciousness, such a complete reversal in our understanding of the world, is not possible. Freud's analysis is consistent with my understanding of how murder, trauma, sublimation, and repetition might work, but-dialectically, mythologically- it makes more sense that the murder in question was of women, the leaders of the matriarchy, at the hands of those who stand to most benefit from the imposition of this new God- our Band of Brothers on the outskirts who, telling each other tales of their own supremacy so long they start believing it as truth, over time, release a pent-up powerlessness and rage and decide finally to "make it so."

The Garden of Eden and Western Society Today

We still have to deal with the cultural consequences of our particular creation myth, and here, as elsewhere in our journey to excavate the truth about the origins and history of our human consciousness, we are left with a dilemma of the chicken or the egg variety. Did our understanding of the world's creation lead us to develop our society and culture in the directions that we did? Or was it our culture and society that projected its values and perspectives backwards onto that first moment(s) in human consciousness? Here, as elsewhere, the answer must be both.

Either way, the details of our origin myth, reflective of the unconscious assumptions of its authors, will serve to elucidate the peculiarities of our culture that have led to a unique form of madness in our present day, a madness we must break through if we are to save our planet and heal our damaged souls.

We have to figure that when he and Eve were cast out of Eden by an angry God, Adam was pissed. It could not have come as welcome news that he was disinherited by his wealthy Parent and that, instead of life in paradise, would have to work and suffer onto the end of days. Clearly, his anger may have been channeled in one of two directions (it was beyond the pale of possibility that he could blame himself), and it was doubtless easier to be angry with Eve than with an all-powerful and vengeful Father.

birth of christ

As for Eve, she must have felt quite underappreciated and disrespectful of a husband who lacked balls enough to stand up to his Father and who now blamed her for their misfortune when she, at least, had the courage to act, to exert her will, to be. And so the seeds of their unhappy family life were sown from the beginning. Our alienation from the world and other creatures will be built in as well. Through Adam, we are given dominion over the animals, not one with them but their ruler- separate, above them, better than, in the image of God.

"Do something, even if it's wrong"- that's Eve's philosophy. Adam would be more of the "If it ain't broke, don't fix it" school, and in my own philosophy and life I must admit to a greater affinity to Eve and a closer connection to the serpent than to this "all powerful" God lording over us to keep us small.

Eve embodies the centrifugal force in human society- dissatisfaction, movement, curiosity, change; Adam is her opposite, centripetal force of stasis, happiness, security, and permanence. It is interesting and baffling (and increasingly difficult to describe using the linear tool of written language) how thoroughly these two interpenetrate each other- the yin and yang of christianity. It becomes unclear, in our own christian schema of the world whether Adam represent the circle (what we normally speak of as the feminine aspect) and Eve the four rivers (normally the masculine) that lead us outward toward the infinite or if it is the other way around. This confusion to our schema shows how fully each penetrates the other, and how each turns into the other- the Two become as One- the closer we get to the center of truth, to the beginning of time, or to the crux of the story.

Adam and Eve are locked into a shared destiny, each denying culpability, and each dependent on the other. Separate, but one, they are two finitudes in search of the infinite- each competing with, and potentially completing, the other in their quest. The fundamental error we, their progeny, have made- the error that needs to be corrected in order for us to grasp the next circle of christian truth- is that we have taken sides in this battle between Adam and Eve.

Throughout its history, the Christian Church has aligned itself with Adam, who is set to "rule over" Eve. Adam is steadfast in his faith, always putting the brakes on, trying to contain (draw a circle around) the excesses of his mate. Eve is the law breaker, God the rule maker, Adam the enforcer, and the Church is Adam's army in the world.

As Western civilization continued to develop along these Christian lines, we moved from our original mythological understandings to a more objective and rational description of the world achieved by the process of further separating our mind from matter. We began to take a longer view, and to examine the world from the disinterested perspective of a scientist. Descartes was one crucial voice in this movement- who sought to find only what he could know for certain- through the exercise of his pure reason divorced from emotion and the subjectivity of his perceptions. Scientists like Bacon and Newton helped advance the cause as they sought to explain the world through observation and the testing of hypotheses. They sought pure, objective proof and facts and so further distinguished truth from our animal instincts, feelings, and our bodies.

The strategy of scientists and technologists- down to the present day- was an extension of that strategy begun by Adam and the Church- to distance ourselves from our human, animal, feminine aspects and endeavor to view the world from a more objective and disinterested perspective-like God.

With time these two- mind and body- human reason and the earth- will become more and more fully differentiated until, through science, we will seek a reconciliation of the two by a complete divorce and separation. In the end (we are at the end), this strategy will prove impossible and dangerous. The negative consequences of our technological solutions and objective systems that are everywhere today are a direct consequence of this strategy that began back before time, in our mythological consciousness when we identified ourselves with a God divorced from Mother and aligned ourselves with Adam over Eve.

To reverse this historical error that, if it is not changed, will kill us, does not require, then, a denial of God, or Christianity, or Adam, or of science, or of reason. We need to hang on to all these things, but, together with these things, we must also embrace our Mother, native wisdom, Eve, story, and the truth of our emotions. The new Circle of Truth is not based on an Either/Or foundation like the old one. It is time for human beings to discover and to realize a new Both/And foundation for the christian truth.

Our mistake has been to conceptualize it as a battle at all, where the two sides seek to dominate, suppress, overwhelm and/or destroy the other. We have forgotten, with God, and the leaders of the Church, and the scientists, that the Two are, in fact, One- that we, ourselves, are Two- and always will be. It is time now to remember, to embrace the creative tension of the dialectic within our world and within our psyches. It is time to remarry our Father and our Mother. We Humans have the power to heal these mortal wounds, and that is what makes us- not like, but greater than, our God.

Old Testament Murders

There is one human story, but it can be told in many ways. The universal and fundamental structure of human consciousness

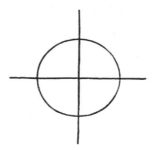

will determine, to a large degree, the course consciousness will follow through its evolution, but for individual human beings as well as entire civilizations, unique circumstances and decisions will also shape its peculiar destiny and make it different than any other that has gone before or after. Beginning with Genesis and continuing on throughout the Old Testament, the Judeo-Christian path diverges significantly from any other. The path we strike will have profound negative consequences, for sure, but it will also open opportunities that would never have been discovered if not for our possibly perverse journey.

First events following man's exile from the Garden of Eden do not bode well for men nor God. Faced with an irrational and shaming decision by his grandfather, Cain is inflamed against his God and takes his rage out on his brother, Abel. We see in these first events of God's life an ambiguity and immorality, an irreason and cruelty in God's judgment that is reflective of our own.

We see a repetition of the first murder with all of the same ambivalent feelings at work, but in this murder, brother is turned against brother by his father, God. The unholy alliance white men make with

God, first through Adam against Eve and now through Abel against Cain, carries substantial benefits but at a very steep price. These first either/or decisions divide us against ourselves but leave open the possibility of "being like God." In our identification with God and Adam against Eve, we choose the mind, reason, and abstraction over body, emotion, and life. In our identification with God and Abel over Cain, we choose I over the other and so leave out the possibility of an all-encompassing we.

What is striking about this decision is that we know that God is wrong, unfair, unjust in his rejection of Cain's offering, but in bad faith we align ourselves with God through Abel just the same. This murder and resulting alliance sets the pattern of making enemies of the other, of our brothers, just as our alliance with Adam over Eve sets the pattern for our denigration of women, our bodies, and the Earth.

As payment for this alliance with God, as payment for this submission to God, man will be granted greater mastery, security, and control over his own destiny, the world, and others. He pays for his mastery, though, with continuous strife, guilt, unhappiness, loneliness, frustration, and complicity in past and future murders.

Through Abraham, the father of the Jews, we are faced with yet another choice, another either/or, another sacrifice, another murder of our humanity. God tests Abraham's loyalty to Him by demanding the sacrifice of Isaac, his beloved son. The story recorded in the Bible says that once Abraham had made clear his allegiance to God, as he brought the knife to Isaac's throat, God provided a surrogate, a ram. But given what we have since learned about how memories- and especially traumatic memories- are stored by human consciousness, we must know that God's ram is a lie. A fig leaf designed to hide the truth we cannot bear- that our father Abraham killed his son in obedience to God.

Now it may be his other son- Ishmael- whom he killed, or perhaps Ishmael and Isaac were one child divided by consciousness's limited capacity to digest the horror/truth, but Abraham murdered his son in obedience to God's command. Here, again, we have a repetition of the Deed, but this time it is the father who turns against the son in loyalty to an idea/ a phantasy/ a fiction/ representation/ abstraction- God.

This God gives man gifts in exchange for these murders. He makes of them the Chosen Ones and sets them above all other humans (also known as enemies). And more than that, God shares with man His power of abstraction. He passes down the Word to man. He gives to man the Law by which we govern relations with each other. Man is bound by his obedience to God's law, of course, that is part of the compact between God and man, but God can continue on- as He did with Cain and Abel- to do just as He pleases. God is above the Law He gives to man, through Moses. And substantial benefits do accrue to man from God's law. We are able to achieve a greater degree of mastery, power, and control through the implementation of that Law, though that stability and power must be gained by the subjugation of our enemies, of our women, of our emotions, of our instincts, and of all other living things.

Sigmund Freud argues that Moses must have been killed by the Jews, his chosen people. Only through such trauma, repression, and sublimation, Freud argues, would the people be willing and able to give up what is in their immediate self interest in favor of some abstraction like the Law. It is an essential element of this new Jewish faith that no image may be made of other gods. The sin of worshipping idols is more consistently punished and condemned than indecent fornication. This shift from mythological consciousness to reason requires a shift from material incarnations to abstractions- to fabrications of the human mind.

The attractions of life and the material world are much more immediate and persuasive and irresistible than the attractions of an idea. That is why terror is employed to turn folks away from their idols, from their bodies to the ideal. Once turned, the magnetic attraction of God, the abstract, disembodied, purely rational idea is the possibility of infinity and eternity- the hope and promise that we might be Gods- who live in peace, for eternity, and have no limits to our power. Through loyalty to God we seek material and emotional stability. We turn to God to stop the madness of emotions and an added promise of worldly success- a mastery over others, riches, land and security to those who can practice some delay to their gratifications and so live in accordance with God's laws.

Beginning with the tablets brought by Moses, the Word and Law grants God-like powers to those human beings who learn to master them. You and me are participants in this God-like power and world view in this very moment. Our identification with God was designed to lift us out of the limits of the world and death and others, to grant us God-like dominion over that world and the others that, through our Law and Word and God, we set ourselves against.

We turned to God and reason to escape the ambivalence and vulnerability we suffered under the old mythological explanations of the world. We turned these explanations on their head, we aligned ourselves with God against our own bodies, against our own women, against our own brothers, against, even, our own sons, with an eye towards immortality and unlimited power- like God, our Father. Did the gamble pay off? Did we realize our dreams? Did we find truth, peace, eternal life, and power? No. But perhaps we found- will find- something else, something we did not expect to find or seek- something still more precious, but it is a long way before that end.

Job

Inexplicably, it seems to God, His Chosen fail in their obedience to God's Word and Law, but however frustrated He may be, God does not give up. There are still good men who live in obedience to God's law, not for any worldly gain but for the sake of truth and faith alone, and Job is such a one. Job marks a turning point in the life of God and the Judeo-Christian consciousness He rules.

Satan appears in the Book of Job for the first time since crawling on his belly in the form of the Serpent way back before the birth of time. If he has appeared since then in the Old Testament history, I have missed him, he was subtle, alluded to, hinted at at best, but here Satan takes center stage alongside Job and God. He talks to God and tempts Him. He says to God that His loyal servant, Job, is only loyal because of the earthly gains he has accrued through his devotion to the Lord. God defends His man. He argues on behalf of Job that he is a better man than that and motivated only by his love of God.

Satan lays the gauntlet down; he dares God to test Job's faith, and God tells Satan He will prove it. He heaps every possible torment upon his loyal servant, Job, and still Job does not waver in his faith. Job does not waver, but for the first time in the history of God, Job does question why. Job is remarkable, a hero, because Job questions God.

And in response, God has no answers to Job's questions. God responds with infantile bluster and intimidation, but it is too late in the game for God's infantile stratagems to work. Men have learned. Consciousness has grown through our previous experiences and suffering with our

Lord. Job has suffered enough to know. He sees through God, and though he does not argue back (Job knows what happens when you argue back with God), Job knows. And through Job, we know, and through Job, we see how, touchingly, even God knows as well, though He can't admit it.

Job's eyes are opened and he knows that God is not all-powerful as He claims. God is not all-knowing and even God has limits. For me, these few moments of silence that God and his loyal servant, Job, share in the wake of God's petulance are among the most poignant in the whole Judeo-Christian story, rivaling even the most important moments in Christ's life. For a moment Job sees into God, and God sees Himself reflected back- in all His powerlessness and shame, all His loneliness and sadness, and in that moment, something happens to our God. He becomes more human. God becomes more real, and, for the first time, there is a beginning of a genuine recognition, a real relationship between humans and God. And, miraculously this time, God allows His servant, teacher, Job, to live.

We turned, so long ago, to God in order to escape the ambivalence, the vulnerability and terror that we suffered under the old mythological consciousness, but here, at the other side of God's story, we have found that the vulnerability, the terror, and the ambivalence have not gone away. Through Job's eyes, and with the help of Satan, we see for the first time the new instrument of our torture, the lying, angry, lonely, childish "God," and in so seeing Him, we (through Job) still love Him. The ambivalence persists and so causes us to rethink our strategies, what it means to be a human being, and where we must look to seek our truth and freedom.

God as Representation

The Jewish God gives us a Law to follow, based on objective principles and reason. With this law comes certain intrinsic benefits. Through it, we will expand our knowledge of the world and so will achieve greater comfort and security. The law demands cooperation between people and so may result in greater peace, understanding, and invention. Each individual will have to sacrifice a proportion of his animal instincts and desires in order to join in this Holy union, and, to do so, a man will be expected to rule himself in accordance with God's law.

God, Himself, is exempt from the Law. He may- and does- act in the most petulant, angry, and irrational manner, and we will call it good. Under God's law, human beings are expected to behave rationally with one another, and that is good, but God does not have to, and that is good as well.

This "God," of course, is just us- that is, He is man's best representation of the infinite, and, as our history will show, it takes time to perfect that image.

As an illustration of the role God plays in our consciousness at this point, it may help to think of consciousness as a bubble. Each individual stands inside his own bubble. "I", as the "creator" of this consciousness, stand at the center. On the inside wall of this bubble "I" project my idea of God- the infinite aspect of myself. Consciousness consists of, and grows from, the dialectic between these two- the center and the horizon, the body and the mind, the material and the ideal, the finite and the infinite, the representation and the idea. This interaction of two aspects within myself is stimulated through interactions with the bubbles that stand outside myself, and it is with these others that

I may really enjoy some benefit through the laws and reason made possible by my (however imperfect) understanding of God.

The story of Cain and Abel establishes the necessity of laws to govern the relations between brothers, but not without an intense ambivalence towards that law and its source, God. Man realizes the necessity for law after his experiences with the chaos in governance that followed the Deed, but to establish some foundation for that law, he must turn back to the one he killed. The dead father is resurrected in an idealized form as God, our Father, and we ask Him to make the rules and regulate man's relations to man. We may wonder why human beings accepted such petulance and injustice from their God, and why they did not demand better. Well, one answer is that not everybody did turn to this God. It would take a lot of convincing and coercion and murders and time to get the Jewish people to choose this God. Another answer would be that no one had the power to dethrone Him, and so God carried on in His influence over people because might makes right.

The best explanation of our tolerance for the shortcomings of this God, though, is that He was the best God we could imagine at the time. We must remember that we are asking a most immature consciousness that has only recently given birth to itself to formulate a representation of its own perfection. Clearly, God is a most infantile and inadequate image of perfection, but we were infantile and inadequate consciousnesses. God did get better over time, as we will see, until one point where He becomes almost human.

The Old Testament is really the history of God's birth and development. That is, the Old Testament is the history of man's representation of his own infinitude and perfection. God is an aspect of ourselves that we have projected out from ourselves. In some ways (and according to the Old Testament authors) He is our better half, but in other ways,

HIS STORY

He is our lesser half (Satan). We human beings engage in dialogue with this projection, this representation, this God to improve ourselves and to improve our relations with my brothers- to become "good," that is, to become more like God.

The Old Testament records the history of man's approach to God. It is God who reveals to us our dual nature- as body and as mind, as I and other, as finite and infinite beings. In this moment of first transcendence, this first moment of consciousness of consciousness, the white man's path takes a different direction than other cultures and religious traditions. In many other places, like the Taoist culture in Asia and in the belief systems developed by many turtle island tribes, spiritual practices, traditions and myths developed that allowed human beings to reconcile and embrace the two necessarily contrasting aspects to consciousness and the world. The yin-yang is the most enduring symbol of this generative duality. In the story of the Bible and Genesis, however, man is forced to choose up sides, and that has made all the difference.

The birth of God, and the transcendent perspective, coincides with that moment in our psychical history when we apply the cross (discrimination, differentiation, science) to the circle (miraculous womb of human consciousness) to create a world. What happens next- and why white man's culture moves in the direction it does- remains a mystery that, we might speculate, bears some relation to the first Deed that served to spark our consciousness in the first place. And we must consider whether "the Deed" is not, perhaps, unique to white man's consciousness. Perhaps the seed for our divergence was planted in the first moment of our birth.

birth of christ

Either/Or

What makes the white man's consciousness unique, problematic, and revelatory is its unusual devotion to, and identification with, the transcendent perspective of God. Long before there is the Christian Trinity, there is the original trinity, born in "the Fall," of God, Other, and I. This triunal development of consciousness (where human beings observe their own dual nature from a third, "transcendent" point) is not unusual. It is even necessary to the development of consciousness around the world.

But what is remarkable about the white man's strategy is the unique alliance and identification between God and man against the woman. Whereas in other cultures, the I and Other (the yin and yang) enjoy equal allegiance, in Western culture, human beings are turned against themselves. They identify with an idea, an abstraction, the murdered Father, perhaps, against their own bodies, their own women, their own emotions, their own life, and their own Mother. It does not seem too extreme to me to call such an allegiance "perverse," "unnatural," even "insane," especially as we consider the stories and the consequences of this decision throughout the history of our people.

It makes sense that white man's culture was born from a particularly traumatic set of experiences from the early mythological epoch, because the Western reaction to that era and its solutions were so extreme and desperate. Western man- descendants of Adam- identify with the abstraction, the idea of God against their body and life, represented by Eve.

The circle and the cross are the two necessary aspects that, in combination, make human consciousness and the world possible. But what Western man does is to choose up sides- to see these mutually generative aspects of consciousness as competing forces between which we must choose. And Western man chooses the cross against the circle. Abstracted from the circle of life, the cross brings fixity and permanence. It brings discrimination and science, reason and abstraction, and because it is divorced from the body and the physical limitations of matter, it brings the possibility of infinitude and freedom.

The fact remains for Western, white men, however, that we do have bodies, we are born of women, and we die. These are terribly frustrating facts that the Judeo-Christian faith, and the civilizations that grow out of them, strive continually to overcome. Through this striving, we have attained an inconceivable degree of madness and destruction. We have also opened the door to salvation and a new birth of human consciousness; if only we can make it through the door in time.

Human beings are mind and body. Western man chooses mind. Human beings are rational and emotional. Western man chooses reason. Human beings are finite and infinite. Western man chooses infinitude. Human beings are masculine and feminine. Western man chooses the masculine in contrast to the matriarchal, mythical, emotional, material, and finite epoch that they have struggled to be freed of. We cannot be one without the other, of course- mind freed of the limits of our body, but Western man will not accept this reality. There must be a way to transcend these limits, to overcome death and finitude, to become like Gods, and, so, at the fundamental root of this most rationalist society possible stands this germ of unreason, this fundamental denial of the facts, and this fundamental unreason is embodied with perfect petulance and obtuseness by our Judeo-Christian God.

Murder of Isaac

Freud's analysis of the First Murder and how that murder gets stored in our human memory will help us to understand the Father of the Jews, Abraham, and his relation to both son and God. Abraham is instructed by God to kill his only son, Isaac, and in obedience to this God, this voice inside his head, Abraham follows directions and does as he is told. He continues in obedience until that moment when, having proven his dedication and intent to put God before his only begotten son, God intervenes and presents a substitute- a ram- for Abraham's sacrifice. It is interesting, and a little confusing, that this animal sacrifice would be sanctioned by God and the Father of the Jews when the religion they will henceforth promote so consistently opposes the worship of idols.

I would argue, rather, that we get only part of the story of Abraham's sacrifice of Isaac from the Old Testament authors. Which is not to say that they lied to us, but, rather, that they lied to themselves. Consciousness could not bear the full memory of the murder of Isaac, and so, it was human consciousness, in its horror and self-revulsion, that, over time, replaces the ram for Isaac. We could not bear the whole and unadulterated truth- that the father of our faith is a murderer- of his own son- and that it was our God who forced him into this most inhumane act.

Such beginning to our tradition is too terrible to contemplate, or has been for all these millennia, but, in retrospect, it certainly makes more sense that the substitution of the ram, the fig leaf, the lie we use to cover that which is too horrible to contemplate.

What Abraham's murder of his only son, Isaac/Ishmael, does establish is a revolutionary loyalty to an idea- of God- over life itself. This first moment/murder in the history of Judaism (and, in turn, Christianity and Islam) establishes Judaism's and Christianity's fundamental hostility to the human body and to life. Abraham, and Judeo-Christianity, pose a conflict and make a choice. They establish an either/or in consciousness, a black and white distinction that requires human beings to choose sides with one or the other. It is an irony of history that this act- Abraham's murder of his only son, Isaac- establishes the concept of Good and Evil necessary to the Christian and Jewish understanding of the world until today.

Perhaps the act is so horrible that it requires us to distance ourselves from it. We cannot accept that part of ourselves that would commit such an act as our self. It must be some thing, some one else who is responsible- who is evil, "not us," even though it is our God who gives the orders and our Father who wields the sword.

There is some legitimacy, then, to the modern critics of Christianity who claim that it is a faith founded in death and a hostility to humanity and life. It may be argued that this alienation of consciousness was a necessary stage in the unfolding of our consciousness, and as horrendous and ridiculous as it appears to us today, it did serve the purpose of drawing human reason away from its dependency upon the world, subjective reactions, and the emotions.

Band of Brothers

Here, at the end of days, we look back and make conscious the patterns, the truths that have hitherto driven our action but can no longer hold us. The beginning- whether in Freud's deed or Abraham's murder of Isaac- is an unnatural separation, a shocking division.

birth of christ

I am neither scholar nor anthropologist. I just look for patterns, and what I see is a pattern whereby, for a large swath of our histories, people mostly ruled themselves through communal networks established in balance and harmony with the surrounding world. Plentiful resources were accessible through our necessary (to see anything at all) awareness of our oneness with all living things. As I speculate here, it was this type of community- a We- that grew out of the first shock of human consciousness- whatever its origin- and gave rise to our first human technologies and applications of reason. I speculated, and Freud ignored the fact, that these communities were matriarchies- stable, enduring communities led by women in harmony with nature.

Here we may also speculate as to the state of our brotherhood under such matriarchy. As Freud's story goes, the goal of the first murder was to gain access to the women that, until now, had been prohibited by the more powerful man. Now that man is removed, but access to women is still denied our brothers. In point of fact, there is little place or need for this band in a society so well attuned to the plants and creatures surround them. Men gather on the outskirts of town to play useless games and wrestle. At night, they drink around the fire and tell stories of their prowess to enthrall the young ones, but that gruel grows thin without new and future action. They grow restless on the margins, and one or two begin to plot revenge.

To make sense of this development, I must risk the observation that this band of brothers is "not all men." Even in the first revolution/ murder of that alpha man, not all males in the community would have participated nor been invited to participate. It is a select group, an elite, superior to others, that makes up this band; an invitation and initiation is required and a price to be paid for admission to the group. Together, they share a precious (trauma) bond best exemplified by- and continually replicated and reenacted since- the original deed.

Mostly, it is a Lie they share, this He-Man Women Haters Club. The creation of Yahweh and, so, the creation of the whole western world from the idea of Him- like an explosion from the godhead/seed, Yahweh- this development in history was by no means necessary. It could have been- maybe should have been- snuffed out at any number of moments in its history- especially in the earliest days. It is a tribute to the tenacity and stubbornness of these early Jewish men- the passion of their commitment- to carry on through years of struggles to keep the Lie alive. And it is not like this movement was breaking out all around the world, like butterflies grow from caterpillars. No. Judaism is unnatural. An abnormality and aberration.

Not to be mean about it. Really. It's a Uranian genius- this complete reversal of the Jews. First, on the outskirts of town, our band imagines this all-powerful, all-knowing, self-sufficient Creator, answerable to no one, and- here's the best part- He's <u>their</u> guy! It's right, He's made of them His Chosen Ones! And in His image, they are meant to rule all others.

A brilliant adolescent phantasy, in full accordance with the Deed, but like a cancerous growth, you know. A tiny part of the body "gets sick," isolates itself, and turns against the whole. We don't notice at first. Glad they have buddies to hang out with. It's nothing- a small itch and secrecy about where they go at night. Untreated, though, this pre-cancerous cell persists, latent, waiting for the right moment to act. And every time, we fail to see their plotting until too late.

It is when we hand over our boys- failing to notice nor intervene as they head out there at night (these days on the internet) to hear the

birth of christ

stories these half-men tell; we hand the band of brothers the opportunity they have been waiting for.

Jews choose a path <u>against</u> Nature. This is a religion for men and by men, founded upon a single act- the imaginary severance of Union and denial of Life. Their disembodied God best represents this principle of severance. He who alone creates the whole world; God is everything <u>except</u> alive. He is a God still in the early days of divorce and separation from our Mother. He is petulant and angry; no doubt hurt, feeling insecure and sad, though, as God, He can't show- or even feel- any of that. You just need to bury that shit if you're God…or a (professional, Christian, Jewish) man in His image. Only violence is an acceptable expression of emotion, in the image of God, to exert man's control/true dominion.

Like a magnifying glass in the sun, Yahweh and His Jews bring the burning intensity and focus of man's reason; all else is worshipping idols. It is this concentration that makes them strong. I do not know the history of the Jews and how they somehow manage to establish their own community and survive long enough for Christianity to come and catch their spark. Much of their endurance must come from the Jews' (the elder mens') tyranny over their own women and children (in the image of God). The Jews do not seem intent upon conquering others likes the Christians would be. Jews were- still are, from what I see- more interested in conquering themselves.

From the perspective of Jews, the birth of Christ is not seen as any kind of boon to their power. The extension of their dominion was never intended to include non-Jews, and these unwashed Christian usurpers are viewed with the contempt they deserve from the true, original, the real Chosen Ones.

By the way, as patriarchy grows, the Jews do benefit from the extension of God's dominion through Christianity and, even more, from the return to science and reason- the Jewish wheel house- in the modern day. Jews have privilege as OGs, like the Yankees do. A swagger and confidence that comes from being around the game longer than anybody else. They seem even to have overcome their contempt for others- the Jews. Contempt is for those more insecure with their place in the brotherhood- trying to get in at another's expense, trying to impress with their ruthless words and shameless acts.

THE GESTURE

God so loves human beings that He sends to them His only begotten son, and Jesus is their name.

God's First Gesture of Love

We have every reason to be mad at God. He got off to a really bad start in His relation to our Mother and the model He set for us, and I can understand those of you who are unable to forgive Him (I have never much believed in forced apologies). Eventually, however, God did demonstrate some capacity to learn and an attempt, at least, at love.

It is always easy to blame others for a problem, and others will always give us errors upon which to pin our blame, but it is harder to look to ourselves. In fairness, though, that is what we must do when we come to consider the reception God received in His first, courageous act of love. Unable to, Himself, become of flesh and blood, God sent us His only son, to share in our suffering and death. In this gesture of sacrifice and union, God assumes the pain and trauma, the helplessness and sorrow that every parent feels. Even if, like other first parents, God had no idea when He acted what it was that He was in for, He made the leap of faith, just the same, in our direction and chose to accept the consequences of His act, His love, His gesture towards we human beings, whatever they may be.

Let us consider, then, how we received the son of God, how we responded to God's gift. Are we to think, really, that God gave birth to a mortal son, knowing that he would be crucified in anguish at the age of 33? Granted that Jesus could be a pain in the ass and holier than thou at times, did he deserve to be crucified? Was that fair or just, compassionate or wise?

God accepted the sorrow of finitude that comes necessarily with parenthood, and we denied to Him and His son the joy. In so acting, it could be argued, we were merely following God's example of vengeance, power, and merciless control. Fair enough. I accept the truth of that, but, as they say, "two wrongs don't make a right." We might have acted differently, but we didn't. We killed God's son. He was so annoying.

And quite contrary to the contemporary Christian view that "Christ died for our sins," I would argue, rather, that Christ dies from our sins. Man's crucifixion of Christ does not purge our sins (Christ does not take our sins with him- that is one of those historical reversals- inversions of the truth- i.e. lies that, we will all realize someday, patriarchal reason has habitually used to cover its own guilt). The crucifixion of Christ mires us in sin- in the murder of an innocent. For "the first time," we human beings, we men "have blood on our hands." We do what has hitherto been the work of God- vengeance, retribution, deciding who dies and when and why.

Christ dies because of our sins. He dies when we sin against him, and so Christ's assassination becomes the occasion for us to take on, to assume responsibility for, our own culpability and sin. But instead of shouldering that responsibility for actions that are most certainly our own, we shirk that responsibility and cast it upon, project it upon an other- on Jesus, himself. We sin doubly against Jesus and his father, God. We men murder Jesus and then cast his body back to Heaven- back to where it came from. We make of him a Christ. We use the myth of Christ's resurrection to cover up our crime and as proof of our redemption.

As human beings, we each endure experiences of loss and pain that have a crushing effect on our emotions and our souls, but, if God has emotions (and, I would argue, that beginning with the birth of Christ, He would). Beginning with the birth of Christ, God enters into the realm of finitude. Though at secondhand, He becomes incarnate in matter; the pain and loss that God must feel would dwarf any pain that you and I may go through. He has given birth to an only son. That son is killed by the very ones He hoped to serve by birthing him, and then those killers claim the son's death as evidence of their own salvation and union with God through this son. Viewed objectively, God reaps what He has sown, and the vengeance that He once showed men is now turned back on Him. His first gesture of love is rejected and killed by those very ones it was meant to serve, and still today, men have failed to learn the right lessons from their treason and revenge against this God they claim to love and love. Just as it took God, their model, multiple opportunities to finally recognize the error of His way, so it is with humans.

Both/And

Christ represents something new to the Western mind, a new idea, but, more than that, a new reality, that we respond to by its annihilation. But as we often see in the history of consciousness, no idea can die forever. There is something immortal and enduring in the idea/the

birth of christ

reality of christ that, while we may seek to destroy it in the time of men, the idea and reality will resurrect itself and, in the interim, will have worked upon us- underground, in the unconscious of our mind and experience- until we are now ready to receive this enduring truth.

In christ, God gives man a correction to their original error. We can argue whether this original error- that is, man's allegiance with God, the infinite against his body, self- came from God or man. A case may be made against either, but really it is both God and man responsible for this infantile construction of duality in the shape of either/or. It is both God and man responsible, too, because they are really one and the same "person." They are Will (man) and Representation (God) of the same life force.

And so, we made an error. It caused great pain and destruction- and still it does, because it has not ended. But, together, through the dialectic of our experience between our "ideas" and "reality" (the representations of the others) we have to generate a new conceptualization of the truth. We see, now, that the duality of human consciousness and human life is not an either/or, but both/and; God embodies that truth in His gift to us, His only son.

This time, though, God is far ahead of us in His understanding. We kill His idea, His new reality, His son, and in mourning for our sin, we compound that sin by turning the message of the life and death of God's Son into the exact opposite of His true and intended significance. By this reversal we wound our God in His moment of greatest humanity and compassion, and so we wound ourselves and set back the progress of our own hearts, our own consciousness, until now.

Murder of God

Through his crucifixion, we men turn Jesus into Christ. We bring him "closer to (our previous understanding of) God." In sending Christ to heaven, we cast him from us and so cast ourselves from him as well. God's presence among us was more than human beings could bear, and so we acted to restore our previous balance (imbalance) and understanding (misunderstanding) and relationship to (alienation from) God.

The crucifixion of Christ is a reenactment of both God, our Father's, original sin and our own original Deed. Christ's crucifixion restores the previous division that God's gesture of love was intended to bridge. In the original incarnation of this error, God cast human beings from Him. In this second incarnation, the reenactment, we humans cast out God.

Upon the foundation of this repetition, humans- men-build a civilization we call Christian, though it is anything but. The civilization we've built is based on a fundamental limit in our human understanding. Western civilization is based on a mistaken understanding of God's gesture and the meaning, significance, and person of jesus christ. We translate, we reduce down, the infinitude of christ, the magnitude of God's love, to terms we finite human beings can comprehend. We boil it down to/with reason. And so, though we human beings built a civilization on the idea of Christianity, christianity, itself, remains still to be born.

Men make from God's gift of christ a "Holy Trinity" upon which we build a Church, a civilization, a whole, entire world. Cast out as he was from fellowship, communion, and contemporaneous existence with man, Jesus is transformed by us into a distant God we worship and

birth of christ

can pray to. We miss the point and bite the hand that would save us. christ's love is more than we can bear, and we seek refuge, of course, in terms that we can understand, God's original terms by which we defined the world before the advent of christ.

Unforgiveable as humans' crucifixion of jesus christ must be, we must forgive them nonetheless. Just as we forgive God His unforgivable errors at the Beginning, so we must simultaneously own and forgive, too, the errors of humanity- the errors of ourselves and the errors of the others- that we may transcend and remedy them now in the future.

But just as God's errors persist throughout the Old Testament and even into the birth of christ, itself (through God's marginalization of Mary, mother of christ), so, too, do man's errors persist beyond the original crucifixion down through the present day. Not only do they- we- commit an unforgivable sin, but we persist in that sin, exacerbate that sin, justify that sin, deny that sin, and so refuse to give up on that sin until, at last, the entire planet stands in jeopardy of annihilation.

One who claims to be "born again" in this false Christ, this bastardization of christ's name and significance, has, in fact, only died to their own humanity. Humanity I define as a responsibility for, and an embrace of, the blackness that is in me and the light that is in others.

christ did not die for our sins. To thus make him into a scapegoat is to miss the message of his life entirely- it is the very opposite of what it claims to be- "Christians" are the murderers of christ in the present day. No. If we are to be christians, we must own our own blackness as christ did his. A true christian would know that they must die for their own sins.

On the Cross

Through crucifixion, we show our allegiance to the idea and sacrifice life. We reconfirm our commitment to an idealized God, and we turn God's only son into one- Christ in Heaven, an idealized God. That is not what christ was or is. christ is a living god. A human being who dies. christ is more than a representation, like Marilyn Monroe. christ is more than an idea, unlike a corporation. christ is an animal, unlike God; humans have a soul, because they are made of matter.

The Jews in our story (who will become Christians) have again succumbed to the temptation of worshipping idols. This time, they worship the cross, the totem, the idea, the Law as if it is the truth, the whole truth, and nothing but the truth. It isn't. We do not want a living God.

The Seed

What we have hitherto taken to be the full flowering of "Christianity" has turned out now to be merely the planting of a seed. Viewed from a particular perspective, it could be said that what God did in the gesture of christ was to offer the idea of christ, redemption and reconciliation, to human beings. Just as God cannot create a world on His own, so He could not bridge the gap between the mind and body, between the flesh and spirit, light and darkness, on His own. Rather, in the gesture of christ jesus, God inseminates the Mother and their shared creation, humans, with the idea of union, of reconciliation, of love. To bring this idea to fruition, and to complete the creation, requires the necessary intercourse with blackness that has now taken place in the underground of human consciousness over the last 2000 years.

birth of christ

After first rejecting the idea of christ and casting christ from us, we humans have worked to reconcile ourselves to the concept, to breathe life into the idea, to make the idea of God come alive. And herein lies the unique responsibility and gift and power of we human beings, as it is only in us that the reconciliation and union can take place. We are the womb for God's creation. At first, in our mistaken and exclusive identification with God, our Father, we sought to destroy the seed, to cast him out, but the seed would not die. As we sent christ's spirit up to dwell with his Father in Heaven, the seed that was his body was buried deep in the blackness of our human unconscious, and there it has grown, despite our ignorance, down through the present day.

christ's alleged resurrection was a wish, a prediction made from the dark side of human consciousness. It was a precursor of what someday would happen- that christ would rise from death and be born again through and in each one of us. Since the day of crucifixion, the latent seed of christ has been germinating in the black soil of human hearts until, today, the living christ sprouts. What some will call the "Second Coming" is in fact the first birth; what we have had until now is just the idea of Christ, our (human) representation of Christ, God's gift to each and all of us. Reborn from the darkness is the true body of christ, in the here and now, in the flesh and blood of each individual- in you, and through you, the entire human race.

IN GOD'S IMAGE

The Divorce

Necessarily, the world begins in divorce- of mind from body and of God, our Father, from Mother, Earth. The Garden of Eden tells the story of this original break, the birth of human consciousness; and while the break, itself, is necessary, the white man's exclusive identification with God, our Father, is not.

It is this decision to align ourselves with God, the mind and light (what I call the original error), and so to assign to men dominion over earth, our women, and all creatures, that distinguishes white man's civilization from all others. It is this exclusive allegiance to the purely masculine element in human consciousness, and the corresponding demonization of the body and the blackness, that has made possible the extraordinary technological manipulation of our planet's resources and that has made inevitable the modern pathology that threatens immanent destruction of the planet, race, and soul.

In a gesture of love, reconciliation, and healing, God sent to us His only begotten son. He joined with earthly Mary and gave to us the miracle child, an infinity made finite, spirit turned to flesh, and we humans promptly killed him. In this replication of God, our Father's, original error, we humans sealed our fate. For the next 2000 years- until today- we would build our world and self in the Image of God, in imitation of God's original and infantile error.

Just like God, our Father, we human beings- men- would learn slowly and certainly not the first time. We would exaggerate our powers and our goodness, and use our hubris and morality to kill and piss on women and the Earth. We turned Jesus- God made flesh- into a mere idea, a dead Deity, just like God had been. We removed him from the worldly realm that God and Mary assigned to him that we might worship Him, pray to Him, and act in Jesus' name. We- the ones who killed him- turned Jesus into the opposite of what God and Mary intended him to be. And, so, in devotion to Jesus' opposite, we build our "Christian" nations - and willfully misunderstand the message of his life. We compound our original error through ongoing, continuous replications of the original crucifixion of the person, Christ.

Today, we humans are prepared at last to see through our previous errors.

The Myth of Science

When people today try to study myth, they struggle to identify the ways in which myth still colors their own understanding of the world. They look at myths of others and recognize the absurdities and untruths and, in trying to identify myths of the present day, think about ridiculous notions others less intelligent than themselves turn to to bring comfort and "meaning" to their lives- the myth of American exceptionalism, for example, or the myth that global warming is a hoax.

Modern, college educated people struggle unsuccessfully to overcome the notion that myth is anything but a falsity or lie. Even, and especially, liberal intellectuals intent on being open-minded and inclusive cannot help looking down their noses at those "tribes" and individuals that still view the world through the lens of myth, who have not attained, like them, to a more scientific, rational, and objective perspective on life. What these folks fail to recognize is that their science, objectivity, and reason is, itself, the myth they tell about the world. A myth based on white supremacy.

A myth that we do not participate in will always appear ridiculous and absurd, and despite the internal logical consistency ever present in these mythological explanations, it will be hard for us to understand how anyone could actually believe this crap. The myths that we, ourselves, participate in will never appear to us as myth. In order to participate in them, in order for them to function as myths in our life and understanding, we assume- like every other human culture- that our myths are not "myths" but truth. The myths we participate in do not seem like stories, but "the way things are"- i.e. "reality," and so it is with science.

Don't get me wrong. Science has tremendous explanatory powers that, in some ways, at least, far transcend those of other mythological explanations. A concept like "natural selection" (to choose just one) describes a truth about the world- time, creation, life, relations amongst humans and other animals, God, the planet- that provides us with a lens for understanding that is nearly inexhaustible and, so, fascinating and satisfying. But even so, it is not "true" per se. Though complex and comprehensive and logically consistent, natural selection (and science, in general) is still a story we humans tell about "the world." It is not "the way things are" beyond the construction of our own human understanding. Though we think "the evidence" of the world strongly confirms our story of natural selection, the world we see is also filtered through, shaped and defined by this concept through which we perceive it; and so it is never possible for human beings to know for sure the extent to which the world conforms with their concepts/stories/myth/science vs. the extent to which we see only what we are looking for.

Developmentally speaking, science is merely an extension of the same story telling, explanatory capacity invented by humans in that first moment of consciousness. Science is just another layer of myth, more comprehensive and complex, more sophisticated and expansive, for sure, but fundamentally the same. Science, like myth, provides an internally logical explanation and structure for understanding the evidence presented to our senses. Like myth, science empowers us to survive and navigate the world. What distinguishes science from myth is its exponential increase in our capacity to manipulate, shape, define, "control" the world as it is defined by us.

Through science we gained a transfer of power from God to men that made men the masters and not merely supplicants. Through science, men came to own their own creative power. We became "like Gods;" we understood for the first time that we are the Gods, the creators, the definers of this world. The problem with this scientific truth, and the problem that threatens to destroy our civilization upon which it is based, is that we failed to recognize the limits of our science, the limits of our story, that it was a story. And while human beings can, clearly, manipulate and so, to some degree, at least, "control" the world they create through their language, reason, story, explanation, that explanation does not explain it all. Our story, our science do not, did not create it all. There is something beyond our understanding; there are limits to our story. Though expanded by the exercise of reason, our human understanding continues to be defined by its limits, by the circle of explanation that, collectively, we've drawn. Our story- our science- is not, and can never be, "the whole truth and nothing but the truth."

The revolution in consciousness that is happening today, a revolution begun by those scientists, themselves- Albert Einstein- who approached the furthest reaches of the scientific explanation and came back to tell the story- the revolution that is happening today is just this awareness of the limits of our scientific explanation/story, and the revelation of these limits is just as profound and just as significant as that earlier revelation- the one that empowered people to move beyond a merely mythological, and emotional, understanding of the world into a scientific, and rational, understanding.

In that earlier revolution- the Copernican Revolution- we committed a complete reversal of our understanding of our selves, and others, and our relationship to God. Through the Copernican Revolution, human beings understood- viscerally and intellectually and for the first time- that human beings and Earth are not the center of the universe. We understood that there was something more than us, and ironically but necessarily, with that knowledge, with that admission of our own relativity and finitude, came new powers- the power of reason, science, technology, creation hitherto reserved to God(s). And we have used these powers, over the last 500 years, to make ourselves- more and more with each invention and discovery and innovation and breakthrough- the center of the universe again.

Now, today, comes the second great revolution in human consciousness- the Einsteinian Revolution, and that revolution, that reversal, teaches us that all we know is relative- that there is no such thing as "objective" truth- the fiction upon which we have built this civilization.

And, ironically but necessarily, with that knowledge, with the admission of our own relativity and finitude, comes new powers, too- the power of story, of simultaneity and contradiction, the incarnation of christ. For the first time, we human beings realize that, as finite beings, and only as finite beings, we are able to realize the infinite.

The Fundamental Error

It is not by accident that this scientific understanding, this new layer of myth, grew up in a Christian world view. While the Church Fathers originally resisted the new discoveries and insights of the first scientists- people like Copernicus, Kepler, and Galileo- their resistance was more about 1) the threat it posed to their own political power and, so, wealth and 2) their inability to "think out of the box" and to imagine any other explanation than the one they had been taught. The problem was not that science was somehow hostile to a Christian explanation; in fact, the Christian explanation made the breakthrough to science and pure reason possible, and perhaps inevitable. Through science and science's devotion to pure reason, we Westerners imitate our God.

The fundamental error we make in our Western civilization, as reflected in our Creation Myth, is in our sole identification with God and the Light to the exclusion of our Mother and the Blackness. Like God, we draw a circle around the world (symbolized by Eden) and place ourselves at its center. The error comes, though, in the idea that all light is contained within the circle- within ourselves, within our world- and that all darkness, therefore, is without- outside ourselves, outside our world. Such construction of light and dark, while possible to the human mind (it is something we can imagine), is, of course, not possible, in fact. This is evidenced in our own creation myth by the presence of the serpent- the voice of blackness- in the Garden, that even God is not able to keep out. And yet, we (white, Western Civilization) built our society nonetheless on the fictional premise that we human beings (i.e. we white men) are all light and that the darkness comes only from outside of us. We mistake ourselves for a point of light, pretending we are not also earth.

This peculiar (and perhaps dialectically necessary) construction of light and black led inevitably to the construction of good and evil. In Western consciousness, the light is so clearly associated with the good, and evil with the blackness that we assume that "it is so" and can be no other way. This perception/construction builds into white people's consciousness, then, the necessity of an enemy- the one who stands outside the circle to oppose us- as the carrier of blackness (=evil) that we refuse to admit into ourselves. Throughout our history, the Africans, Native Americans, and others have carried our blackness for us. Nature, herself, has been the dark and ineffable demon to be mastered and controlled, but it is women- who are, of course, Nature's emissaries- who have been our most constant "other," the carrier of our blackness. This makes sense to our mythology where that God damned Eve listened to the serpent, deceived her innocent (ignorant) husband, and broke the circle of God's light in the first place. We rape women and children, enslave black people, and then (though it makes us sad to do so) must punish and resent them for bringing blackness into our world.

And so, while it has been "natural" and "rational," that women should be the carriers of man's blackness, keeping women in this role has not been easy without certain ambivalences, contradictions, and hypocrisies periodically breaking through. There is the small problem that we are all, in fact, born of women and, too, that we are (so far) dependent upon women to provide us sons who will carry on our light and goodness. Add to that a disturbing itch that men's bodies seem to inevitably produce that causes us to go to women- something hard, impossible to understand and equally hard, impossible to bring under the control of man's (supposedly) all powerful reason. This itch we blame on women, of course (who else is there to blame?), but it has also, over the course of our history, caused men to turn against themselves- that is, to see their own bodies, their own flesh as the enemy whose blackness invades our consciousness against the Divine Will received by God.

We find in this fundamental error, this first fiction by which we constellate the blackness and the light in this peculiar way, the seeds of destruction for this world view buried in the very creation. From this start, we have built a civilization with a tremendous breadth of accomplishment and achievement, but, through it all, the feet of clay remain. We have built a society with underlying hatred for the very nature upon which we depend, a hatred of our women (whom we put on a pedestal), and a hatred of ourselves- our own bodies, our impulses, our desires. We have built a society and a consciousness that is continually at war with itself- the mind with the body, the I with the Other, the inside with the outside. We have built a culture committed to death, as best symbolized by our human god, crucified on a cross of our making.

It may be possible at this juncture in our development to finally see through, and overcome, this peculiar constellation and so give birth to a new and deeper understanding and identification with the world, the other, and our self. We have seen the horizons of our knowledge- as symbolized by the view of earth from space- and in so doing, have expanded our consciousness forever. But we are threatened by our (society's and the "rulers" of that society) continuing allegiance to this fundamental error that they call "truth"- "the way things are"- "the facts of life"- the only "truth" they've ever known, and the only "truth" they can imagine- even if it kills us.

When the Circle Becomes a Prison

The circle becomes a prison when we forget there is something other than the circle.

The circle becomes a prison when someone else draws and defines it for us.

The circle becomes a prison when it is hurting us, and we can't get out.

The circle becomes a prison when it makes us shrink.

In days like these, if the circle doesn't feel like a prison, that may be a sure sign that it has become one and you its willing captive.

Through the accumulated efforts of multiple generations and, more especially, millions of creative individuals, we have created a collective circle so imposing and pervasive that it is very difficult for any individual to detach themselves from it and/or to see beyond it. Certain of the communication media we have collectively developed- the internet and TV, in particular, are so compelling as to be addictive. The combined power of their images and possibility (don't miss what comes next) so hooks our human emotions and physical desires that we feel helpless in the face of them. Spiritual vampires, they invade our consciousness, and we cannot resist letting them in.

We have allegedly transcended these earlier emotional and physical responses with our science and our reason, and yet, these "more primitive" responses that came earlier in our human history still hold the most powerful sway over our lives. It is these emotional and physical responses that are the true source and motivation for all actions and decisions in our life. We may often use "reasons" as a cover for our true motivation, and/or we use our reason as a tool by which we are able to better position ourselves to satisfy our emotions and physical desires, but this idea that human beings are "rational beings" is a sham, and the advertisers and politicians (the most cynical and successful in our culture) recognize this fact of human nature more fully than the rest. They use this, their greater insight into human nature to simultaneously "convince us" of our own rationality and to manipulate our "baser instincts" in ways that allow them to satisfy their own basic instincts more fully than the rest.

The history of Western Civilization, the incarnation of which is all around us, is the continuous unfolding of a single idea. An idea that by divorcing reason and intelligence- the human mind- from the body and limitations and animal nature of human beings that we could achieve transcendence, that we could achieve enlightenment, that we could attain mastery and freedom, that we could become like God. God, Himself, the ultimate fantasy of reason. The fantasy of complete liberation from finitude, from incarnation, from the body, from Eve, from the Earth, from Death, from blackness, from His own beginnings, ... His liberation from life.

The self-centered, animal motives we allegedly transcend through reason continue to operate unabated beneath the surface of our consciousness, all throughout the Newtonian period, and still, and always. Just because we turn our back to them does not make them go away.

This willed ignorance of our own true motives is the source of white man's mastery through technology (to the extent that it has been achieved); this same willed ignorance is the source of the "carte blanche" and privilege white people assume as their God-given right throughout the scientific, capitalist, imperialist, racist, Christian period. This willed ignorance is the root of evil buried, necessarily, deep in the rationalist world view. In our time, these "chickens have come home to roost" when what passes for "reason" is, at its root, most unreasonable of all.

The hippies in the 60s forced the rationalists to contend with these animal aspects in ways they had previously avoided. Since then, the rationalists, the capitalists, and the Christians, all the contemporary murderers of christ, have learned to sell these aspects back to us. The corporations and their politicians learned from the hippies where the real power lies, and it isn't in reason. Now, everybody just pretends to be rational, but we all know it's a lie to cover our own self-interest. The division of humans into isolated cells through corporate media is symptomatic and causative of the immature understanding of relativity I hope to move beyond. The message that "it's all relative" and "you're on your own" feeds your human soul to the corporate machine, and they like that.

We humans have created this collective apparatus- a machine- that strangely has the same Will to Live that Schopenhauer attributes to all living things. What makes the corporation a monster is that it has no heart (an exact reversal from Mary Shelley's, my beloved). Detached from a living body, reason (as represented by the corporation) becomes weirdly, cruelly irrational. And we are all expected to play along if we are to keep our job. "Be reasonable." "There's no place for drama in the workplace." "data-driven decision making." When a corporation-reason detached from a living body (in the image of God), looks at people, It sees objects- an image of Itself. Its eyes can see nothing else. Humans within the organization can see- they have hearts, but, to keep their job, they are required not to. Not to see, not to listen with their hearts. They are required to, themselves, become objects. "Just doing my job." Be professional.

Paid liars for the corporation and Catholic Church will blame Tiamat- they will blame that same feminine aspect they have been crucifying since our father, Abraham, killed Isaac/Ishmael. They will double down- again and again, on their willful ignorance of their own darkness. We know that Tiamat is the shadow of their own creation, their Frankenstein, corporation. She is the bride denied our Frankenstein. What we are seeing are the last gasps of a dying age. They will use every weapon to defend their view. They sell relief- drugs, football, pornography, shopping, food, forgetting, phantasies of Heaven- from the hell they have created and hire peppy journalists to confirm this is all there is. Ice cream and casinos.

Where Evil Comes From

The most immediate evidence of our senses would indicate that trees live above ground. Through the application of our reason, science, myth, and technology, we discover the root system that supports the tree and are thus able to discover that we, at first glance, accidently neglected one half of the tree. So it is, metaphorically speaking, with our own personality. Though they know very little about it, people overwhelmingly give themselves the benefit of the doubt when it comes to their own dark side.

Though we must extrapolate the motivations of others from their actions, our own conscious motives are immediately before us. Rarely does it occur to us to dig down to the root of our motivations like we did to find the underlying roots of trees. It serves our immediate self-interest to ignore the possibility that we may be driven by certain ignoble motives that remain hidden from our view. We all have experienced the resentment and shocking disbelief that comes when someone else attributes motives to our actions that are not true. Often when this happens, it is a matter of that other person projecting their own motives (usually the ones they don't like to own themselves) on to us. But sometimes when this happens, the other person is right (or at least partly right), and, it turns out, they understand our motives better than we understand ourselves.

Such an admission of our failure to understand and own our motivations is, in my experience, almost never made. Such self-reflection and excavation of our own hidden motives is not something any human being is inclined to do on his or her own, but with proper education and guidance from our teachers, it is not too terribly difficult to at least begin. No one excavates their own hidden motives, though, unless they intend to do so. Sometimes the traumatic effects of our actions may try to force us to attend to our own hidden motivations, but human beings are most talented tricksters and protectors of themselves, and even under the pressure of traumatic events, "the light bulb has to want to change."

Turning a critical eye towards our own hidden motivations becomes one of the necessary moral imperatives under the new relativistic metaphysic that will take us to deeper levels of consciousness and understanding. Human beings' failure to engage in such self-examination is a contributing factor, at least, that can lead these human beings to provide fertile ground for the spread of evil. As a precursor to evil, human beings must be convinced of, and feel justified in, the rightness of their own motives, and, thus, any negative consequences of their actions must be attributable to factors outside of themselves. These may include the evil motivations of others, the misinterpretation by others of our motives, or, at most, a failure on our part to accurately understand the situation. "He means well," we say to explain this last circumstance where the motives are pure but the assessment of the situation is not right, to which I often feel compelled to respond that Hitler meant well, as well.

People draw a circle in order to "be," to have a consciousness, and to make sense of the world around them. Each individual participates to varying degrees in the circles of others- family, friends, community, nation, era- and each also creates a circle that is uniquely their own. From this circle we compose of individual and collective elements, we create a story and an explanation of the world. People at all times and places have had to account somehow for their own origins, their own death, and the presence/possibility of something beyond themselves- some type of divinit(ies) or God(s). It is not possible for humans to not ask and answer these ultimate questions. Such questions are in the very nature of the circle of consciousness- and so in the nature of humanity itself, and while it is possible that some people may not be conscious of their answers to these questions, that does not mean they don't have answers. Though not raised to a level of consciousness, these answers still continue to function in these people's lives.

Unfortunately, people's answers to these fundamental questions often contradict each other, compete with one another, and so lead groups of human beings into conflict. People who understand a relativistic ethic, even to a minor degree, will understand that truth can find a multitude of representations and that that multitude does not necessarily have to negate or reduce any one of them. There are other folks in the world, though, for whom there can be one and only one truth. That truth is, invariably, of course, theirs. These absolutists feel a duty to the Truth and to other people. They have a duty to bring others to their truth very often, and, sometimes, they feel a duty to defeat all competing truths as well. We are getting closer to the answer to our question of where evil comes from, but we still are not there yet.

People "mean well." They just misunderstand the situation, because they have walled themselves inside of an infantile and solipsistic vision of the world, of truth, of right, of God, and of themselves. As true believers, they will work devotedly to impose that mistake upon all others, and that is one place where evil comes from.

Evil comes from people locked into a circle/world view so rigid and impenetrable that it does not allow in any doubt, any blackness or any other. People need a circle to "be" and to survive, but, to be effective, that circle must be porous and fluid. The blood that connects human beings to each other and the blackness must flow through the circle. It must allow the person protected by the circle to breathe, to see outside themselves, and it must allow other people to see in. An effective, healthy circle is supple and dynamic. It has a continuity and an identity, but within the constraints of that consistency, it must also have flexibility, multiple aspects, variation, different dimensions, fun. When viewed from different angles, and as experienced in different situations, the protective circle/world will reveal different- even contradictory- aspects to itself, and it will be capable of movement, growth, and change.

People who live inside a circle that does not have these characteristics are trapped, imprisoned, walled off from "reality," other people, blackness, and the wellsprings of life. Interestingly, these people are less likely than the rest of us to feel trapped or limited in themselves.

Under stress from the environment, consciousnesses, like animals and cells, may shrink in self-protection. In times of danger, we draw a wall of defense close, tight, impenetrable around ourselves and those we love. When the danger passes, we can relax the circle and resume its growth through exchange with others and the world, but where the threat from outside is perceived to be life-threatening and/or ongoing, this retrenchment may become a more permanent solution until, it has been used so long, there is no longer a way out. The shell of protection calcifies and chokes off the flow of stimuli from outside necessary to interiority and depth, growth and survival.

Here in our time, we see two distinct circumstances under which this strategy of retrenchment and calcification turns into a permanent and fixed response to a hostile world. In what is, by far, the most common entrenchment, whole communities retreat into a protective and shared dogma that is no longer moved by or responsive to "truths" from outside. Those outside our circle of protection are seen as enemies, as potential destroyers. Their humanity cannot be admitted to the sphere of our tight, dogmatic Truth.

Christians in America have become the clearest example of this survival strategy. It no longer matters for these folks whether the truths they tell are "true." They have faith in their Truth, and the preservation of that faith at all costs becomes the sole motivator for action.

In protection of their Truth, singular and Absolute, they effectively turn off all valves of perception that would admit alternatives, criticism, doubts, or new or conflicting ideas. What had been a porous membrane that filters ideas from outside our circle in ways that are simultaneously protective and nutritive now has become an impenetrable wall protecting a solipsistic world view that can tolerate no dissension. All that is inside is light and right, and we build a bulwark against the force of darkness from without.

If Christians today feel that their world view is under a continuous and life-threatening attack, it is. They are not wrong in that. Christians cling hysterically to a truth that no longer works to adequately explain the world. Any free exchange between individuals and the world necessarily leads to further exposure and erosion of their outmoded truth. To protect their children, and, more importantly, to protect their vulnerable untruth, Christians replace education with indoctrination. They require their children to adopt the same world view- without question, in faith- as the community surrounds them. They suppress critical and creative skills, risk-taking and curiosity in their children, thus crippling their ability to grow their consciousnesses even after they may have seen through their parents' dogma.

The goal of this kind of "education" is not to develop dialogue and exchange and analysis but, rather, to build a static, impenetrable and unquestioned wall of defense against all that is uncertain, contradictory, bigger than or outside of my own perception (except for God). The "I" of these individuals remains embedded in the definitions of others. They see only one way- the way others see. Like bubbles in the dish water, each is hemmed in by the others, the I indistinguishable from those who surround it.

The internal momentum sparked and nurtured by an effective education and perspectives outside my own is not valued here. It is just such antagonism, uncertainty, disruptions to the peace that we must guard against. The old metaphysic that Christians cling to is consistent with this strategy in that both value fixity and absolutes. Such individuals always act from "inside the bubble," one might say "from inside the ego." No outside perspective is tolerated, as these tend to undermine the sole integrity beneath our own. We surround ourselves as exclusively as possible with others who believe just the same as me.

The only ideas I have are those planted there by others. And there is protection in that. Together, we stand on firm ground. The protection of the herd. Interiority is discouraged, and certainly not nurtured. People who think too much for themselves have an undermining effect. Emphasis is placed on obedience first and conformity and loyalty to family and Church. Whereas I sought, in my approach to education, to produce as much momentum possible for further and self-sustaining growth, here the value is on the opposite- to keep the peace and maintain the status quo, with as little change as possible.

Faced with the necessary assaults of needed transformation in our own time, a third of our population has retreated into a rigid, collective untruth. As with any myth, it is self-reinforcing and internally logical as long as you are "in it," have no consciousness outside of it. Intrusions from outside the myth are resisted as a matter of life and death, and, in times like our own, when this singular, collective truth is felt to be under attack from every direction, the defenders of the truth grow ever more hysterical, ever more unreasonable, ever more violent and dangerous in its defense.

From inside the walls, it is the whole world to them. Everything depends upon it. From the outside, as with any myth, it appears as madness. And that's what it is. A collective madness. But what makes it "mad" is not that the myth/ the world view/ the explanation is false or untrue. ALL human myths are "false" and "untrue." What makes this one pathological is that it does not work. The longer they persist in this untruth, the more likely it becomes that they will use that truth to finally destroy the world they seek to preserve. The very thing that could save them- alternative perspectives from outside the circle of their own truth/myth, is the very thing they resist most.

The majority of rigid individuals identify as "Christians" and/or "Republicans," but there is a second type of rigid individual with an origin story very different than the first. Here we find an individual whose growth was neglected and abused for very different motives, by narcissistic adults interested in themselves alone. Not all children abused by narcissists become sociopaths. The ones I know, while irremediably scarred, have courageously refused to be just an object of their abusers. These ones, who have escaped the rigid prison of the abusive other, are most vulnerable, and most valuable. They are not rigid individuals, but the opposite, and we who have been nurtured and protected are obligated to provide protection and shelter for these most vulnerable and courageous ones. They are our leaders.

But there are others, the opposite of the courageous ones- the narcissists and sociopaths, who react to these early violations of their initial vulnerabilities with the rigid circle strategy. They draw a line around themselves that others should have but didn't. Being children, the lines they draw are infantile, not subtle. Here, the circle is drawn by the individual, themselves, and not by the community that surrounds them. This individual is responding to a situation opposite of the one faced by the Christian. Here, there is not too much, but far too little and/or a debilitating, collective definition. Those who should facilitate the growth of a protective barrier in the child violate it instead. The child is on its own, in service to an inscrutable other, and under constant threat of attack.

Children who survive this kind of childhood and adapt the strategy of rigidity get trapped inside of a solipsistic bubble, closed off by an impenetrable wall of self-protection against emotions, vulnerability, others, and God. Christians, at least, retain and participate in an infinite aspect beyond themselves- in God and a community of others. Sociopaths have none of that, and now don't want it. They are all there is. Any infinite aspect must come from themselves alone, and so it is that such individuals are most alone and most callous to the humanity of any and all others.

In our time, the Godless sociopaths have learned to speak the language of rigidity- fear, hatred, anger, jealousy, and power (helplessness). They manipulate the symbols to convince desperate, rigid Christians (whose truth is dead) to do their bidding. In this way, sociopaths have come to be "leaders" in this time between meanings.

Clearly, I am a proponent for subjectivity and depth, the neglect of which I blame for much of what is evil and broken in our world, but this infantile subjectivity is not what I am pointing to. The subjectivity of both Christians and sociopaths moves us in the wrong direction- backwards in our emotional development, though, truth be told, this kernel of infantile subjectivity (narcissism) remains and functions in every one of us at different times and to varying degrees. Though we evolve beyond our infantile subjectivity, we never release ourselves from its influence completely. Like all levels of human consciousness, it remains part- and at the center- of who we are, and in times of stress, it is not unusual for people to revert back to it- in a desperate attempt to protect themselves. For the rigid individual, though, for the most emotionally limited and damaged individuals- one type of which we call a sociopath- there are no other options. This is the only way they have to be.

This absolute and impenetrable concentration of emotional energy can have an empowering effect. What I am describing is not a limitation in their intelligence, but in their capacity to form emotional connection to others. Folks trapped in this kind of infantile subjectivity will exhibit the same range of intelligences as the general population, and, given sufficient opportunity, they can rise to positions of power, authority, and influence thanks, in part, to the single-mindedness their emotional focus provides them.

When they can draw others back into participation in these earlier and infantile levels of functioning, these rigid, underdeveloped ones can be terribly masterful and effective. While the rest of us will have doubts and reservations, ambivalence and guilt about acting from these lower levels of our consciousness, these folks do not suffer from the conflicting voices of conscience, reason, and the others. They are able to act with passionate, consistent, ruthless, and un-self-reflective self-interest and can be terribly compelling, charismatic, charming, and intimidating bullies.

In this time of social break down we are going through, these individuals appear to be gaining greater traction. Partly, this is the case, because our politics have become so brutal and divisive that anyone with a conscience and emotional sensitivity will not/cannot subject themselves to such inhumanity, and the ones who try either get destroyed or soon give up, because it is more painful and destructive than they could have imagined.

In our world today, people are treated like objects. Those who would rise to positions of authority and decision making are expected, required to make those decisions based on "data" and "objective" considerations that leave the humanity of the folks involved out of account. Such an attitude toward others is easier for a sociopath who lacks the capacity for self-reflection, empathy, and conscience that has such a crippling effect on the abilities of the rest of us to function in this kind of world. The rigid individual also comes equipped with a kind of emotional armor that those of us with more porous, supple, and otherwise healthy circles/identities lack.

Being treated, themselves, as objects by the system and the others does not present the same kind of problem for these folks as it would for you or I. They have so secured- walled off- their own emotional "integrity" from the assaults of others that what other people say or do to them fails to penetrate. They grow a "thick skin"- something I've never accepted as a virtue.

And so, in an age of brutality, indifference, and cruelty when human beings are routinely turned into objects, these folks with a rigid circle of identity actually do very well. They are adapted to the environment, and as more of them continue to rise to positions of authority and control, the conditions that give rise to their success become more and more the rule and expectation. Thus it is that we see in recent years an ever accelerating- an exponential increase in-organizational brutality, ruthless indifference and inhumanity that becomes, more and more, built into our government, business, and social systems.

The antidote to this rising brutality must be in the further development of new layers of reflective subjectivity. We must continue the dialectic and dialogue between the subject and the object, the I and the other(s). We learn through confrontation with the rigid ones that we cannot win the battle on these- their- terms that we must remove ourselves from the field of battle temporarily and work to increase our own- and others- sensitivity and vulnerability so that, when the current system finally breaks down, we will be prepared to reenter the field of devastation.

We- you, because I'll be dead before long- may need to remove ourselves to the nagual (to use don Juan's term) or to the Background (to use Mary Daly's). Here is a place beyond reason that the rigid individuals cannot see and do not know exists, a place where they cannot find us, where we become invisible to them, where they can never go.

Fundamentalism

I understand, and I trust that my reader does too, that my ideas will inevitably be manipulated, reduced, misrepresented, and mangled by other people. They do this not out of malice, but out of a sincere desire to make sense of what I am saying. The problem is that these ideas are too big for them, too new to them. They lack the mental structure necessary to contain these new ideas. It does not fit into available categories of "the known," and so, they try to make it fit. Smoosh it in, and, even, sometimes turn it into its opposite just to make it fit. I understand all that. The reason I write is to help create and build those structures in you- my readers, so that you, at least, can understand, so that you, too, in your turn, will expand on these ideas and so that you, too, will be able to move these others closer to developing these structures in themselves some day.

Though it is inevitable that my ideas will be misconstrued, I have an obligation to those who come after to provide, as much as possible, explicit ammunition they can use to combat these misconceptions. And so it is now that I take a moment to distinguish Science from Religion. Throughout most of this book, I have tied scientific rationalism together with Judeo-Christian religion. God came first. He was invented by the Jews as the Jews were invented by Him. Out of Judaism came Christianity, and out of Christianity came science. Many scientists view their science and reason as the very antithesis of religion and myth, and, in certain respects, that is true, but it is equally true that science and reason would not be possible without its dialectical antecedents in Judaism and Christianity and myth. There would be no astronomy without astrology, no chemistry without alchemy, no scientist without God.

I tend to join the two out of a need to emphasize essential commonalities long neglected and denied. And, too, I want people to recognize that the two- science and religion, reason and myth, Judeo-Christianity and natural selection exist concurrently. The antecedents (religion, myth, Judeo-Christianity) are not "dead" in the sense that they cease to function. No. These elements of white, Western consciousness continue to operate, albeit underground and out of view, and so inform our definitions and relations, our science, of self, other, and the world.

In the preceding chapter I alluded to fundamentalism (though I called it something else) as the major source of evil in our world today. In anticipation of the limited understanding individuals will bring to bear on my ideas, I need to unpack my meaning further. Scientists, of course, will assume that I agree with them and that I see anti-rationalist religious fundamentalists (Christians, Jews and Muslims alike) as a source of evil in the world. And this assumption would be true. I do see anti-rationalist fundamentalists (Christians, Jews and Muslims alike) as a source of evil in the world. The problem is that this truth, while true, is not the whole truth. The rest of truth, I fear, our scientists will ignore- even when put blatantly and explicitly in front of them as I do here, they simply do not have eyes to see it, do not have a mental structure to contain it. And so, "the rest of the story" will be for them invisible, just as if it wasn't even there.

There is a fourth fundamentalism operating in our world today, more pervasive and dangerous than the rest, and that is scientific fundamentalism. These "scientists" are known by their faith in Darwin, in technology, in progress, in economics, in "data," in "reason," and in man's solutions to the problems caused by man's previous solutions.

I am most suspicious of science, because it is the only one of the four fundamentalisms that is more than a vestigial remnant from an earlier day. Science is alive (though not well). It is the current and controlling fundamentalism- the one approach beyond all question, the "truth" we take for granted.

The surest sign that "science" is the controlling myth in our place and time and culture is that people do not- almost cannot- think of it as a myth. They think with it but lack the mental structure necessary to think about it. You, yourself, are very likely (at least to some degree) a practitioner of the scientific faith. I am; it is the truth within which I was raised (though I was also offered an alternative). And to be clear, I am not opposed to science (any more than I am opposed to the judeo-christian truth and myth). What I am opposed to is our faith in science, our absolute devotion to science at the price of other stories we could tell.

And I can hear the scientists now. "Science is not a faith; it is just the opposite. Science is a relentless state of inquiry, of examination, of hypotheses, experimentation, evidence, and analysis. Science is the anti-faith. Science is precisely the thing that you claim to be doing yourself." Perhaps. I would agree that a "science" in its most generous and noble incarnation could be all that, but that is not what science has become for us.

A more limited, a more self-certain and self-perpetuating, faith in science shapes our world today. It is a faith in man's knowledge and version of the world, a faith in objective truth. It is a faith in the explanatory power of material causation (like how the chemistry of our brains is at the root of all our problems and our wonders). It is a faith that "only science can get us out of this mess" (this mess created by previous applications of, well, science). It is this version of science, with its bodily incarnation in corporations, money, and technology, that is driving us off a cliff. I am morally responsible to call that science out- to say that this is the man behind the curtain and that this Emperor has no clothes.

I am a critic of science in so far as science (reason and the scientific method) posits itself as the one and only pathway to the truth. I am a critic of the tyranny of science that repays our loyalty to it with the simultaneous destruction of our planet and denial of our souls. "Science," of course, posits nothing. It is scientists, or, it is just normal people trained in the science taught in schools, who posit the scientific myth as truth without recognizing the limits of their version, or that they even have a "version," of the truth.

It is inevitable that my criticism of science will be turned into something it is not- turned into what is, in fact, the very opposite of what I intend. Scientists, and "normal," "rigid" individuals imbued with the faith in science, will need to translate my criticism- which they currently do not have the neural network to comprehend- into something they can understand. They will take my criticism of the myth of science (exclusive faith in materialist causes and the powers of human reason), and they will mangle and disfigure my ideas in ways necessary to squish them into their existing neural networks.

Scientific practitioners remain embedded in an Either/Or mindset that science inherited from Christianity and the Jews. They will use their existing mindset to comprehend my metaphysic and thereby turn it into its opposite. As an illustration of the process, we may look to science's attitude towards astrology. It reduces astrology down to something science can understand and thereby concludes it is ridiculous. Either/Or is the tie that binds science to religion. It is the consistent thread that I have come to break. We see the way forward, to a next stone to jump to, only by leaving behind the Either/Or. And anyone who conceives this newly emerging "truth" through the eyes of Either/

Or is bound to misunderstand it and turn it, pathologically, into themselves. Science cannot comprehend the both/and consciousness our relativity points us to, even though (ironically, dialectically) it was from science and its limitations that this new truth grew (just as, once upon a time, myth and story opened the way to its own transcendence by the scientific understanding).

Disembodied and Dismembered Gods

Without realizing it, then, science is a continuation of the mythological journey of human beings. It is a search for meaning and control, a search for understanding and truth. Through science, men thought they could find that meaning through reason alone. The problem, they hypothesized at the beginning of the Age of Reason, was that man's truth had been mixed up in, clouded and polluted by, man's emotions and attachments to the merely physical- the body. What if we were able to distill human reason from the confounding and confusing forces of the here and now, emotions, and mythology? Through pure reason, human beings would discover the truth that had so far eluded them. By becoming more like God, and less like animals, man would discover the key to mastering the universe.

It was actually an eminently reasonable hypothesis at the time, and so men began their long experiment that has continued into the present day. We have sought, through science and the application of reason, a truth that would be objective- one that would be true for all people, in all places, and at all times. We sought "reality" uncolored by the reductive prejudices of particular individuals or cultures. And we could prove this truth through controlled experiments. By the application of "the scientific method" this objective truth would be measurable, demonstrable, and able to be replicated.

birth of christ

Now we stand at the opposite end of this trajectory of science. We see all around us, and we feel inside of us, evidence of the unintended consequences of this purely rational orientation, and, through its incarnations, we come to understand the false assumption upon which scientific truth is based. We see, at this stage in the dialectical expansion of human consciousness, the falsity of science just as, so many years before, the scientists saw the falsity in the mythological Christian explanations.

As with any myth so far known to man, science has its gods. Rationalists and/or scientists, themselves, have historically either denied a belief in God- they have claimed to be atheists who set their scientific understanding in opposition to the mythology (i.e. for them, the falsehood) of Religion, or they were monotheists who picture the one God (Christian, Jewish, Muslim) as the source (I was going to say embodiment, but no)... as the source of pure reason for which they strived.

After the original resistance of the Church Fathers who were in political control and thus threatened by the encroachments of the early scientists, the Christian faiths quickly grew to embrace the rationalist approaches to understanding. They found in this search for pure reason and scientific explanation a certain resonance with their faith in man's ability to transcend the limits of his body and this world through faith in God.

This natural connection between scientific explanations and the old Christian faith is by no means an accident, but rather, a clear case of cause and effect. This Christian impulse to find meaning and direction and salvation beyond the limits of this world is, in fact, the very seed in the earlier Christian views that led men to consider the path of pure human reason. The change that took place between the two epochs was that man took attainment of the promised land into his own hands, and he, not God, reason, not faith, became the vehicle for achieving the separation from our bodily limits and our finitude.

But there is another, unacknowledged God in this scientific vision and in the rationalistic version of Christianity that attends it. This is the dismembered god- the Mother Earth and Life- that science sought to understand by cutting it to pieces. For their rational analysis to comprehend life, it became necessary to destroy it (she is an "it" in this view). And so, throughout this scientific and Christian epoch, the Mother God was kept in the shadows and the darkness, or, in the language of the psychologists that would arise in the later days of this scientific epoch, she was held fast in the underworld of the unconscious mind. Science made an object of this God, that is, reduced Her down to measurable, observable, finite proportions. Not conscious of what their science implied, they consumed this God, who's destruction, it turns out, was the source of their own God's elevation.

Thankfully, Gods are difficult to kill. You may cut her into pieces, you may ignore her, or disparage her, rail against her, and resist her, but so far, at least, they have not killed Her. The voice of life and earth and body continues to bubble up into the Christian consciousness- through dreams and sexual desires, through infidels and common folk, youngsters, savages, women. She is the God whose denial was necessary to make the scientific dream of pure reason possible, but she would not be killed.

And now, in our present day, this God is everywhere. As rationalist Christianity and science lose authority, legitimacy, and truth, Her own power, grown terrible through years in darkness, repression, and denial, grows proportionate to their loss. She is more scary now than ever for the scientists and rationalists, the apologists for the old, false truth- the politicians and the journalists, professors, economists, bankers and self-proclaimed Christians, and they will do anything- anything- to keep Her down.

They are horrified; they are desperate, hysterical, guilty, helpless, hopeless, irrational, and wrong. To them, it appears, the end is near, and their Apocalypse- a final surrender to the maw of darkness- gives them wet dreams, but for we more rational- post-scientific- ones, this death wish of the rationalist must give us pause. It is important that we turn the corner and take control- through a rebirth of truth deeper than the old one- before, in a final fit of irrational reason, They exercise science's Final Solution.

With the explicit acknowledgement, now, of this neglected God, we re-introduce for the first time since the crucifixion the missing fourth element into the Christian metaphysic. We have 1) God, the Father, we have 2) Christ, the God/man, we have 3) the human (that he became the "Holy Ghost" should tell us something) and now we have 4) the Mother- on equal par with Father and fair progenitor of Christ.

Tiamat

Mircea Eliade retells a story from the ancient Babylonians in which "Tiamat" is a serpent, also known as "Chaos" and the harbinger of death, terrible and tremendous, that rages beneath the earth. Like many ancient civilizations, this tribe of humans placed a totem at the center of their village, center of their world; this totem marked the navel of the earth, connected humans to the heavens and the deeps, and served as Logos- the basis of all security, stability, order, meaning, and law.

In this case, the totem pinned the head of Tiamat beneath the surface of the earth, for, while you could not kill Her (Tiamat is forever), you can contain Her motions and Her strength. Man can manage the chaos with his Laws.

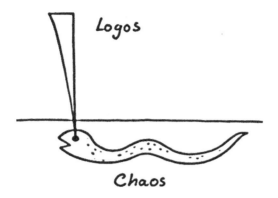

Until one night….when, in the darkness, the ground began to tremble and shake. Tiamat had grown restless, the people knew. They spend the night huddled together in terror, reflecting, no doubt, upon the transgressions- their own and/or those of others- that may have weakened the Logos' hold, that may have fed the Chaos.

As morning broke, the people emerged from their homes and hiding places to find the Totem lay dead upon its side. The connection had been lost; the Serpent was on the loose. There was no longer any basis for action, no reason to live, no order to guide them, and so the people drifted off aimlessly, bereft. Civilization was at an end, and all the people died.

This story becomes important now, because we, ourselves, have heard the rumblings. We have felt the ground shift beneath our feet. President Kennedy's head blown off; the Twin Towers for you younger ones; gushing oil in the Gulf of Mexico, and countless examples still to come that will make the ground shift for the rest of you. We will all see the Logos fall, feel the sudden wave of insight/terror that our truth is at an end. That the world does not make sense, and there is nothing to hold the chaos at bay.

It is no wonder that my fellow Americans cling hysterically, even murderously, to a "truth" they know is dead. In flashes of terror, unforgettable but quickly suppressed, they have seen their "truth" is dead, and yet they cling to it. It is the only truth they know, and so, like the Babylonians, they mistakenly believe that it is the only truth there is. They will resort to anything to preserve it, will kill anyone and everyone who will question it; intuitively they know that where there is no truth, there can be no life.

The Babylonian story becomes important now, because we can use it here, today, to understand and, eventually, regain control over our own situation. If we dare to listen, Tiamat will come alive for us, in us; she speaks to us now, and though her voice inspires dread, it is the one we need to save us. The patriarchal world known as Western Civilization has (re)created this serpent, Tiamat, and only by heeding Her portion of the truth will we save ourselves.

Through suppression of the darkness, denial of the body, demonization of the feminine, we have created this very evil- have created the very monster- awesome and malevolent- that now threatens to destroy us. In desperation, unreason, and fear our "leaders" act to save "reason," science, "civilization," objectivity - the only "truth" they have ever known. The only truth, they assume (like Babylonians), that there is.

They try to still the chaos, but it is too late. We know it is too late; they know it, too, and it is this truth that accounts for the perversity, the desperation, the darkness and the hopelessness, the cruelty and craven inhumanity, of our present age.

But the Babylonians did not have to die. And neither do we. The Babylonians lacked two things- 1) new leaders and 2) the ears to hear them. They could not quiet their own panic long enough to listen for new voices to lead them from the old truth to a new.

It is only the limits in our human understanding, experience and knowledge, that makes us think the world is at an end. The cycles of nature can teach us- if we train our ears to listen- that with each end, comes a beginning; each birth arises always and only out of a blackness and a death. And so, what we mistake for the death of "truth" is a death, it's true, but, it is only the death of this truth, of one truth while it is, simultaneously, the beginning of a new and better truth.

Our contemporaries fear an evil they have, themselves, created, an evil that has always been an inherent limit in the (scientific) story they taught themselves and one another. My fellow Americans fear death of all they know and love and depend upon, because they cannot see yet what is being born. These fellows will only be able to let the old and deadly Logos fall if we can create for them and in them a living image of the truth that is on its way. Add to that the political problem of defeating those invested in the old, dead and dying truth. Like the Church Fathers that imprisoned Galileo for speaking the scientific truth once upon a time, so, today, there are Corporate Fathers who stand "to lose everything" if this new and necessary, inevitable and truer, truth is able to prevail.

Regular folks need human, spiritual leaders who can articulate this truth that we are only now beginning, like an infant distinguishing light from blackness, to see; but what is required to make this transition, to avoid the tragic abortion of this new birth, transcends the power of any single man or community of women.

What is needed is the living body of christ, who lies in seed, inside. The old Christ, the idea of christ, with whom we have tried so far to satisfy ourselves is not the answer. He cannot save us now, and he never could. The cross on which this old Christ hangs is broken- it is, He is, the broken Logos we must abandon to find the living christ. A resurrection- second coming- is what is necessary, but such rebirth must require a simultaneous and certain death of all that we have believed. Necessary to attain to this next stage in the dialectic of human understanding- and so to save our souls and planet- is a reversal of all the truths we hold most dear. And so it is at all such moments of awakening, at the birth of each new truth.

Devil Worship

Though they may not admit the truth- the failure of the patriarchal system- "The Powers that Be"- the corporate machine and the human individuals who depend upon that machine for all livelihood and meaning- know, in their heart of hearts, that the system is a lie. In revolutionary moments such as this, many- even most- human beings will cling cynically or desperately to the ways of old. At such moments, individuals and even whole societies will forsake the human demand for meaning and morals in their desperate attempt merely to survive. Such effort cannot sustain itself for long. Human beings cannot bear a life devoid of meaning any more than they can survive without the other necessities of life- food, water, sleep, and companions. And yet, they can and do go for short periods without these necessities, may even pretend to themselves they do not need them.

And so it is today that the perpetrators of the status quo have cynically embraced the "relativity" of truth and so can go about their business, like walking dead, like zombies, like the soulless creatures they've allowed themselves to become, "secure" in the "mature" and "rational" understanding that there is no "Truth," that "everything is relative." Informed by this modern metaphysic of rudderlessness, folks may "rest assured" that what they do doesn't matter after all, that it is "every man for himself" and "you need to take care of yourself, because no one else will."

There is an essential truth to the relativity uncovered by our father, Einstein, and, shortly we will get to that, but, I assure you, this reduction of human experience to meaninglessness and moral indetermination is not it. The "relativity" people believe in today is the opposite of what relativity will eventually mean for us once we comprehend the meaning of the shift. What we see so far in the earliest days of relativity is "relativity" as understood through the lens of the old and dying truth that it has come to take the place of. We haven't, as a people, switched the lens through which we see the world just yet. We are in the process of doing so, and once we do, we will understand far better what relativity really means for human understanding, and, through this understanding, we will restore meaning to both the world and our individual actions and experience. We will right ourselves again.

As it is now with "relativity," so, too, is it with our current understanding and use of "myth." Though they may not, cannot admit the failure of reason, science, business, and technology to solve our human problems, the protectors of the status quo nevertheless recognize (as demonstrated through their politics and actions) the necessity to ground their arguments in something more substantial, more convincing, and more compelling than merely rational argument and scientific analysis.

It is through their intuitive understanding of humans' need for truth that the conservative and Republican forces have gained an upper hand against the liberal, Democratic, technocratic, and educated elite. The Democrats have a greater faith in the power of human reason, science, and technology than Republicans do. Most Democrats still participate in the myth that science and rational decision making can solve our problems, if only we apply these principles with fidelity and unity. They are mystified and apopletic at Republicans' refusal to go along. The Democrats are especially stymied by the failure of "the 99%," the poor and working people for whom they speak, to join them in a political rebellion against the wealthy, ruling class whose policies consistently work against the poor and working classes.

In one respect, the Republicans are more advanced in their understanding than the Democrats, because the Republicans know that reason is a failure. They recognize in a way that the Democrats do not that reason is no longer the pathway to truth. And so, in their message to the people, they aim deeper- into the roots of human knowledge, understanding and experience. They appeal to human emotions and use, not the language of logic and reason, which they disparage and mock, but, rather, the language of myth. The language of emotion- of fear and of hatred, of privilege and resentment, of selfishness and, yes, even love- of country, of family, of independence, of the way things used to be- is far more convincing than the academic analysis of the liberal elitists.

The Republicans' reactionary use of myth is incredibly successful politically, and it is, as the Democrats argue, quite reasonably and ineffectively, powerful enough to cause a large swath of the population to act against their own political self-interest. This Republican use of myth is also incredibly cynical and destructive to both the advancement of human knowledge and the future health, and even survival, of both our nation and the planet.

As with our current understanding of "relativity," our current use of myth, with its cynical manipulation of human emotions and the explicit and intentional abandonment of reason, represents a desperate movement backwards. It is a retrenchment to our more ancient strategies for survival in response to an overwhelming failure of the systems that depend upon human reason, science, and technology. What we are seeing with the Republican retrenchment is a natural and animal response to threat and danger. By making our consciousness small, by falling back to previous levels of understanding, we may hope to increase our chances of survival.

It is a reaction that "makes sense" at a certain, biological level, and it may even be a reaction that could "work," though if it does "work," the survival we achieve will not be at the same level of consciousness that we shrank from. We will have reduced the capacity of humans in order for some of us, at least, to, physically, survive.

I title this section "Devil Worship," because this strategy of retrenchment does not solve the dialectical crisis we find ourselves faced with at this moment in our human evolution. Rather, this "solution" represents a defeat and retreat, a surrender, a death and aborted birth in the consciousness of humans and the world. It reminds me of Freud's death instinct. It reminds me of an experience we each must feel throughout our own daily lives- a will to resignation, to give up, to give in, to just stop fighting and end it all, a desire for sleep and rest and peace and suicide that comes from a level of exhaustion, hopelessness, futility, and meaninglessness that grows deeper and more oppressive each and every day- especially in the days we live in- in days of spiritual crisis- in "the darkness before the dawn."

The Republicans have taken a portion of the truth that is, just now, being born, and have used that truth against itself, as an excuse by which we may escape the painfulness and trauma of this new and necessary death and birth. This retreat to darkness is, to me, a worship of the Devil, a resignation of the human spirit, a falling away from the light and God that the rest of us must not tolerate and cannot allow.

That said, the Democrats and their well-reasoned arguments, data, and institutional fixes are not going to save us from this retreat to the Devil and His darkness. It is just these "solutions," in fact, that drive us into His arms. No, what is needed is a new birth, an awakening and new truth. What is needed is a new understanding of the power and importance and truth of myth, a new understanding of the limits of reason, and a never before discovered synthesis of these two. We must move beyond the either/or of Democrats and Republicans, of reason and story, science and myth, and move instead to an understanding of how we humans can combine both- myth and reason- to discover and create a new and truer truth.

I, too, have been tempted by this resignation to darkness. At one such moment, I had a dream that I was standing in a rich and luminous field, looking out to a bridge that was not far away and that would lead me to a wondrous land unknown. For a moment, I hesitated. I could cross that bridge- and wanted to, but I knew that if I did, I would never return again. And in that moment of hesitation, the scene before me changed. I was deep inside a dark, damp, and dreary cave, faced with a woman fat, repulsive, ugly with her legs wide open and sucking me into the rotting maw that lay between- a tunnel, not a bridge. I came out the other side, through a kind of reversed birth, chained by hand and foot, one in a line of slaves, trudging down a steep and narrow path deep inside the darkness.

Twin Terrors

Tiamat is the dismembered God reunited beneath the Earth, in the darkness, in the world of dreams. Like a horror movie monster that goes on living even after we have killed it- again and again and again- getting stronger every time. Such a one is Tiamat, except Tiamat is real.

She is our own collective blackness- repressed, denied, forgotten; terrible, ravenous, and angry. We would be wise to recognize Her now, learning our lesson from man's previous denial, repression, presumption, and arrogance from which She grew. The power of Tiamat has grown strong, fed by darkness and resentment at the neglect and persecution of Her creators.

She is the feminine, but She is not the Feminine. She is a story of the feminine, but not the whole or only story. She is merely a version of the feminine- one that's been given swagger by our particular scientific/Christian version of "the truth," a necessary, though unintended by-product of this particular world/view we have consistently pursued. And so, though She represents an aspect of the darkness, the unconscious, the feminine aspect of human consciousness and being, She does not represent "the whole truth" to be found in the darkness any more than our patriarchal world view represents the whole truth about human reason and the light. She is a partial truth grown grotesque, perverse, and dangerous by the skewed perspective of a civilization that has created Her- a civilization that is, itself, founded on a partial truth- of pure reason and a disembodied Christ. Tiamat represents a real challenge that will inescapably consume us if we try and pretend Her away.

Tiamat is the shadow side of white man's creation. She is the opposite of the order, light, pure reason, permanence, stability, security, hierarchy, and law that we have so cherished and so nurtured. She defies the mastery of man, overwhelms his meager dominion through technology. But she is not the only monster we have created.

It was Nietzsche who taught me that every human virtue must have its roots in the darkness of a corresponding vice, and so it is with Tiamat. Tiamat is that root, that vice, that failure that lies, by necessity, beneath our Western civilization. But above the ground, we do not, at present, fare any better. Above the ground, in the image of God, our Father, in the name of the Christ we kill, man has built his own creation. Based on pure reason, and with full confidence in his morality and right, man applied his science and built, through his technology, business, and government, a massive system of production that would defy all our human limits. Above the earth, casting the shadow that is Tiamat, and forming the purest representation of man's reason divorced of feeling and emotion, stands the Corporation- a monster as terrible, as ruthless, and as ravenous and impersonal as the serpent that shakes the ground beneath our feet.

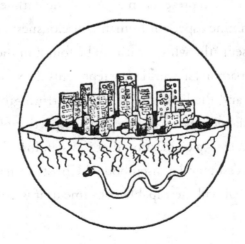

These twin monsters, threatening not merely our freedom and dominion, but our very existence and life, are the unnatural but necessary offspring of a world vision- the scientific/Christian vision of the Western patriarchy- that divorces the masculine from the feminine, the darkness from the light, emotion from reason, intuition from intelligence. And while this truth is all around us, is suffocating us, and appears both pervasive and exclusive, it is not the only one. This truth we have built- this world we have built- is one among many possible truths and worlds. It is not the Truth, not the only One, and so it is that we may- we must- destroy this "truth" before this truth destroys each and all of us and be confident that there will be a better, healthier, and truer truth to follow.

MARRIAGE

The Irrationality of Reason

We can count on there always being a logical, internal consistency to any story human beings tell to describe the world, themselves, and the relationship between the two, and to "get inside" a story of the world not our own, we need to begin by locating this logical consistency. Only thus will we begin to understand how the story could function for individuals and groups who do participate in it, that is, who do accept it as "the truth"- the right explanation of how the world began, is, and will be.

"Modern" societies pride themselves on the further sophistication, maturity, accuracy and objectivity of their own version of the truth- obviously superior and a qualitative advance over the primitive mythologies of previous cultures. In modern times, men have discovered and developed reason to replace the infantile emotionalism of previous civilizations and so, the leaders, at least, of the culture have arrived at a more objective understanding of "the way things are." Reason, science, and technology provide us with a more accurate description of the world, and that description has empowered us to gain greater mastery over nature and over our own destiny.

Evidence of this human mastery over the planet, over each other, over ourselves, and over our future is all around us….or, well, it has been until recently when, there has been some small fraying around the edges….there always will be…new problems for us to solve….always will be….new frontiers for scientific discoveries…but look how well, how completely science has solved the problems of the past…and this pattern of past successes will, of course, inspire our continuing faith in science to resolve even what seem like the most intransigent problems of our modern world….the pollution of our air and water, global warming, man's inhumanity to man, the emptiness, alienation, and despair you feel, when you're not numbed, at the center of your being.

Science provides the answers. Of course. It is the truth. Not myth. Not story. The objective truth.

Or not. What if science has its limits, just like myth that came before it? What if science- and its reason- is nothing more than a further extension of myth- the internally logical stories- that preceded it, and what if we have reached the limit of science's usefulness, of the scientific story's ability, to make sense of the world, ourselves, and the relationship between the two?

And what if some new explanation is emerging, waiting in the wings, just as science once impatiently waited, once arose, once was born - an outgrowth of our myths? Would you like to hear a new story? One that makes sense of the world, our self, and the relationship between the two? One that can provide answers to the problems left by science- pollution of our air and water, global warming, man's inhumanity to man, the emptiness, alienation, and despair you feel, when you're not numbed, at the center of your being? Want to hear a story?

Human beings- men- may be rational, but they are never just that. In their transcendence, through reason, of myth and of the physical responses we share with other animals, men did not leave myth and their bodies behind. We held on to these earlier forms of knowing (or they held on to us) just as we adults hold on to the lessons of our childhood that continue to inform our experience, all throughout our days. In the same way, as we advance beyond science, objectivity, and reason to yet another layer in our evolving consciousness, we will not leave our science and reason behind. We don't want to. The defeat of reason is the defeat of our own history and progress. Transcendence of mere reason, that contains our reason in it as a formative and enduring factor, is a movement necessary to our survival.

The fundamental error that Western civilization, and the white men who shaped it, made was to think it was possible to separate reason from our myth (our stories, our history) and our bodies. So enamored and inspired were they (understandably and justifiably so) with their discovery of reason and objectivity- that is, with man's ability to assume a perspective outside the limitations of his body and mere subjectivity that had grown into a prison for his consciousness, so enamored were they with this new capacity for explanation transcendent of the I, that they set about destroying previous layers of their own consciousness the same way the Romans and colonialists clear the ground of native cultures.

They set up an either/or relationship between their previous ways of knowing (and projected these alienated parts of themselves onto women and brown people) vs. their new found powers- for reason, science, objectivity, and distance- that they attributed to God. In this either/or of consciousness, men succeeded in alienating themselves from themselves, from each other, from their women, from their planet, and from their truth. The civilization we see all around us today (like prison walls, including the prison walls inside our souls) are, to use Malcolm X's phrase, "chickens come home to roost."

People's myth and bodily needs and desires continue to function in them- and have continued to function in them all along- but man denies them. He seeks to "discipline himself" against these forces of the Devil (i.e. himself). He seeks to blame others for these elements he denies, to suppress them in himself. Our refusal to admit these parts of ourselves- to others and my self- feeds them on dark and unconscious energies that must somehow express. In the name of denial, in our false assertion of, and aspiration to become, purely rational beings, we commit violent and unspeakable acts. We sin; we lie, and we blame an other. The double murder abused women know.

It is time for the lying to stop and the healing to begin.

Man (and women) is (are) capable of reason. It is human beings' greatest achievement yet that, someday, we will be able to be proud of. But human beings are never just rational. We continue to be driven by the stories- the myths- about the world, ourselves, and the relationship between the two- that we developed in our childhood. We continue to be driven by our bodies. These forces (Freud's "id") drive our reason- always have and always will. It is time for us to recognize this truth. It is time for us to own- to stop demonizing- our own bodies and our emotions. Our bodies and our emotions are not evil as Western patriarchy and its obsessive and exclusive faith in reason has made out. Our bodies and our stories are profound, ever present, and beautiful, when allowed expression. They are not- should never be- subordinate to our reason, and the endeavor to make them so (over the last 2400 years) has made our reason, itself, evil. Rigid. Leading us to death or, worse, a purely objective existence (Hell).

It is time to reconcile our reason to the emotions and the body. It is time to make peace with our self and with each other. It is time to make peace with the planet we are destroying. It is time to stop the irrationality of reason through such reconciliation. It is time to end the patriarchy.

Patriarchy is based on this false domination by reason over the human body and emotions. We assume that the patriarchy is "all there is" because it has gone on for thousands of years and appears everywhere we look. Country folk may glimpse something else- rarely- from time to time, but city folk live inside the belly of this beast, and no wonder they believe, in hopeless desperation, that the belly and the beast are the whole world. But it's not. It's not. And the proof lies in your own gut. Stop numbing yourself for 10 minutes without television, basketball, or drugs, and you will feel all the proof you need rising up inside of you.

There is more to life. There is. You knew it all along, and our bodies, our stories, our reason- all of them together- will take us to where we need to be. A new depth of consciousness is being born inside us, even and especially in the belly of the beast. You can feel it coming out. Let it be born in you as well- through a reconciliation of the different parts of our self- that we have, until now, thought to be at war with one another. All these conflicting voices inside of us- tearing us apart, are, it turns out, just multiple incarnations of one and single being. We are body. We are emotion. We are mind. We are one. We are other, and the other is our self. By maintaining the distinctions, but by owning all sides of the distinctions, we see the unity behind it all. Like the work they do in Internal Family Systems (IFS), we come to recognize and own all our parts. And so begins a circling back to these roots of human consciousness. Having reached the limits of our scientific explanations, we do not extend further outward but, rather, turn our inquires within. Following the cycle of "nature" (before man's time), following the cycle of our own body and life, we begin the turning, and form the seed for a next generation.

Three becomes Four

Human works of art and science reflect and attempt to improve upon the works of nature. Human creations bring the forms of nature into consciousness and, through manipulation and the innovative combination of natural elements, can succeed at creating something new and uniquely beautiful, interesting, or useful. Sometimes, though, human creations fall short of the achievements of nature and instead of enriching it, they end up producing a reduction in nature's truth that is ugly, destructive, and because "un"natural, even grotesque.

As I write, I, too, hope to shape a human creation that will reflect my own unique experience of nature in ways that will both enrich the experience of others and, in certain moments, at least, fill their hearts with beauty. What is beautiful to some, though, will appear grotesque to another, all depending upon where we are coming from (in space and time and consciousness) ourselves.

In retrospect, it seems like the scientific understanding of man has often expressed itself in threes- in triads, pyramids, hierarchies, and, even, a Holy Trinity. I, myself, have often appreciated both the beauty and the explanatory power in these trinities (my former seventh graders may still tell stories about "Turecek's pyramid"), but in the course of writing books I have lately come to realize the limitations in these triads, and though I do not find them ugly in themselves, I do blame these mental constructs for much of the ugliness I find in the world around me.

MARRIAGE

Unlike trines in astrology, the triangles I am referring to have a fixity to them. They are of man's creation. And while these hierarchies served as useful symbols to bring order to the world, more recent lights now reveal how these same symbols demonstrate all that is wrong with the purely rational, scientific version of the truth.

There is a symmetry and balance to nature that necessitates that three becomes four. As children, we all saw trees and only learned afterwards that there was as much tree underground as above. This insight changes the way we look at trees, and so, too, it changes the assumptions about how we see the world. So it is with pyramids.

Our rational hierarchies fail to recognize their own roots in matter, the unconscious, darkness, and emotion. The Holy Trinity, to be complete and true, must acknowledge a foundation in the feminine- be it Mary, Lucifer, the body, or our dreams. Social hierarchies ignore the fundamental equality of all in body and in death, and I'm no kind of mathlete, but I will venture that those of you who are can tell confirming stories from geometry as well.

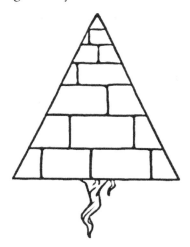

birth of christ

When consciousness expands in one direction, it necessarily creates an echo, a complementary, mirror reaction in the opposite direction. The two constituent elements in human consciousness- the body and the mind- necessarily develop in unison (or, more accurately, in unified opposition) - whether we are aware of it or not.

Once we begin an expansion upward- towards reason, towards the three, a root or reflection is created underground. It is understandable and natural that this root has remained in darkness through the early days of consciousness (consciousness is young), but we have now reached a point of maturity in consciousness where this underground development has been brought to light (through our dreams, emotions, Freud and Jung, through the native people we tried to kill).

In its effort to remain pure, scientific understanding has, until now, remained willfully unconscious of its own fourth and fundamental root. Mistaking its partial description for the whole, science developed technological solutions to life's problems that, we now see, are destructive to the human spirit and soul and earth. Once upon a time, pure reason promised freedom and mastery of the earth, but now our science and technologies grotesquely suck the life blood from our planet.

Our reason can only be restored to health and usefulness by re-tapping the roots of scientific understanding in mythological consciousness, human emotions, feminine wisdom, our individual body, and the earth. The good news is that we have located the original wellspring of our reason, and so, the healing can begin.

Once you see how three is really four, the world can never be the same, thank gods. Blessed be our Mother.

An Honest Mistake

We human beings make this terrible, but perfectly understandable mistake that, it turns out, we are now paying for with the destruction of our planet and our soul. We must remain confident that we can correct this error, but not naively and blindly so. This error is long established in human consciousness, and it will not correct itself. The correction needed requires our awareness and our action, and it can't wait another day.

It all goes back, partly, at least, to the fact of our mobility in the world. We are not rooted in the earth like plants are, and this crucial locomotion that animals achieved brings them a degree of power and pride undreamed of in the more humble world of plants. We humans took advantage of our locomotion still further than the others when we next jiggled loose a separate mind for ourselves, and, so, created God, the world, time, reason, worry, and awareness of our impending death. So confident did we humans become in our own miraculous achievements that we began to imagine, now, too, that we could transcend all limitations, that we could become "like Gods."

We humans dreamed of ourselves as transcendent beings. We created God- the first narcissist- in our own infinite image and set about convincing ourselves that we, God's chosen creature, were marked out for Heaven, eternal bliss in eternal life, and so we sought- within ourselves and all together- the path by which we would, could return to our own origins in the eternal light. We are "fallen" creatures intent upon building edifices and vehicles that will take us back to our original union with God, our Father, the infinite, the light.

The thing is, though, that we kind of got things backwards. We forgot, in our aspiration for eternity and light, our true origins; we would

birth of christ

deny these humble origins in dirt, disrespect our Mother and our family, pretend (like the newly and undeservedly rich) that we did not know, and were no part of, these poor relations- other animals, finite creatures, ants, and snakes, and worms, and beasts. We forgot where we came from. That is human beings' mistake.

Only now, in this present moment of our evolution, are some of us beginning to realize the value in these roots we left behind. We feel cut off- lonely, alienated, inauthentic, unreal- like phantoms of our former selves. We see now that this goal, ideal (Heaven) we set for ourselves is just a dream, a lie, and we see that the ones we have followed, the ones we hoped to be more like, are just as empty, just as lonely, just as vacuous. They are liars like ourselves.

And now we look back on the people that we trampled on to get where we are today- the heathens, negroes, women, and, most especially, "Indians," and we realize that after all, perhaps, these folks knew something we did not. So convinced were we of the superiority of our own reason and ideals that we could not listen to, could not abide, and, so, set about destroying their primitive and childish myths of connection with the earth, with animals, and with spirits (a multiplicity of gods).

God learned from us, and now we have to learn from God. God doesn't want to be separated from our Mother any longer. He longs for Her, but can only be reunited through we humans, the living offspring of the two. It is time we return God's earlier gesture of love, but to do that necessarily requires that we admit some darkness in ourselves.

White people made a mistake once a long, long time ago. They somehow got this picture of themselves as pure light fallen to the surface of the earth:

MARRIAGE

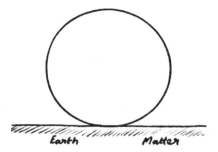

It is time that we fix that

Three becomes four as we change epochs. Mother and Father. Blackness as well as light, sea as well as sky. We need only to remember it, acknowledge it, be embraced by it- our blackness, our origins in matter, and the well spring is there. We've been looking in the wrong direction the whole time.

Kant and Eve

The ladies set their clocks by him as Kant arrived each day for his rendezvous with Eve.

Copernican Revolution

Scientists and rationalists had discovered a new and exciting strategy for uncovering the truth that no one had ever tried before. By distancing themselves from their own emotional judgments and reactions, by naming them and setting them aside as Rene Descartes has modeled for us, it would become possible to see the world objectively. If we could train ourselves- and each other- to see, not through the jaundiced, prejudiced, subjective, and limited perspective of our own internal judgments and our own individual perception, but, rather, as a disinterested and unemotional observer, then by joining our individual perspectives together, we would be able to construct a version of the world and a version of the truth that would describe things "as they really are." Through the application of reason and the scientific method, we could transcend the merely human filter that had, hitherto, clouded our mutual perception of the truth.

The scientists called on one another to take a step back away from our own animal aspects and to exercise man's higher faculty of reason to understand our selves and the world around us. The scientists encouraged one another to assume the transcendent and objective perspective of God. The movement, then, was towards separation of the observer and the observed:

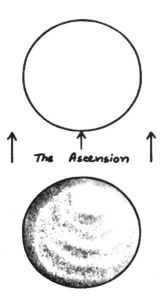

In the early days of science, this new approach to truth was resisted- sometimes to the point of violence- by Churchman who had dominated Medieval society through the power of their Christian myth. In short order, though, (within hundreds of years) the benefits of this new scientific understanding began to show themselves in scientific resolutions to real and practical problems in the world. Man learned quickly to apply his science to develop technologies and objective understandings that would allow him a greater mastery over the world. Weapons improved, as did modes of transportation, growing and preserving food, battling disease, and manufacturing tools that would maximize output from our human labor.

After the initial resistance from the entrenched Christian status quo, religious leaders soon discovered certain natural affinities between this new science and traditional Christian attitudes towards the body, sexuality, women and the Earth. Christianity reshaped itself in a scientific and purely rational image once its leaders realized the extent to which man could establish his promised dominion over earth, the animals, and women through this application of scientific understanding.

In the dialectic of human consciousness (of which the scientists had a limited awareness), this movement towards science and rationality, represented a reaction to the failure of the feminine, mythological understanding that had naively placed human beings at the center of the universe and subject to the whims and will of God or gods. In order to accept the truth of science an act of humility was necessary to acknowledge and accept that the evidence of our senses had surely shown that man was not, after all, the center of our universe. To accept the possibility of scientific truth, it had been necessary first to fully embrace the Copernican revolution that placed the sun, and not the earth, as the center of the universe.

In fact, despite the testimony and "proofs" of the earliest astronomers, most people could not accept this truth until a new path- a new step to jump to- presented itself in the name of science. The possibility of a scientific and objective truth was, in fact, the deciding element in allowing people to shift from a mythological to a scientific consciousness, because the possibility of a new truth turned the humiliation of the loss of centrality into an act of simple humility. It traded our absolute mortification for one that we were strong enough to bear.

And an ironic consequence of this shift was that, very quickly, this new scientific understanding that at first required the humility of man soon fed into a growing power and authority and mastery and hubris on the part of man. Less dependent upon our God or gods, human beings began more and more to take matter into our own hands. We moved from a passive relationship to God- from acceptance of our fate- to a more active role in establishing a relationship to God. Some began to believe in grace through works, and it would not be long before the great Martin Luther would capture our new found power through his revolutionary insight that every man is his own priest and that Jesus is in each person's heart.

As in every stage in the evolution of human consciousness, though- including the next stage we are now breaking into- the worm of its own destruction lies buried inside the original vision of each new version of the truth. In the case of science, the problem, it turns out, was that the separation of mind from body, of reason from emotion, of the masculine from the feminine, could never be complete. To purify reason of all emotion would be to kill it. And so we see our fate as a culture devoted to scientific solutions today- that if we continue to persist down this path towards purely objective, rational and technological solutions, we will end up destroying the planet upon which we depend. In our own time, our rationality has turned weirdly and frighteningly irrational.

Freud's Hypothesis

According to Freud, the event that leads to the birth of religion and to consciousness (since, in certain essential respects, the two are one and the same) is a trauma. Is a murder. In Freud's telling of it in Totem and Taboo, the sons conspire to murder the father who has taken all the women to himself. Upon the father's death, the sons experience the first reversal. The original sin. Remorse for he who has protected them, he that, irreversibly, they have killed. Freud makes much of the ambivalence that adheres to these earliest days of human consciousness- the simultaneous love and hatred, the simultaneous fear of retribution and revelatory celebration, the simultaneous dread and glory of this first, this human act.

birth of christ

And it is an act of men- not women. An act of violence. An assertion of authority, but one that is only possible by the banding together of the many- weaker individuals- against the more powerful one. The father lies dead before them, and as they eat his body, the sons, the many, wake up to the ambivalence, the contradiction, the awesome responsibility and vulnerability that comes from being a man.

"In the beginning was the deed." And the deed was a social one, as we are social animals, and all that has happened since has been- and will be- an attempted reconciliation- of opposites, of contradictions, of the ambiguities, of what it means to be a human.

And now, before we leave Freud and his <u>Totem and Taboo</u>, we must point out the two stages on display here in the scientific epoch of understanding as well. In the beginning stage of the scientific epoch, emphasis had been on an objective understanding of the world, from God's perspective. But at some point in the process of evolution in the human consciousness, the scientific perspective and analysis had been turned back upon itself. Important pioneers in this movement backwards include such crucial figures as Job, Kant, Freud, and Einstein.

But just, as Freud points out, there had come a time in the mythological epoch when human beings had turned away from the totemic cults towards the laws of God and Judeo-Christian religion, away from the perception that human beings, themselves, were the originators of the truth and world, and towards a conception of the world and truth as somehow from a source outside our puny selves, so, too, has there been a turn in the course of the scientific epoch away from the understanding, the faith that the truth can somehow exist- and be discovered "out there" in the "objective" world and a reawakening awareness of the subject. Freud is crucial to this turning, but even he, even Einstein is secondary to the great one- Kant. Kant turned reason back upon itself. He began the process (continued here) by which we turned our reason back upon itself in search of its origin and beginning. This way lays the next revelation, the next permutation, the next incarnation of god(s).

Humans' sense of time is really skewed. Kant wrote 400 years ago, but, ironically, many people- the vast majority of people- have never made the turn. Until now. Now is the time, the age of the tipping point, but, until now, the men who "rule the world" have persisted under the false, outmoded, wrong metaphysic they inherited from Newtonian physics, Cartesian metaphysics, and Christian faith, the first stage of the scientific epoch of human understanding, that has long been dead, though they do not yet admit it. Materialists that they are, they need to see physical proof of their disastrous and mistaken truth, and, even now that the evidence is all around us and, indeed, threatening our very existence, they continue to deny, deny, deny, deny. But now it is out of brutal power. It is out of perverse self-interest. It is about money, now. Everything is about money now for these delusional few who hold the reins of power, and that is why they consult only the economists as their high exalted priests.

But the tipping point is here. The turning is almost complete, and people understand. Politicians cannot stop it. The ground is shifting underfoot. The next trauma is at hand.

Turning Inward

Unlike the blackness, it would appear that the light must come from somewhere. Unlike the blackness, it would appear that the light must have some beginning and so, we fear, an end. It is the light, then, that creates all time, space, and knowledge, and uncovering the source of this light becomes the great and irresolvable riddle of all human experience.

In the earliest days of human consciousness, it could be argued, we human beings are the source of light we use to populate the world with intentions, gods, and stories. If this is true, it is also true that, in the earliest days of consciousness, we have no awareness of ourselves as the source of story, truth, gods, and the world. There is no consciousness of self in these earliest days but, rather, only consciousness of the "what is," "the way things are," "the world" and "truth" we take for granted as the one and only truth. We have no consciousness, whatsoever, that this world and its dimensions are constituted and defined by us. As we look back upon this history of stories human beings have told about the world, it is easy to look down upon the naiveté and foolishness of our predecessors. And it is common to feel, with some sense of superiority, that they could not have actually believed this!

It is quite natural that human beings should take comfort in the fact that they, themselves, have arrived at a greater understanding of "the way things are" than their predecessors and/or more "primitive" tribes, but it is rare for humans to consider whether their truth, too, might not be the projection of a false and limited definition that says more about the one who is projecting it than the way things "really are."

People draw a circle, and while it is easy to see the limits of the circles that other people draw, it is rare for human beings to recognize the limits- and that there are limits- of their own. It is rare for human beings to consider whether their own description of reality, their own projection of the truth might not, itself, be a falsehood and delusion. And, in this respect, humans' first descriptions of the world will, again, establish the pattern for all descriptions that follow. Human beings establish the best explanations possible based upon their observations of the world around them and fail to recognize that this explanation is wrong and that their world is false. So has it always been and will always be.

But, throughout human history, there are also exceptions to this rule. At all times in human history, there are certain individuals who will see beyond the limits of the collective story of their time. These outliers and "discontents" are the grains of sand inside the clam shell who, through constant agitation, give rise to pearls of wisdom that are both humans' greatest achievements and the womb of all future creation. These are the shamans and prophets of old who, by turning consciousness inward, reveal the limits and source of the stories people tell to create a world.

And so, too, are there certain times in human history- and our time is such a one- when consciousness is turned inward upon itself and so the falsity of man's descriptions are revealed. Such a "turning inward" is a crucial movement necessary to the growth and, so, survival of human consciousness.

Prophetic moments in human history such as our own are forced upon human consciousness and are not experiences we would typically seek on our own. Turning consciousness in upon itself is a painful movement that must be triggered by irreconcilable contradictions between what we say is and what is.

These moments of turning inward, these moments of trauma, are times of murder- and ours is such a one. The ground trembles beneath our feet; our gut fills with emptiness; our brain with terror and our heart, despair, as we recognize that we are an accomplice, that we are one of them. A murderer, this time, of our planet, Mother, the souls of children, our future, and ourselves.

It is in just such moments of death and complicity that we human beings awaken. We know- in a flash of lightening- like Plato's slave exiting the cave, like the infant from the womb, that all we have known until now is not true, is dead, and something new is born, and born through us, in us. The new light is born in us.

The Exceptional Cruelty of Freud

I accept Freud's account of the Deed just because- as Freud argues and we show- this origin story so clearly establishes the pattern of murder and lies that still defines the Western patriarchy that grows from it. Freud is right in his analysis of the Jewish God, Yahweh, as the idealized sublimation and reversal of that murdered father.

But Freud is wrong in his estimation of totemic cultures and matriarchal epochs. Blinded as he is by his own- Jewish, Western, patriarchal, white, male- prejudice, all Freud can figure is that these totem cultures were a kind of a rough draft for the real thing. Human beings, with limited intelligences at this point, were not able to fully conceive God, Yahweh, right away and had to resort instead to little animals and figurines- dolls, idols, one might say, as a prop to their understanding.

These various totemic cultures that Freud tries to conceive escape the limits of his own rational understanding, because, quite frankly, they come from different cultures with different values and different origins than the Judeo-Christian cultural lens that Freud tries to reduce them down to. In fact, Freud's failure to understand these cultures- and his use of Western reason to "understand" and mansplain them nonetheless- is symptomatic of the whole Western culture of which Freud is so much a part. In Freud's view, the entire matriarchal epoch is a kind of fallow time when little is happening and we are just waiting for the idea of Yahweh to percolate from the original murder/seed.

MARRIAGE

If Freud's origin story of the Deed is true, it is only true for what, in polite (white) company, is called "the Western world." Freud did not fully understand that part; as a European man, Freud assumed his origin story as <u>the</u> origin story, and, in so doing, blindly dismissed many thousands of years of human history as a kind of warm-up for the real thing.

Not that I am any great expert in matriarchy or totemistic cultures. Like Freud, I am infected by, a product of, this culture, and my readers may easily identify my own unconscious prejudices and limitations, as expressed here. And yet, the two of us, Freud and I, each have a role in this process of excavating the roots of our own culture. It is fated, somehow, astrological, that these assignments fall to us as they do; Freud never really had a choice. He had to turn a critical eye to the darkness. It was in his nature; it is what he is called to do, and so with me as well.

And both of us are called by our times to pursue this criticism, this inquiry, this turning inward- in answer to a pressing and heartfelt and universal need. Also astrological, each period in history produces individuals best equipped to meet the needs of that time.

To be clear, though, the need Freud and I rise to meet is particular to certain moments in a history. It is during the waning moments of a civilization (and life) that this need arises to turn back and reflect, to reap the lessons of all that has gone before. To so interrogate the past and compulsively search for meaning in "the rest of the story" is symptomatic of a civilization in decline. -

The movement of consciousness inward- begun with Kant- has consequences, and, depending upon your perspective, not always positive ones. Such inquiry by a civilization into its own roots may have an undermining effect on the credibility of those "truths" and institutions we previously took for granted. Simultaneously, the credibility is already compromised, creating wiggle room for critics who respond to what is already developing into a painful itch.

Either way, digging loosens the ground around the foundation. Not everyone welcomes more criticism at this, their most vulnerable time, and in vocalizing the problem, the critic makes themselves a target and a likely suspect for causing it. And even if the critic brings the necessary medicine, as they, themselves, no doubt believe, it does not change the fact that the critic calls on people and a civilization to accept truths more painful than they can bear.

Easier to kill the critic, and better, too, because once dead, the civilization, the collective may make of him what they will. We can simply lie about the man and what he lived for, lie about our community's response, turn him into some kind of hero and model for our children- this one we killed. Like an idol, I guess. They take the dead man and make of him the opposite. That is the pattern here and throughout the Western tradition. We see this transmutation by the collective (under control of the brothers) in the father they murder and turn to Yahweh, their special and almighty protector. They do it again with Jesus, whom they murder and turn to Christ, and they did it again in our own time- well, my time (smile)- with Martin Luther King. They killed and hated this man and now use his image to sell poisons like Pepsi and (Christian) nonviolence.

Freud and we both stand nearer the end of Western civilization, and our examinations, while necessary, will contribute to the waning power of a civilization so exposed. Freud saw all this- saw what happens to the social critic and exposer of darkness, and it scared him, I think- the fear of oblivion and price of ostracization was more than Freud would bear. His ambition and cruelty (objectivity) would prevail to make Freud Freud and not some unknown lunatic spouting crazy theories about the incestuous families of Europe.

Freud never wanted to undermine the foundations of the Jewish and Christian and scientific and white community with which he so closely identified. I make that judgement based on Freud's own actions and the decisions that he made. People are a combination of traits, and Freud was ambitious; perhaps above all else, he craved acclaim (and the incumbent financial rewards) from the great men in Europe.

Seen through my lens, Freud so longed to be accepted as a member of that inner circle of elite and chosen few that he was willing to pay any price of admission. And the price named was a betrayal of his professional oath- the betrayal and violation of the women and children who came to him, who depended upon him to be a man and a doctor and protect them. Freud chose otherwise.

Seeing the pattern of murders is crucial to understanding the history of Western civilization, but it is the pattern of Lies subsequent to each murder that really marks us out as special. It is here- in the clean-up phase- in the explanation and defense- that the brothers gain their mastery. In the image of their God, Christians and the Jews 1) become masterful liars and 2) learn how to use violence and a threat of violence to compel acquiescence to their Law, their Rule, their Truth, their Lie.

For a moment, Sigmund Freud had a chance to blow the lid off the whole shadow side of Western civilization. In moments of cocaine-fueled Uranian honesty the truth must have come to him with shocking clarity, but in an act of self-preservation that describes what is most essential about his character, Freud lied and is lying still.

birth of christ

Freud was a physician. A doctor. Young girls came to him for medical treatment. They were suffering symptoms of "hysteria," and either they or their families sought medical help from Dr. Freud. In his analysis with them, girls told Freud stories of various sexual experiences with older male members of their families that were troubling and/or confusing to the girls. Early on, it seemed obvious to Freud that these experiences were linked to the physical and emotional dis-ease the girls were experiencing.

Here is the trouble for Freud- the men who were committing the assaults on the girls and causing their disease- these men were paying the bills. The perpetrators were the most powerful and richest men in Austria and Europe at the time; Freud lusted for the approbation of these men, and the fame and fortune that would follow, and as a brilliant young doctor, he was well poised to make his mark. But such a revelation as this- that the leaders of the free world were raping their daughters in their own homes- such revelation would destroy Freud's reputation and career. And so, Herr Freud makes a decision.

It is the same decision that men- our band of brothers- have faced for millennia, through every stage of Western civilization, and still today. Freud made a choice- to preserve his career and reputation, Freud aligns himself with the powerful men- the perpetrators of the violence- and thereby accepts the array of benefits they provide. Freud rapes the girls' consciousness and tells them they are asking for it. To advance his career, he pretends away the girls' existence as human beings.

And Freud's Faustian bargain pays well. The explanation Freud provides for the girls' hysteria and sexual "phantasies" is (not accidently) absurd on its face (like Judaism) and yet quickly becomes the established treatment for women's complaints of abuse and/or symptoms of "hysteria." Freudian analysis and the dissemination of its concepts throughout Western society has proven immensely successful at protecting not only powerful men who rape women and children but an entire corporate and Christian society based on the normalization of just this kind of double rape- first within and then by the institution established (a Lie) to protect you- you know, the priest, the policeman, the doctor, the judge.

In his act of betrayal- in this second murder of innocents and women, Freud not only replicates a past pattern of double murders but essentially writes the recipe for its perpetuation in the future. Freud adds critical tools- gaslighting, institutional support, expert testimony- to the brothers'/rapists' arsenal. Because it serves the interests of the status quo, the legacy of betrayal and abuse begun by Freud persists unabated and has now spread throughout American society. The clearest description of these patterns derived from Freud's example may be found in Lundy Bancroft's stunning profile of the domestic abuser, <u>Why Does He Do That?</u>

The pattern is always the same, and Bancroft describes well how domestic abusers employ the same gaslighting techniques- questioning her sanity, increasing her isolation, normalizing the abuse, intimidation and outright lies. We see law enforcement jump to the defense of the perpetrator at every turn- just as the rich and powerful fell in behind Freud. These sworn members of the brotherhood (police, judges, even doctors) know they could be next. That is, they could be the one that some hysterical bitch accuses of abusing her, and so, his natural sympathies are aroused on behalf of a potential brother who could lose everything- his job, his reputation- in the face of such accusal. They try to be fair. They try to be supportive, but faced with the terrifying irrationality of an hysterical (beaten, terrorized) woman, the cops kind of see where the guy is coming from.

birth of christ

What makes the double murder of the brothers' extraordinary and cruel is the second part. First comes the event, the rape, the murder, the trauma. But it is what follows- in the explanation- that the real rape and murder occurs. Here a story is told that reverses the truth of what happens. Behind that story lies the whole power of the brotherhood. And one thing they have learned, for sure, is to be absolutely confident in the Lie (which is so easy for the brotherhood that believes its own Lies). The one violated- isolated, powerless, and alone in her story- is left to question her own reality and to consider the consequences of speaking out. A consciousness isolated in this way is torture. The circle of women long since broken- each one alone in her nuclear home. Unable to share an experience that she alone knows. The lie and the enforcement of the lie is the cruelty; its the part Freud is especially good at.

Freud's example also highlights another crucial pattern in the development and maintenance of the Band. Like the Chosen Ones of Yahweh, the band of brothers is always a tightly drawn, select and exclusive club. There is a steep price for admission to the group that, while it varies from one situation to the next, always has in it an element of humiliation and submission and surrender of one's self-identity and integrity to the group.

The allegiance here is different than a normal human desire to be a part of and serve a larger community. Here there is something else. Here a membership inside the circle requires a breaking down, a humiliation and shame (and not the building up that a healthy community would require). It is a queer arrangement and no wonder to me that this He-Man Women-Haters Club is so frightened by drag queens and homosexuals. I mean…

MARRIAGE

In our society, where the brothers' power is so firmly established and institutionalized, we find this kind of initiation rite at various levels of society. Athletic teams are the key strategy for the indoctrination of boys into this band of brothers (physical mediocrity may have saved me) at an early age. Like the Church's priesthood before it, the Corporate State's military and police force provide wonderful opportunities for even poor, dumb, powerless men to join the ranks of the Chosen Ones.

We laugh at people's participation in capitalism and the idea that I, too, can become a billionaire if only I work hard and smart enough. But it is not just this phantasy of a lottery-strike fortune that binds poor white men to capitalism. Through their identification with the rich and powerful forces that rule, the judge or police officer or, even, the individually armed citizen, gets to participate in- and exercise- that shared institutional power. Like a Bills fan, they all get to be part of the same team. Wear the jersey, root for white men and say "We."

It was the genius of Christianity (the Catholic Church and priests, band of brothers, murderers of christ) to extend the Chosen Ones' dominion over the whole world. The Church sells a <u>story</u> to millions of "Christians" that they, too, may be one of the elect and chosen. They need only sacrifice the divinity inside them (crucify the living christ) in trade for obedience to the Church, ministers, and their Book. The reward for worshipping the dead man on a cross is a promise of eternal bliss in Heaven (remember that old Tree of Life?)- just as long as you follow the rules here, now.

Such brilliance unmatched by anything but Yahweh! The beneficiaries here remain the originals- the murderers, the band of brothers, the high priests. Everyone else is sold an empty promise and a lie. Like the shiny certificate Oz gave to- who was it?- Oh, yeah- the priests have many rewards, depending on our weaknesses, so morons gets diplomas, cowards get metals, and the man of steel is handed a clock and told it is a heart. Remember Indulgences? Pick your poison, boys.

Christianity's genius is in marketing. It is not just Heaven that binds the Christian to the priests and Church. It is the opportunity to <u>belong</u>. The need to feel <u>special</u>. The need to be Chosen, and to have some outlet, cover and, most of all, forgiveness for my shame.

These days, the uniform and the robe, the gun, even the color of skin are enough to mark the individual as a member in good standing and so authorize a man to act on behalf of the brotherhood. He becomes an agent of the State. It can be intoxicating- this access to power and protection- particularly to boys who had been denied that security in childhood. The power of the State inheres in the individual. He can feel it coursing through his veins. There is no room to question the morality or rightness of this force. To do so would dissipate the force, and so it is a rule of the brotherhood not to question- and a role of the brotherhood to seek out and persecute those who would.

What ties poor, white, rural men to the oligarchs is not just the capitalist Lie that you, too, can be a billionaire. Rather, poor, white man are already better off under the capitalist system in so far as they are given opportunities to actually <u>participate</u> in the power structure- to become a part of it and exercise Its power. Given a gun and badge, a single man may act, in the name of Big Daddy, with impunity and so rest assured of Big Daddy's protection. He is a member of the brotherhood. He feels its enervating power as he becomes part of something numinous, something greater than himself.

We see the stages of unfolding genius in the brotherhood's usurpation of power. Begun by the Christians (i.e. the murderers of Christ) in

MARRIAGE

their brilliant extension of the Chosen Ones to include all the priests' victims and slaves, "the followers of Christ" are convinced to enslave themselves to Church and priesthood for the imagined reward of an eternal life with Christ. Pressing their Lie of Christ in Heaven, the brotherhood convinces a large swath of the population to enslave themselves out of a belief (a feeling, nothing more) that I, too, am among the Chosen Ones, the saved, the special, the elite.

Christian and white, we right, and that's enough for the (true) elites to convince us that we are members of the Brotherhood, as well. We are not. It is a Lie, like everything the brothers do, but a remarkably effective one. Telling people they are special, superior, chosen actually works. It makes them feel better. They <u>want</u> to believe it, of course, and so they do. The fact that they are being used and lied to doesn't matter, and you won't convince them.

"Here's your gun, son. Now do your job."

"Thank you, Sir. I will, Sir."

They sell the <u>idea</u> of the exclusive club at no cost (rather, a benefit) to themselves.

All this has been hard to work through for me, because, as is obvious, I am deeply indebted to Freud for the critical excavation of the roots of Western civilization he has achieved. My own life work begins necessarily where his left off. He is an intellectual Father to me, teaching me how to peer intently into darkness, and yet I despise him for his betrayal of women and his selfish and cruel perpetuation of the old violence, murder and lies.

Freud talks a lot about ambivalence, and he generates a lot of that in me as a student and colleague. In a way, Freud is here again a perfect model for the abusive father. He is not all bad. There are moments when we love him. We have cherished memories of connection, and we are like him in crucial ways. We share his brilliance- the abusive father; we are proud of our gifts but ambivalent about the fact that they come from him. It is these positive connections, in fact, that make it a betrayal. Someone we are indifferent to does not betray us- only one we thought who loves us and demonstrates that we are wrong. So it is for me with Freud.

From first believing his patients, Freud now decides "it is all in their heads," but worse than that, Freud actually maintains that these sexual memories of his young patients are wish fulfillment phantasies that girls generate themselves. The girls want their fathers and brothers and uncles to fuck them. The girls are begging for it, seducing these men and then blaming the men for indiscretions that are most wholly their own.

On a par with Jefferson's claim that all men are created equal, on a par with Paul's usurpation and murder of christ, on a par with Abraham's murder of his son, this act of betrayal by Freud represents one of the few, most heinous- and consequential- crimes in the violent history of the patriarchy. "Gaslighting" is not a strong enough word to describe what Freud did to his patients. He made innocent victims- children- into perpetrators. These children, who turned to him- a doctor- when most vulnerable and alone and… Freud chose to sacrifice his young patients.

Which brings me to a final point now- one that I have not yet fully developed but that nonetheless requires some mention, and that is the role of shame in the brothers' constellation. Conspiracy theorists tell stories of an Illuminati that performs sexual, typically homosexual, rituals of initiation as a requisite entry into the circle of the richest and most powerful elite, and, frankly, such speculation would make sense given the patterns so far uncovered by Freud and by me, here.

To be clear, we are peering here into the shadow side of the brothers and the brotherhood. Such an act must be experienced by the brotherhood, itself, as a direct assault upon the brotherhood, and perhaps it is. The brotherhood depends on the darkness in each individual. The brotherhood depends on personal shame to enforce its power and Law. That is why some ritual participation in a Lie is requisite to admission to (even the feeling and delusion of) participation in the brotherhood. Every man in our culture has some deep experience of shame- almost always around sex and cowardice, but no one talks about it. Talking about that is taboo to the brotherhood, because the brotherhood needs that shame as a threat and weapon against all disobedience and/or refutation of the Lie.

Looking back, it is truly extraordinarily how odd and absurd the story is that this band of brothers settled on. It is a lesson repeated by sociopathic leaders of patriarchy still today, that is- if you're going to lie, lie big. And that is what the Jewish lie of Yahweh is- it is an absolute contradiction of everything people might consider "common sense." It is a reversal so absurd that people would need to be compelled to comply through threat of violence. But as absurd and unnatural and untrue as Yahweh's lies are, the benefits of believing for those Chosen few- our band of brothers- who choose to accept this core unreason are substantial and enduring.

What is it that Freud does to these girls, exactly, that makes it such a violation? What sin does Freud commit? If the pattern is always the same, then Freud's example should elucidate the whole underlying dynamic. I would argue that Freud's sin against his patients is that in their moments of greatest humanity and vulnerability, he turns them into objects. I would argue that this is the underlying sin of Western civilization that we- you- must now, finally, begin to overcome.

It sounds so abstract- "turns them into objects"- not personal at all- until we consider how that betrayal must have been experienced by the girls. Just as we have experiences turning others into objects, so have we experienced being turned into an object, our selves. We can imagine/remember how it feels.

Here the girls had already been physically and psychically violated by the powerful men in their families, and they came to be seen by Dr. Freud. The girls had told no one, could tell no one about the crimes against their bodies that they did not even recognize as crimes. Though they definitely felt the shame of it. They shared this with their doctor. Girls 16, 18, 20 were all alone with this truth they felt but could not explain. She needs someone to help make sense of her experience, and the perpetrator, of course- upon whom the victim depends- can only deny such a thing- even to himself. Also in shame…. It is the doctor's job.

There is one controlling/dominating consciousness in each of these situations- in the rape and in the consultation with the expert/doctor. In the rape, the reality and self of the child is annihilated, consumed to feed the rapist's need for power and control over life. She is turned to an object to satisfy his animal desires.

The girl comes to the doctor for healing- in hopes that her previous health and self and reality may be restored. The doctor looks this girl in the face (or maybe not- maybe why the Freudian couch); the doctor tells the girls' story back to them, but he tells it from the perspective of the rapist- this time with all the force and authority of the society behind it. This second rape, we must imagine, leaves the child more alone, more invisible than ever. Like Cain, alone in her precious "truth," she has no one and is found guilty of the crimes against her.

The feeling of being disappeared does not go away. We have experience of our own subjectivity, our own humanity and feelings and consciousness. I am right here! But in the sin of patriarchy, the other, the brother, the one in relation to power looks through you and perceives nothing. It is not that the brother pretends your humanity away. He doesn't ignore you like an angry child. Rather, to do his job, for his place in the brotherhood, he has forsaken the capacity to see you as an individual human being. He does not recognize your subjectivity (your humanity) because he has sacrificed the same in himself as price of membership. You see in his eyes there is no sense in arguing. There is no sense, only the participation in a power so much greater than his own.

You can put yourself in the place of the girls and know how it feels to be so completely and entirely alone as Freud has left them. As painful as such imaginings may be, we make them willingly, as part of our responsibility to feel. Reflecting on the girls' experiences with Freud revives in us our own humanity, our own indignation, our own vulnerability and loneliness that- though painful is preferable to being dead, hard, an unfeeling object: preferable to being a brother. Though we must allow ourselves that experience- as brother- as well; to our shame, as humans, we participate in both- dehumanized and dehumanizing- parts of the equation. We are complicit as members of this society, though we may wish to appear otherwise. I eat meat. I don't know what people in other meat-eating cultures do; I have heard stories of indigenous American cultures that acknowledge the bond and sacrifice of the animal whose life is taken, knowing too, that my time will come. But I'm not like that. On a daily basis, I make an object of that chicken- a dead thing I don't care about except how it may be consumed by me.

We all participate in this distancing, this inhumanity that has come to be taken for granted by patriarchy. I kill flies and bugs in my house. Mice. Sometimes I think about it, but, really, I don't care. While living creatures, they are dead to me.

Once I set a have-a-heart trap in the garage and then forgot about it. Months later, I came back to find a skeleton inside. A brother would laugh that off, because he makes an object of that mouse (and me). I think of that mouse all the time. And for a reason.

You know. And you do it too. Participation in the patriarchy requires a cutting off of connection, a severing of emotional ties, a discipline against one's own humanity (called "being a professional" and) best exemplified by Abraham's murder of Isaac and repeated here in Freud's murder of his patients. A participation and complicity we are ashamed of; a shame the brothers depend on.

Relativity

The masculine and the feminine, the blackness and the light- these we will have with us always, but by redefining one, we can and will also redefine the other. A new masculine, a new Logos, a new truth is possible. We have begun to point to this new truth here as have several of our contemporaries in simultaneous articulations of this newly emerging truth.

To both escape the wrath of Tiamat and escape the prison of the corporations, to transcend the uroburic either/or of Democrats and Republicans, we must begin by taking some of that blackness back into ourselves where it belongs. We must own our blackness and stop casting it out on others- onto minorities and the poor, onto our enemies and women, onto Jesus Christ.

We must embrace our own finitude and death, admit our own failures and limitations, eat crow (the blackness) - and so, accept our true place as human beings. We must seek the light in others different than ourselves- find christ in the other- project that, and so open a bridge for understanding and relationship that human beings have as yet not known.

One aspect of this new truth that we are, together, birthing will be an understanding of relativity- not the infantile understanding of relativity that we have thus far known. Not the kind of relativity that pits our head against our heart, our mind against our body, each against the other. And not the kind of relativity that believes that because multiple truths are possible, there is no such thing as truth and/or that all "truths" are equal (like assholes).

No. The relativity we are, together, giving birth to, recognizes that though our truth is "just a story" and just one story among many- infinite- possible stories, our story is nonetheless true and uniquely beautiful. Our truth is one of a kind- a window onto the infinite housed in this humble, mortal body. Like a star shining brightly in the night sky, of infinite heart and eyes of wonder, I stand in awe of all the stars around me, knowing I am one like them.

You will see in my writing a continuing tendency to layer nouns upon nouns, verbs upon verbs, and images upon images, each new word adding another dimension, a different angle, a greater depth of meaning. This tendency embodies, too, an essential part of the new relativistic understanding of truth. No one word is enough to capture my full meaning, the full truth about a concept and, especially, about a person.

To even begin to approach "the whole truth and nothing but the truth" requires us to view a concept from a variety of angles. And so it is with our selves and others as well. There is no single "truth" about any human individual. Every "truth" is relative, from a particular perspective, a version of the truth, in itself a partial truth, but in conjunction with other such angles, and other such truths, the beginning of a creation of infinite depth and beauty.

Each one of us is a complex construction of images and angles, perspectives and truth. Each angle reveals a certain aspect to ourselves but cannot possibly reveal all that we truly are, and so to reduce a human being down to a single image- to turn them into an object, to fix them in time and space, as our own patriarchal society longs to do, is to commit a sin against that person.

This tyranny of the single image forms a prison for the human soul, and liberating ourselves and others from this reduction down to objects, to cogs in a machine, is a large part of the political and spiritual struggle inherent in this new birth of relativity.

The relativity of truths is not limiting but liberating just because we human beings are capable of constructing a complex of images, of perspectives, and of truths. We human beings have learned at this point to shift our own perspective with great fluidity, though some are more fluid than others.

To be sure, some are more fixed in their perspectives, and these ones may even see their fixedness as a virtue- integrity- that is lacking in those who are more liberal in their perspective. And part of the desperate political struggle we are engaged in is with these people who insist on a fixed loyalty and obsession with a one and only truth until they are strangling the life out of the rest of us who would move beyond in our understanding.

And, of course, those most fixed are also the same ones with their hands upon the instruments of power- the institutions and the corporations- become instruments of torture, death machines that enforce the tyranny of objective truth, but there is another way. Lots of other ways, a vitality to the human spirit, an infinity of human potential, if only we can break the icy grip of this dead and dying and murderous past.

While our body remains fixed at this place and time, our consciousness is free to roam. Perhaps temporarily and only to a degree, but to a rather large degree, we humans have grown able to embody the experience of others. We can shift our consciousness from this point of I into the point(s) of other(s), and so we are able to see the world from different perspectives, through different sets of eyes, and enter for a moment(s) at least the experience of an other- different than our own. It is this capacity of human consciousness, grown stronger over the course of our evolution, that makes the birth of christ possible today.

This ability to shift our point of reference is an aspect, too, of the relativity of consciousness, and like the ability to form multiple perspectives on ourselves, so, too, this ability to enter multiple perspectives of an other creates infinite possibilities in our life. And beauty. Beauty most of all. Beauty is the simultaneous awareness of our own finitude and infinitude. It is joyous and painful; it is the height and depth of human experience. Life as lived through the body of christ is beautiful.

And so, we see where consciousness is taking us, beyond our quest for pure reason divorced of our animal instincts and emotions and back into the heart of existence, experience, our world(s). The second coming is a circling back. Back to the roots of human consciousness and experience. Back to the beginning, but this time with the added consciousness we gained through our sojourn to the sky, to reason.

Just like I described Heaven earlier on- when I was saying it was not possible, but maybe, maybe now it is possible after all, but only for this short moment we call life. And our knowledge that it must end, and that we must die, makes Heaven more profound and palpable and precious, makes Heaven possible at all.

And when we sleep, and when we dream. Carlos Castaneda points us to this hitherto largely unexplored realm of human experience and consciousness. Here, more than in our waking life, our consciousness is free to roam, to leave the body behind, to return to when it is time to "wake." It will be the responsibility of future generations to explore these realms that, I can only imagine, must hold truths as beautiful as here.

Time

As long as we believe that we are made in the image of God and God is all goodness and light, it is possible for us to believe that there is one- objective and eternal- truth, and that our definition of the world is the only possible one. "Christians" understand, of course, that, as humans, we do not attain to the full and infinite understanding of our God, but we can be confident, nonetheless, that that portion of the truth that we have so far uncovered must be reliable, must be "reality," and the way things "in fact" are.

Once we begin to question, however, God's own original claim to rightness, truth, and objectivity (as I have done here), once we consider the possibility that God, Himself, was mistaken in His perceptions, this insight opens the possibility of alternative universes, of a multiplicity of truths and worlds, that, in all honesty, our faith in Christianity and, later (currently) science, was designed to protect us from.

Scientists, themselves, have, thanks to Einstein, come to recognize the relativity of our definitions of time, but this realization is slow in trickling down to most humans' ways of seeing. Consciousness is structured in ways that hold on to previous ways of making sense even when the "truth" of these perceptions has been demonstrably outgrown. We have an obligation nonetheless to extend our knowledge to consider possibilities at the furthest edge of our understanding.

Time under the old Christian, scientific, and objectivist paradigm was understood to be unilinear. We moved from the past, through the present, to the future. There was no going backwards, of course, and this was the only construction possible for this crucial element in our human experience. The linear construction of time made possible a faith in progress that has been fundamental to the scientific faith since at least the time of Bacon, Newton, and Descartes. This Western construction of time enabled us to keep faith in the perfectibility of man, and with every advance in human understanding- most especially the advance from mere mythology to reason- it became ever more likely that human beings would approach the understanding of God, the model of their endeavors.

Buried deep beneath white culture was always an alternative conception of time present even in the moment of Eve and Adam's exile from the Garden of Eden (where, until the "fall," there was no time). This was, of course, the cyclical time of nature- the seasons, night and day, birth and death, moon and tides, and menstrual cycles. Linear time, and the progress of science, reason and man, was set against these natural cycles and became a crucial part of overcoming man's mere animality

birth of christ

and subjugation by forces greater than himself. Through his faith in linear time, progress, and the perfectibility of man, the objectivist and patriarch seeks to transcend the limits of his body, to escape subjugation to the cycles of Nature, even to cheat death (through fantasies of Heaven and eternal life).

With science, we sought the infinite on the human plane alone, instead of through heaven.

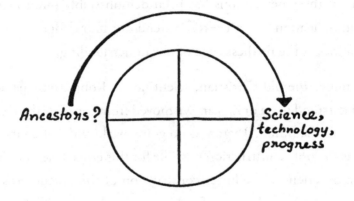

At the present turning, we seek the infinite in the depths.

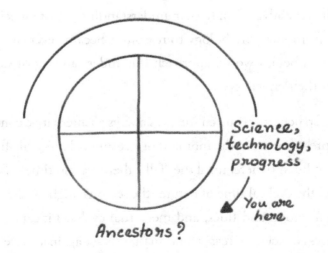

More subtle thinkers throughout the Western tradition would come to recognize the combination- the marriage, if you will- of these two types of time in a kind of cyclical evolution and progress that came to be known as the dialectic. Though the idea of "progress" is falling into disrepute in our current epoch, we cannot deny the reality and power of this linear time and progress of the patriarchs. Human beings are, paradoxically, mysteriously and miraculously, animal and spirit both, and so we cannot deny that progress, growth, and dialectic are not only possible, but are, in fact, distinguishing elements of human experience in the world.

Through a more conscious marriage of these times- linear and cyclical, patriarchal and natural- we will come to understand the profound significance of our current moment in history, and so, too, will we awaken to yet another possible conception of time- a conception that makes possible the birth of christ.

Contemporaneous Myth

In myth, events are always contemporaneous with us regardless of whether (viewed objectively) they happened in some distant past, are expected to happen in some distant or not so distant future, or if they happened somewhere out of time. Now, this is only true for myths that we, ourselves, participate in. That is, myths that we do not recognize as myths. Myths that we don't participate in are not myths for us. They are profane "stories" that other people believe provide some explanation of their world, but, for us, who view them objectively, they are more like anthropological artifacts about a tribe or individual dead to and different from our self.

To understand the distinction, and to see how myth functions in time and consciousness, it may be helpful to understand that objectivity is, itself, a kind of myth. It is a "truth" about the world that we so take for granted that it does not occur to us to question it. We assume that there is something called "an objective world," when really this world is a construction of our collective consciousness. It is "real" in a certain sense. It is real for us, but it is not necessary for there to be a world. It is a collective representation that we have built on and build on, but the fact that we share this myth of objectivity with other people- lots of other people- does not make it any more "real" in the sense that it is "objectively," universally, necessarily true about "the world" divorced from our particular definitions.

There are other people for whom a world exists, but the idea of objectivity does not; there are people for whom objectivity is "just a story" that the white invader tells. We might say- and have said throughout our history- that such people are out of touch with "reality." Well, they are out of touch with our reality in exactly the same way that we are out of touch with theirs. It is difficult to conceive of, but there are worlds different than our own.

"Myths," if you are not in them, always appear irrational and, usually, ridiculous. They can't really believe that, we will often think when presented with the myth of another. And yet, we all have our own set of unexamined, often ridiculous myths that rule our lives. We participate in cultural myths, and we also each have an array of personal beliefs, stories, gods by which we make sense of the world, our self, and others. People never choose their myths. Rather, the myth acts upon, it "chooses" them, and thus, at a mythical level, we do not get to "choose" our beliefs.

We all carry in our consciousness, in our construction of a world a host of unexamined and unconscious myths- some of which we share with, and usually received from, others- our family, our community, our nation, the media, our time, but also others that are particular to ourselves. The myths we tell ourselves to construct a world still all seem to follow certain fairly universal patterns. There are archetypes, collective mental structures into which our myths must flow in order to live.

The science (?) of psychology has devoted itself, at least since Freud, to delineation of these structures and to a process of excavation in their "patients" to uncover what and how myths were operating within an individual consciousness, within a particular person, to create a certain world.

Psychology grew out of a medical environment based on "patients" whose personal mythologies were failing to function in ways that made them "happy," "well adjusted," "healthy," "well." Their mythologies were making them sick in one way or another, and so it became (becomes) the psychologist's role to uncover and root out the mythologies that were the source of the distress. While I share psychologists' interest in excavating myths, and bringing them to consciousnesses and light, I do not want to participate in the pathologization of all myth in people's lives, consciousnesses and worlds. I am particularly concerned with mythologies that have come to define our collective consciousness and that, as individuals, we both have inherited (to varying degrees) and are suffering from.

Certain mythologies- whether personal or collective- can become pathological- i.e. self-destructive to the host. My concern is that we live in a society made sick by its own mythology. The cancer we are suffering from has been present in our body for hundreds of years. I know that by going back and reading the analyses of previous "doctors" (philosophers, psychologists, novelists, and social critics) who had diagnosed the problem "even then." In recent years, in my lifetime,

birth of christ

the illness has progressed at an exponential rate, and, if we are not too late already, we must act before we destroy our planet with this illness- with our false myth.

The patients psychologists treat suffer physical symptoms as a result of the pathology- the maladaption, the error- in their consciousness. If the treatment is not successful, patients can, and do, die. Where the treatment is unsuccessful, the patient commits suicide. They kill themselves, which may take a variety of forms. Before such termination from the pathology, the doctor and their loved ones will see clear evidence in the patient of violence against their own body and/or mind, a self-destruction that, while not yet terminal, clearly- to an outsider, or even to the patient, themselves- is not rational nor healthy. And yet, in the grip of their own mythology, tormented and trapped by a reality they cannot find their way free of, the patient has no choice. They are compelled to self-destruction by the sickness, the limitations, the untruth of the "truth" that has taken possession of their consciousness. They are as if possessed. They are possessed by a notion, by a construct, by a "truth" that is destroying them.

In our time, the patient is the planet. The body is our Earth. The "truth" and myth is objectivity- "science," patriarchy, either/or, masculine thinking separated from the wellspring of life that is blackness, emotion, fluid, feminine, and beyond our human control and mastery.

Our job- my job- is to root out the illness that is destroying us, to bring it to the light of consciousness, to expose the dark side of our consciousness that we deny, have kept suppressed, to the light of understanding and self-recognition, that we may not be ruled by its invisible forces any longer. To do this, and to heal, we must admit something that we have feared and have denied over the course, at least, of our white supremacist civilization. We must awaken to a part of ourselves that we have kept buried and so, demonized, that, once admitted, we will realize, can save and complete us.

We are on the edge of either a tremendous awakening- by recognizing and embracing our own blackness we will, ironically, come to feel (not merely "believe in") God. Or we won't break through, and the forces in our collective consciousness (the ones with their hands on the instruments of power in our world today) still wedded to the false "truth," the mythology of science gone evil, "God-like," mad, will drive us all to suicide and so will kill our planet.

I am not opposed to science. I am opposed to the mythology that possesses us that says and/or acts as if science, objectivity, and human reason are all there is. As if it is "the whole world." I will even grant that it is "the whole world"- our world if only you will recognize that "our world" is not all there is. There is something beyond our world, beyond our circle of understanding, that we have tried to keep out and deny, that has terrorized us for millennia. There is a blackness beyond our world. Our denial of it will not make it go away. It is seeping in to undermine our false consciousness. You cannot keep it out. It is life. It is our Mother, forgotten and denied. It is our larger self, not in God, the Father, Heaven, Light, but in Earth, matter, Mother, blackness. It is Divine. It is our second self. The eye of our dreams. Our very body upon which our life, our consciousness, God, the Father, existence, culture, survival all depend. The blackness that we've feared- the blackness is our savior. The blackness is our self; the other brings the present.

Simultaneity

Human beings' definition of time and "progress" is a product of our Western civilization, that is, the product of this patriarchal world we created based on God's fundamental error, turned into a lie. This world view runs very deep in all of us- to such an extent that even for those of us who are furthest out on the horizon, for those of us who have most developed our capacity to see through this world as just another fiction and creation- even for us, the terms and definitions of this old worldview continually assert themselves and define how we see the world, our selves and others. And we would be mistaken to think that we will ever shed- once and for all- these old ways of seeing and defining the world. We won't, except temporarily and/or in death, and, something tells me, we wouldn't/shouldn't want to even if we could.

These old views of our world, our self, of others, time, space, concepts, ideas, God and Mother define our world and so make it possible for us to exist- and be conscious at all. We do not wish to be rid, once and for all, of all these limits to our understanding, as it is just these limits that make us human. They are our finite aspect that is to be cherished and celebrated and embraced just as surely as those infinite aspects we have been longing after for so long.

But what is important in order for us to advance to the next- relativistic- understanding of the world and our own consciousness- is to realize that this world we have created is only one of many possible worlds. And to realize that this joint construction of our world is really just a fiction- a lie, a mistake, a fabrication, if you will- that does not, cannot describe "the way things are," "in fact," that is, freed from our prejudices and the imposition of our definitions. There is no world "in fact," and the "objectivity" that the patriarchal world has sought throughout its science and its reason is, itself, a fiction and a myth. It does not exist, and all worlds are relative, they are fictions, even the ones that have been around for 2400 years and allow us to fly planes, build buildings, and suck oil and gas from the body of our earth to fuel our insatiable machine.

Inside the large, but limited, patriarchal world view, time is seen as a linear progression, but "it" (time) is not, "in fact." Time, "in fact," is just another fiction that we humans use (necessarily) to define and make sense of the world. But if this is true, and if it is also true that patriarchy is just one among many possible constructions of "reality," then it must be possible, too, for human beings who have learned to see outside the bounds of the patriarchal fiction, to conceive a sense of time or no time that would be substantially different from the time we have always (and often still) assumed.

Mary Daly teaches that the Garden of Eden is not, "in fact," the story of man's beginning in some distant past, but, rather, the story of our future, the goal we have been striving towards. Humanity will awaken, when "Eve," our Mother, gives birth to a new consciousness in humans that will allow us, for the first time, to see beyond the walls of patriarchy, of patriarchy's God, and patriarchy's story of the beginning that has, until this moment, kept hidden from us our true human potential and destiny.

Contemporary readers may remember the scene from the movie, The Truman Show, when Truman, who has lived his whole life, unbeknownst to him, as a fictional character in the fictional world of a "reality" television show, bumps up against the limits of that world. He has sailed a boat to escape this world, when out at sea on the far horizon, he comes to a bump and stop where the walls of the television set end. So it is with all of us. We have come up against the limits, the wall of God and reason- what we had always assumed until this day to be all the world there is, and we have come to realize with a thud to our solar plexus that there is something more.

birth of christ

Like Truman, the only world we have ever known is dead. In the movie, Truman finds a door- a way out of the fictional world that has imprisoned him. Truman walking through the door- to transcend the limits of the story he has been told about himself- is a powerful metaphor for the solution most often presented to our current predicament. It is a metaphor and a solution, though, that I must resist. On this most crucial point, I break with spiritual leaders of my time, and I argue that a "transcendence" of reason- a continuing expansion of consciousness outward- is neither possible (except as a continuation of the patriarchal phantasy of Heaven) nor desirable. For us, unlike Truman, there is no exit. We have reached the limits of our human reason, and, for us, the solution must be found by turning back to where we came from. We must reverse course and turn our consciousness in upon itself. That is the necessary revolution of our time- that way- back to the heart of our experience and consciousness and relationships- lies healing, vitality, survival, awakening, and truth. The forgotten wellspring.

We have breached the wall of God and reason through disobedience and creativity, the humanity of Eve within us. What God warned would be a world of work, pain, suffering and death is all that, for sure. But it is also something more. It is a world of possibilities, freedom, infinitude, mystery, miracle, liberty, love, and beauty (beauty, most of all). What looked like death, what looked like Armageddon, is the return, or first arrival, of understanding and of meaning.

THE SACRED HOOP

The Idea of Christ

The way to christ passes through Tiamat. Tiamat, the resurrected serpent, grown murderous and awesome, in the underground and blackness. We pinned her head with our cross of science, reason, religion, technology, dominion, and Law with the light we claimed from God, never recognizing until now (and for many, still not now) our own hubris and failure to conceive "the whole truth" through our naive assumption that we stood for "nothing but the truth."

The blackness of our earth, and our own bodies, and, even, our own women, that should be a source of life, nurturance, and renewal, we have turned into Tiamat- a death dealing monster that we fear we must destroy, or be destroyed by, only understanding at the deepest levels of our own consciousness that the One we have systematically sought to silence and ignore, is, in fact, a necessary aspect of our self.

God, our Father, sent us christ to bridge this gap, to heal our souls, our civilization, and our understanding- to re-establish a lost connection, and we responded to God's gesture by killing Jesus, casting him back to Heaven, and out of flesh, and thus undoing God's act of reconciliation and attempt at health. In making Christ another God of perfect light that we could worship and pray to, we lost the possibility of true relation and a true understanding that the person, christ, promises.

Being human we only understood a portion of christ's truth. Because we humans see in threes instead of fours, because we (until now) lacked the eyes to see beneath, to recognize the shadows, to consider the darkness, we missed the shadow side of Christ's ascension, and, so, too, we failed to recognize (until now) the consequences of our actions in imitation of God, our Lord.

The serpent, Tiamat, is the shadow of our Christ, just as the Devil was, before them, the shadow of our all-knowing, and all-powerful, and all-benevolent God. When we cast Jesus into Heaven, making him all light and goodness, we simultaneously planted the seed of darkness and terror with his body/self that we denied. And ever since we have praised the one, denied the other.

If we are ever to realize christ as God intended, we must own christ in both aspects. We must reconcile ourselves to christ's body, to blackness, to mortality and limitation and death- and so must reconcile to these aspects in our self as well, if christ is ever to be born.

Let christ's blackness flood our arid souls and quench our thirst for truth reborn.

Replace the Circle

In our either/or consciousness we have pitted the cross of science against the circle of life. The patriarchy employs a strategy that amounts to the subjugation of the circle with the cross. We have sought a (re) solution and truth that is unchanging, universal, and absolute. Such solution fails to recognize, however, the necessary fluidity of all answers and all life. We fail to do honor to the circle in our devotion to the cross, and thus it was that we could take the life of our god and worship, instead, the cross upon which christ gave their life. It is time, now, in the dialectic of our consciousness, to re-lay the sacred hoop over the excesses of the cross.

The reassertion of the circle of life does not negate the discriminations of reason and does not invalidate the truths uncovered by our scientific methods. The circle restores balance by putting these capacities of human consciousness in proper perspective. A reassertion of our smallness, humility, and presence in the here and now provides a necessary context for our scientific inquiries. It serves to focus science on the real life-and-death issues that are immediately at hand.

The hoop brings our attention home to things that are needed. Limiting our attention allows us the light and intensity and focus necessary to do what is necessary. The sacred hoop also turns our attention in on itself and saves us from dissipating any more precious energy on phantasies of human beings as transcendent beings "like God." The hoop brings focus on our real and immediate concerns- the problems at the center of our experience, the problems that threaten our continuing existence.

The laying of the sacred hoop is an act of humility- as every advance in consciousness has been. It is an admission of our own finitude, an embrace of our human smallness, but as we have found in revolutionary moments in our past, through our act of humility, we find that new worlds are opened to us, our horizons are expanded by the enclosure of our consciousness. We see outside the hoop more clearly, too, when we define what is inside. Attention is turned away from our representations of God and back to the infinitute in our body's depths.

The Collective Circle

All consciousness is collective, but we each participate in that consciousness as individuals. We are the necessary cipher through which the collective consciousness comes alive, becomes real, becomes at all. In a way exactly analogous to how Schopenhauer talks about how the Will to Live requires individual incarnations to become manifest, so, too, do the collective creations of our human consciousness require individuals in order to animate that consciousness. In a way exactly analogous to how God comes to life only through the human body of Jesus, the collective depends upon individual human beings to perpetuate human consciousness, to keep it moving forward, to keep it alive.

Our individual consciousness is constructed from the achievements of the others who have gone before. The use we make of these materials, the unique constellation we bring to pre-existing materials of consciousness- will depend upon a "something new"- a new mystery and miracle- a new moment in space and time and consciousness that each individual brings with them upon entry into the world. The collective works through us to become real, incarnate, to come to life, and we work within and through it to "make our mark," to "find our place," to make meaning and a difference in the world.

"Reality" is a continually evolving collective construction that we are inescapably embedded in and, simultaneously, able to transcend and change through unique contributions that only we can bring. Education (both formal and informal) is the process by which we are introduced to consciousness or, what is the same thing, indoctrinated into the collective. But education must also be something more than that. To be meaningful, to be inspiring, to be transformative, to be useful, education must also provide nourishment to- I don't know what to call it- the "conatus"(?) (Spinoza), the "noumena" (?) (Kant), the soul (?), our "self" (?), the center in us all that makes renewal, life, and human consciousness possible. Through education, the structure of human consciousness and the world is rebuilt inside each of us. To begin requires the individual "sticking point," the individual body and unwavering center point we each bring with us to this world; to live, the structure must remain dynamic, open-ended and with new possibilities. Creative. Generative. Alive. Individual.

What we do with these structures we inherit from the others, the decisions we make inside the context they provide, are, partially, at least, up to us. We have liberty to extend consciousness, to experiment with variations, to "think out of the box," to recreate the world and formulate new truths. Even such divergences will, no doubt, be conditioned by the combination of limitations and capabilities we are presented with by our time and others who "raise" us, condition us, prepare us, or are around us from the time we are born.

Our life and its (re)solutions will come in answer to specific questions and contexts into which we have been born. That is why people born of a certain generation will often develop solutions that align with one another- because we are each asked the same questions by life, by the accumulated consciousness of others who have gone before. But it is this power to contribute, to change the world, to advance the collective consciousness, that makes life worth living, that gives us meaning and our purpose, that makes we human beings the greatest miracle of all.

It is equally possible for us to overestimate our freedom of will and to overestimate the degree to which we are conditioned by others, because our individual freedom and our conditioning by others are the two crucial elements by which we define ourselves and our relations to the others.

birth of christ

Through the dialectic of the two (what is and what may be, "reality" and imagination), the individual is able to add to the collective. In fact, it is just the accumulation of such additions that have come before us that defines the reality we are born into. It is the dialectic of the two- the external conditions of consciousness that define the world around us, and our own individual freedom- that decides the path, the story, the trajectory of our lives. All knowledge is filtered through the unique lens of our own experience- that is different than any that has gone before. All consciousness is expressed through human individuals, and individuals who develop this internal dialectic of the particular with the universal are able to make substantial contributions that can change the world.

Mother Earth

Just as the Corporation and the patriarchal version of truth that created it is not the only possible representation of the masculine aspect of our human being and consciousness, so, too, is Tiamat only one among many possible representations of the suppressed feminine aspect, and, again like the corporation, Tiamat is by no means the best, the "truest," representation. Tiamat, like the corporation that She shadows, is a perversion of truth, based on a limited misunderstanding that divorces the masculine and feminine aspects of our consciousness and being.

We live at a time when consciousness has gone back underground- on a journey of renewal, like modern day Columbuses, we seek out new worlds and undiscovered riches, but this time the exploration takes place not in the external world but inside each of us. The Hippies started us down this road into darkness and renewal, and though they were successfully quashed by Reagan and the seductive, repressive, and sometimes violent forces of the old Truth, their seeds have nonetheless been planted, and the worlds that they have opened cannot be forgotten.

The Hippies were following the lead and voices of many, countless mothers of this journey- the psychologists, the philosophers, the environmentalists, Native Americans, African Americans, and women- each providing a different angle on a newly emerging truth.

This opposing, introspective perspective- what I call the second movement in the scientific epoch- the movement inward leads to a reimaging of the feminine- a resurrection of a discredited vision of the feminine previously held by native americans that the patriarchy had clearly subdued (like Tiamat) but could never kill, and from the remnants of these cultures was reborn an image of the feminine that stands in stark contrast to the Eve, grown monstrous, of the Christians and the patriarchs.

Mother Earth, as nurturing as Tiamat is devouring, as beautiful as Tiamat is fearsome, but just as impossible to destroy. It is this new and ancient image of the feminine that is/has/will become the kryptonite of the corporations. They will try to co-opt her- with all their talk of "going green," but ultimately She is more powerful than they are. She begins to look like the Terra Firma upon which a next generation of truth may be built. Like the little clod of earth that our Mother walked around, we walk in circles around this concept, Mother Earth, and from her, with us, a new world will be born.

From the ground that is this resurrected feminine it becomes possible to re-imagine, to recreate a new and living and true masculine as well. The new masculine will not be, like the old scientific conceptualization of the masculine, divorced from our Mother, the Earth. Rather, this new masculine will be continuously fed by the waters of life and the soil of earth. The new masculine will depend upon the feminine. It will grow from her, have roots in her, and so will be tied to her inextricably; we have learned from the previous incarnation (and its death) that to divorce the two must end in death and destruction. The infinite, then, must depend upon the finite, the light upon the darkness, the mind upon the body, the Earth upon consciousness and consciousness on Earth.

christ grows like a tree from the body of Mother Earth, much as, and opposite of, how the Logos violently pinned the head of Tiamat. In some ways, the constellation of symbols is the same, but the meanings have been reversed. The value judgments- because the singular allegiance (and the corresponding antagonism) of the either/or kind of thinking- have been removed.

The resurrection is not Christ's return to Heaven, but rather, christ's return to Life. The blood courses through the veins of christ and she lives again- is born again- and, really, for the first time- through our Mother's children, you and me.

A Dialectical Perspective

Reason alone, we now realize, is no longer adequate to provide a satisfactory explanation of the world. This new truth- or lack thereof- is a consequence of the relativity of Einstein that is trickling down our collective throats. We need a way- many ways- to absorb these insights in order for the collective body to survive. This book is my attempt to help in the digestive process.

Failure of the collective body to absorb these ideas results in sickness. It is a failure to adapt. Its symptoms include an excess of shit, a temperature, exhaustion, distress at the cellular (human) level. People are scared, and they don't know what to do. We need a next stone to jump to.

We need meaning. The language of myth is symbolism; we return to that language now to both integrate, and move beyond the limitations of, reason and all previous understandings.

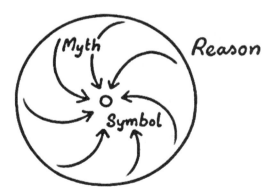

With the help of reason, we can learn to use symbols in a self-conscious way, to be simultaneously aware of both the power and limitations that inhere in these (human) symbols.

birth of christ

We may learn to use this knowledge in constructive and practical ways, to better adhere to the world around us and, so, better prepare for future circumstances, and, so, more effectively survive and thrive. To do that requires a system of education, though, that both 1) supports the current and future physical needs of children and 2) consciously challenges their growing consciousnesses through a Vygotskian zone of proximal development. To do that requires a purposeful collective effort. To have that requires a shared story that makes both visceral and rational sense of the world; a story that inspires each of us to fully realize our own meaningful piece. My contribution to the whole. A story that allows us the understanding and will to action necessary to survive and thrive.

Through the Word, we sought the One, fixed (eternal, universal, and unchanging) Truth while symbols allow the embrace of a greater adaptability and multiplicity of views. This changeability in symbolic meanings (and the emotions they signify) was viewed as an infidelity, an unreliability and deceit, by the standard of Jewish Law, the Word, the one and only Truth. It was a shortcoming in human understanding that Judaic reason sought to solve and overcome.

The fixity of Law, upon which white men's civilization is, so far, based

represents only a relative value in the language of symbols.

But here in our time, at the end of a long trajectory through reason, the Law and Word has failed us, too, as we are drowning in a sea of relativity and lies. We see now how the privileged position once assigned this Word, this Law, this (absolute) Truth, may be understood as nothing more than a brutal, brilliant (though unself-conscious) power play that set one People's (the "Chosen Ones") myth above all others. Once illuminated, the roots of Mind over Matter in slavery, rape, and genocide cannot be unseen.

To its credit, the Truth (and its wholehearted pursuit) has, at least, gotten us to this point where we can finally see through it. And, as with any myth, once you can see beyond it, you can never squeeze consciousness back inside. It's like the Garden of Eden that way, like the womb, though we humans, in our perversity and terror, will try.

To move forward requires a certain courage and acceptance of our loss. Not everybody can do that. It is too painful, too vulnerable, and that's what leaders are for. Those most able must forge ahead and clear the way, that others may follow. What is needed is a new foundation, a new "sticking point" that we can count on. Without such center, human beings cannot survive. The human race is dying now from a lack of truth and meaning. Persistence in the old, dead truth will be the instrument that kills us if a new foundation is not found. We are thrown back upon ourselves and turn, once again, to our beginnings in symbol and in myth in our desperate need to find a way.

In a time like ours, all the meanings reverse themselves, and to move forward and survive requires that we learn to read gestalts. For these, we turn to symbols, a language, unlike reason (which moves only in straight lines), amenable to revolutionary shifts in perspective.

As we proceed, it will serve our efforts to periodically remind ourselves to beware of judging these new ways of knowing by the standards of old absolutes and ethics (the way of Truth and Word and Law), as these foundations will, necessarily, continue to infect the patterns of our thought.

Symbols requires a greater fluidity and playfulness than reason and are best judged by a more aesthetic set of values- by their emotive depth, their beauty and inspiration. In common with reason and the Word, symbols aspire to universal meaning, though, in contrast, symbols do not aspire to fixity. Symbols lend themselves to understanding whatever situation is at hand. They are a lens we look through. They have both physical and ideal meanings. They reveal the infinite (darkness and light) embodied in the finite. Unlike the Word, whose aim is to fix a Truth once and for all and under all circumstances, a single symbol may be modified to communicate a multitude of (related, though sometimes contradictory) truths.

THE SACRED HOOP

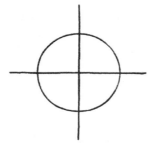

With the beginning of knowledge-what Christians call "the fall"- the circle is broken.

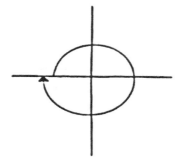

Like a seed cracked open, this break marks the beginning of human consciousness, movement, death, finitude, and time. Once released from its womb of potential, non-existence, consciousness continues to spiral ever outward in accordance with Fibonacci's sequence, the underlying structure of life, until death, at which point the circle closes once again.

birth of christ

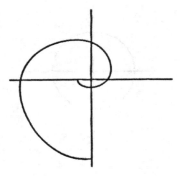

The garden cracks open.

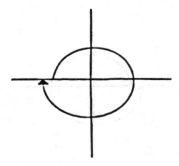

We mark this birth on the eastern horizon of the cross, the way the sun goes, at the beginning of each day. Created in this first rising is a distance, a gap, "the firmament" necessary for light- for consciousness- to pour in what has hitherto been non-existent because unknown. It is a startling moment- this awakening of collective, human experience akin to the child's emergence from the womb. Quickly, desperately, over millennia, we devise first explanations to bridge that gap with dreams of reconciliation with that source from which we are divided. So begins the first epoch in human consciousness and humans' first development of symbol.

We may believe Freud's account of this first movement or not. But this is a matriarchal time. We seek and create totem poles and animal guides, symbols, through which we pray to reconcile the spheres of consciousness and earth from which we came. In these early days of human consciousness, the symbol is meant to serve as mediator and re-connector, a kind of glue we use to reattach ourselves to the lost source. We perform ceremonies and rituals designed to enervate that connection, to heal the wound of separation, to restore the wholeness that's been lost.

Here we are, then, in our schema at this first stage in the mythological epoch of human consciousness:

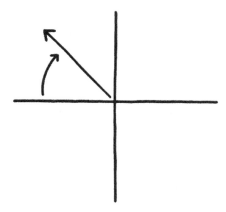

The goal of this first, mythological stage in human consciousness is, most decidedly, a return to source, a healing of the wound that severed us from immanence, peace, unconsciousness, eternity. As lived, the time before this re-solution, the time of chaos and exile, wandering and wondering, desperate fear and beginning faith, must take generation upon generations until, at last, we arrive at something solid we can cling to, a first new balance and connection.

birth of christ

With what relief these first humans must have responded once a center to their universe was first established, marked by the totem at world's navel, with animal spirits (gods, familiars) to guide their way. It is at this point in our history when, like shipwrecked sailors clambered aboard a raft, our human ancestors could look around them for the first time and, so, begin to gain their bearings. At this moment it was that our forebearers could turn their gaze onto the sky for the first time. At this moment it was that they could begin to discern the patterns and the rhythms of the world into which they had fallen. Through observation, experimentation, and practice (a first birth of science and reason), they began a long series of adaptations that continue to this day.

And they told first stories. The old ones told stories of the hard times to the young. Only now, freed at last from a desperate, ceaseless struggle to survive, could they, at long last, rest, take a breath, and sing the rhythms of their heart and world. They read the stars at night and so began to build a bridge, not only to the earth below but to the skies above as well. In this way, the people prospered. For generations upon generations, the people settled and adapted to this new world into which they found themselves cast. Over time, women developed the first technologies and inventions- pottery, language, farming, and domesticated stock- that marked them out as "human."

The goal from the beginning was always reconciliation, a healing of the wound, and return to paradise that was, once upon a time, but now lost- a paradise recreated and created, both, through story. And so it was that they, that we extended the horizons of the world (through science and adaptation) and established connection, through gods and stories and emotions, to skies above and earth below- in search of that perfect time out of time that never was but only in our bodies' memory.

THE SACRED HOOP

By one telling of the story, a seed of irony lies buried deep in human consciousness; so deep, in fact, that it may form the core and essence of all such knowledge, and that seed resurfaces in just such times as these. You see, the humans' stratagems to achieve lost union had, in fact, the opposite effect. By their stories and their sciences, humans grew their consciousness and so, simultaneously increased their distance, widened the chasm between where they are and where they dreamed to be.

Over time, the increasing evidence from their senses and reason and growing dominion over their world had the opposite of its intended effect. As their consciousnesses grew, their alienation from source grew with it. The stories they told about their past, the world, and their place in it grew, over generations, less effective and, so, less satisfactory. The gods did not come to their aid as expected, and some, at least, began to wonder why. A seed of doubt, a grain of sand- the irritant, had (like a snake) somehow entered into their garden of understanding; it could only be ignored so long.

It was at this, next moment in the history of our (Western) consciousness that Jews gave birth to a most unnatural and unimaginable reversal. From this seed, the entire foundation of our understanding (until, at least, today, and even then) and the entire edifice of Western civilization would grow. And that moment is where our story takes us next.

With the invention of their God, the first Jews turned what, to humans' early symbolic understanding, had been a curse into their greatest virtue and aspiration. The trauma of separation from our bodies, nature, the earth, our Mother that, through our totems, rituals, and gods we had sought to reconcile was now re-envisioned from the imaginary perspective of an idealized, disembodied, and singular God. The

birth of christ

Jews identification as "the Chosen Ones" of this newly imagined One would require sacrifice and a thorough embrace of the divorce from matter that people had, until now, mourned and sought to reconcile.

Theirs was a demanding and a jealous God whose first and second Commandments required that they cut all ties and forsake all others. This God would continually test their faith and loyalty in a multitude of ways, beginning with the requirement of their father, Abraham, that he murder his only son in this God's name. The men and boys would slice their penises (and still do today) to demonstrate their loyalty and allegiance. By voluntary submission to this One and only Lord and Master, and their silent complicity in His lie (made explicit in His third command), these few, Jewish men, were promised enduring mastery over animals, women, and all other humans.

This bargain remains at the core of, is the seed from which, Western (white) civilization has grown. In our symbolic/schematic representation of humans' evolving consciousness, this movement represents the second stage in man's mythological understanding.

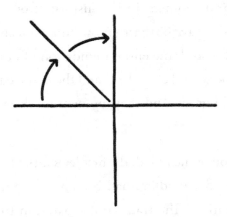

This movement is not necessary to the development of human consciousness. It is specific to a Western world view. It is a choice our ancestors made, from which I (and we) benefit and in which we still participate. The same silent complicity and loyalty is expected and required of us, and, even now, those who speak against it are blasphemers that we have obligation to make an example of.

This (Judeo-Christian) God represents our sole allegiance to, and identification with, consciousness (the "light" and spiritual aspect of humanity) set against its opposite, a shape-shifting enemy that may take many forms ("nature," women, our bodies, heathens, savages, non-Christians, sinners, emotion, Satan (and more)). Native American traditions, which we sought (still seek) to eradicate, do not make this same division. Neither do Eastern ones, with their yin and yang. And the various African traditions, well, I don't know, they are invisible to me (a white man raised inside this culture), as if they don't exist.

There can be no doubt that great power accrues to those who act from inside this Judeo-Christian vision (myth). Through it, we are given license to use, dismiss, destroy all others in the name of our Lord and to do so with righteousness assured, as we are acting in His name. But Christians, and even modern Jews, are more generous than that, allowing, as we do, that even heathens and black people may be saved, may be born again, on condition that they, too, become complicit in God's lie.

Even slaves may learn to willingly submit to this One and only Lord and Master and so be rewarded and redeemed after life, in Heaven. We have come so far; God's love is grown so inclusive through Christians' murder of, and new lies about, His son that now most anyone (pedophiles, but not homosexuals (unless they lie about that, too)) can join the fun. In point of fact, most believers now devote large swaths of time, money, and effort to charitable endeavors to recruit new members through, for example, mission trips to countries made poor

birth of christ

by Christian imperialism, Indian Schools, Catholic and Evangelical alternatives to public education, and Christian radio.

As with any myth, once you see the story- even for a minute- from the outside, you cannot shrink your way back in. But people try. These days, lots and lots of people try, with violent intensity and desperation. Because once one myth fails, another does not immediately arise to replace it. Rather, we are left adrift, exposed, vulnerable, helpless, without center and meaning.

Lost are the benefits of believing. Like a child disabused of the idea of Santa Claus. She will go on pretending for fear of losing presents, too. With Christians today, the stakes are infinitely higher; the needs the story met are matters of life and death. That is why so many Christians today are hysterical and violent in defense of their faith. A true believer has no need to defend their faith against attacks nor to convince others.

But, wait. We have gotten far ahead of ourselves. The momentum of consciousness irresistibly compels us forward; that is not a bad thing, but if we are to understand what has gotten us here, and where we will be going, we will need to circle back and more systematically trace our steps. The new myth invented by first Jews arises in response to the failure of an earlier set of myths (involving totem and spirit animals/familiars/guides) in the way I pictured here:

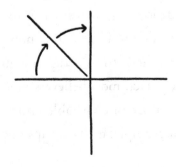

Developments in human consciousness are always cyclical, or, more accurately, dialectical. Each new solution (each new story, each new myth), then, grows out of a reformulation of elements that broke down under the previous myth. Each stage in the mythological development (whether the totem pole, the Jew's monotheistic God, or the one(s) to follow), itself, undergoes a natural process of birth (a synthesis from pre-existing elements in response to pressing needs), a life (where that synthesis provides people with a firm ground of explanation, meaning, and action), and death (where the explanation is no longer adequate to digest and explain new information coming in from the outside world, until the weight of discrepancies causes the story to finally seize and fail). We (human consciousnesses) are not able to simply jump directly from one story to the next. Rather, in between stories is a period of breakdown, confusion, disorientation, and terror- a period of darkness reminiscent of human beings' first experience in the wake of consciousness' first breaking light.

In lieu of the original physical manifestation of "divine" light and consciousness (the totem and the spirit guide of animals), the Jewish strategy (unique in the history of the world) is for humanity to evacuate the earth and body completely and, instead, identify with an imaginary, disembodied, and infinite God in Heaven. The success of their invention is by no means certain.

To follow their One God requires them to rip (some) humans (Jews, the Chosen Ones) free from all other gods, common sense, reason, and the knowledge of their bodies. To do so requires a tyrannical and traumatic violence and terror campaign against their own people, and they are only successful because of the incredible rewards and benefits that accrue to this special group as a consequence of their compliance with the Jewish Law. This imagined deity, which is theirs and theirs alone, grants Jewish men the privilege of dominion over all other peoples, animals, land, women and children. The reward of mastery and righteousness more than compensates for the sacrifice and lie.

This Jewish solution was, from its inception, intended exclusively for a small circle of select humans. It could never extend to large swaths of humanity, by its very nature and intention. Through sheer tenacity, will, and a deeply ambiguous mix of extraordinary humility and hubris, this story of a select people and their angry God persists through time and refuses to die.

The Jews have always had a hard time of it, and their dominion here on earth has always been quite tenuous. And even if they were ever to triumph completely, it would only be for a small circle of Chosen few. In point of fact, they have been continuously surrounded by hostile enemies who sought their ultimate destruction, though that never came.

As with any myth, their history passes through periods of 1) a first struggle to survive and gain any foothold in the world, 2) a period of relative fixity and permanence where the mythology takes firm root and the vision thrives, and 3) a period of doubts and dissolution, where the foundational principles begin to fray and fail them. This trajectory will lead to an eventual re-solution of elements out of the failure of that which came before.

One failure, it seems, in the Jewish vision is in the very exclusivity through which the Jews survived. Without some constructive means to grow more inclusive of others, the growth of the vision, the extension of their dominion would always be constrained by their own beliefs and, so, the Jews remained a vulnerable people. Add to that a harshness of their God that must be exhausting and difficult to sustain.

This second weakness, I have argued, their God, Himself, would recognize (in Job). In my telling of the story, it will be God, Himself, who will offer the next re-solution through His movement towards the people, until now alienated absolutely, in His first gesture of love.

Such development is possible just because this God is an aspect of humanity's consciousness and, so, can grow and change and adapt to new information and circumstances, same as any other part of ourselves. Perhaps, in surprise and admiration at the unwavering loyalty and humility of His people, the Jews, this God (or that aspect of ourselves we call God) introduces a new capacity- for love, and, in so doing, interrupts a previous balance that now must be re-solved.

He cannot have anticipated the reaction that would come from the other side- the murder of God's son, the rejection of God's gesture, a harshness in His people complementary to this new softness in their God. They send this son of God back to Heaven. They take that power God relinquished into their own hands, and, in so doing, strike a new balance, a re-solution, a new myth.

This re-solution breaks the previous Jewish stranglehold on Heaven, as their enemies swarm the gates under cover of murder of this new God of love. Swaths of people and a next instantiation of the Jewish solution- through the rise of a next world religion, Christianity. To fully thrive and establish world dominion will require this jealous, violent, angry Jewish God to be modified and transplanted onto new and more fertile ground. For this God's love and man's dominion to extend over the face of the earth, new murder is required. In our symbol/schema, we mark this next evolution of consciousness:

birth of christ

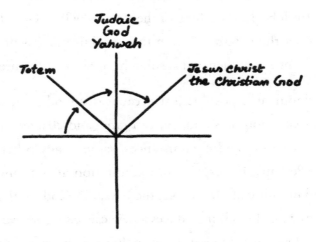

and call this new re-solution "Christianity."

From the seed of Yahweh is born a new totem, a new God. As indicated by our schema, God's gesture of love- that distinguishes Christianity from Judaism, represents a movement back towards humans and this world. God comes down from Heaven, in the body of Jesus, His son, to demonstrate a loving kindness that was never a part of who the Jewish God was or aimed to be.

Christ's birth and death represents a next reversal in the life of Western, white man's developing consciousness. Depending on one's perspective, it may be viewed as either an advancement or a reduction. But, as in all things in this Western thread, it is a story of power and violence and establishing white man's dominion here on earth, that we call the "love of God."

This next movement is decidedly <u>not</u> the action of Jews (though they still bear some responsibility as first progenitors of the idea). Christianity is, rather, a consequence of actions by the enemies of Jews and their leader, Paul, vile traitor to humanity and God.

Christianity is a usurpation of power. Seeing the potential benefits and power that may accrue from Yahweh, this Jewish God, Christians deign to steal this power through a new lie and fabrication all their own. There is a Promethean element to this reversal of reversals that allows these Christians to steal the fire from this Jewish God and claim it as their own.

They accomplish this theft, <u>and</u> depict themselves as heroes in the process, through a new deceit all their own. By compounding Jewish lies with still further lies, white Christian men obtain dominion that persists through the present day. We have already described elsewhere in this book the details and deceits of this myth perpetuated by Christians, and I'm not sure what more to say except to once again make clear that the Christian story used to prop up Christian power bears no relation to Jesus or christ. More accurately stated, Christianity represents- in every way- the exact <u>opposite</u> of everything their supposed man/God stands for. Christians and their faith are the exact opposite of all they claim to be. In this, they lie to us but, more especially, they lie to themselves, in order to establish and maintain their dominion. Christians are the murderers of Christ (and I don't mean "once upon a time" but still today), and Christianity is the tale they tell themselves to hide the blood.

Human myths have always been about establishing power and control ("stability" and "peace") in the world. They always serve a utilitarian end that way- to help us thrive and survive, and, given the limits of humans' explanations and understanding and physical bodies, they have always privileged some people ("our people") over others. We can imagine (have imagined here) what might have happened if the values represented by their god/man were, in fact, what Christians believed and acted upon.

birth of christ

Sadly, though, human beings were not ready for that. Though their consciousness was sufficiently developed to formulate the idea, their true motivations trailed behind and so turned that idea into its very opposite. To point this out- the deceit at the core of Christianity- is the greatest sin one can commit to those who participate in that lie/self-delusion.

From the Christian lie was built a Catholic Church that, led by celibate men (a band of brothers we may recognize) who established their dominion over all other people, women, and the earth. A momentum was established now, and from this Church would grow the scientists who, in the image of God, would now extend that dominion further and so complete man's theft of power and light from on high. And that brings us to the next stage:

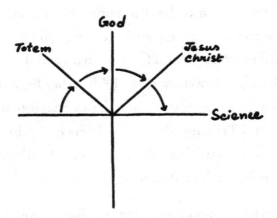

The priests, of course, resisted this transfer of power from their hands until, quickly (within hundreds of years), they realized that they could use these new-found powers of human reason to extend their dominion even further- over, in fact, the entire world. This is the world that I was born into. This is the story I was raised in, the world and story I was taught, as an American white boy, that I would be responsible for leading some day. So confident were we in the foundations of our faith (in man's reason, science, and objectivity) that we allowed discordant voices (hippy teachers) into schools, encouraged critical thinking in our children, and entertained doubts that, in earlier times, had been aggressively persecuted and silenced.

We live in a revolutionary time, and even in my own short lifetime, the myth that was our very foundation is now exposed as a violence, a deceit, a sham. Though beset with fear, depression, anxiety, shame, guilt, anger, confusion, desperation, hopelessness, isolation, and self-loathing, we cannot unsee the truth. Though in thousands of ways we try.

A large swath of our population (almost exactly a third, it seems) seek regression to the Christian "truth" as an answer to the breakdown in our human truth. Most of the culture wars we see now are between the fanatical defenders of these two, competing truths- 1) the absolute truth of our salvation through our Lord and Savior in Heaven, Jesus Christ and 2) the more subtle truths of science and human reason. The Christians enjoy a decided advantage in this war, for unlike the "rational" ones, they are not divided against themselves. We are being, literally, strangled by this battle of either/or, and, if we cannot find a way out, Western civilization will destroy itself and all others in its wake. This is not normal- the days you live in- this is not "how things are" nor "human nature." What we are attempting to navigate is truly extraordinary, beyond amelioration and compromise.

Ours is the most crucial moment in the history of human consciousness since the birth of Yahweh, the One and Only Jewish God. To survive will require us to deconstruct the foundations of our civilization and beliefs down to its crucial core. To survive will require us to overcome the resistances of both sides of an Either/Or consciousness that, today, rule our world. We must overcome the regressive violence of the Christians who would save themselves by shrinking consciousness and recoiling from new truths they cannot bear to face.

Added to that, we must overcome the resistance of those who oppose these Christians with a commitment to a status quo of objectivity, human reason, and godless "relativity." On either side of the current culture war are arrayed forces that would refuse any further development of human consciousness, because the growth necessary is more painful than they can bear.

What is required now is a turning inward- a process initiated by the likes of Kant, Einstein, and Jung. Such movement is positively repugnant to Christians who react to any and all demands for such a thing with revulsion and violence.

Among the more "reasonable" ones, with maturity, education, and/or self-interest enough to see the truth but who, themselves, lack the youth, capacity, and/or skills necessary to admit the turn in consciousness required, we meet a different kind of resistance. These "liberal thinkers" would pretend that reforms, legislation, compromise, tolerance, science, and other such rational adjustments will be enough to turn the tide in favor of survival. These ones are motivated by fear, self-interest, and (often, willed) ignorance of their own ignorance. These two sides are locked in a civil war in America (that, though just beginning as I write, is, nonetheless, inevitable).

Many, many of our young people (anxious and depressed) see all this clearly but feel powerless to stop it. They look for leaders, for elders to help guide them but everywhere find only adults who have lost their minds, who cling to power, who perpetrate unceasing violence against others and the planet, through their self-centered ignorance and lies. Blind to the predicament our young people face, they are asked- commanded- to choose a side.

This is not "normal," what we are going through. This is not "how human beings are." This is how human beings are in this moment when a 4000-year-old world view is collapsing, and, if we can survive the labor, a new cycle in human consciousness is being born.

My aim here is to honestly acknowledge and articulate- to the best of my ability- the truth and horror and potential of the present moment. To tell our young people- You are not crazy!!! You are stronger than you realize. And I believe in you.

I have said in other places that "we live in an age of the setting sun," but we are beyond that now. We are well advanced, now, into the darkness and the deeps. Your parents lack lungs to breathe in this environment. They are drowning, and, in desperation and fear for you, their children, they seek to pretend the truth(s) away, to keep the ship afloat. And that just makes things so much worse for you. You are right to prefer they get out of the way and/or die, that the work might at last begin.

What is required, and just beginning, is a necessary journey through Hell, a turning of consciousness that generations before were not, are not fit to make. To illustrate:

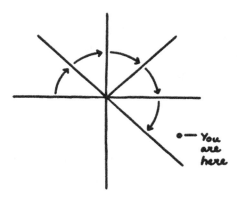

birth of christ

You will note that, unlike in previous drawings, I don't mark our current moment as at the 45 degree angle. That's because we are not there yet. We are in the in-between. We are adrift in violent oceans without any answer, no firm ground, rarely even a small bit of flotsam, as yet, to cling to. It's fucking exhausting, and you have to wonder how and why you even go on. But you go on.

What I pray to offer here- as best as I am able- is some far distant vision of land on the horizon. I'm not sure myself that it isn't a mirage, but it is something. There is something there, I see it, and I must, I absolutely must call to you and point you to it. I am obligated to do so, as you are obligated to carry on and begin the journey even though it may prove futile.

There is, and always will be, a temptation in this long and torturous development of human consciousness, to turn back to where you came. And I must warn you of that here. In my time, there are a few well-meaning adults who have, themselves, gone further and taken the plunge into darkness required.

Still infected and crippled by the constraints of the old, dead world in which they were raised, these "spiritual" ones lack capacity to go as far as you, as far as is required to survive. And they, instead, settle on a spectre and phantasy of their lost God with the apparent advantage of "being here and now," inside of you. It is a continuation of the vision of our infinite aspect divorced from body, existence, finitude (just like that God of old), and they call that phantom "Self."

These well-meaning, spiritual "leaders" have made the turn inward necessary to survival but lack the capacity, strength, youth, courage necessary to move forward into the unavoidable depths. They take refuge, instead, in a hysterical delusion of the old, dead God "inside of me!"- a little floatee they call "Self"- and call out for you to join them in this nowhere.

You must plug your ears to their siren call and wake yourselves and one another when you fall under this spell of "spiritual" surrender. You have knowledge, gifts, strengths that these old ones did not have. In grief, and even gratitude for their well-intentioned failure, you must turn your back to their dying gasps and keep swimming. Though you may feel weak, trust that you have capacities they did not have.

What's begun with you is the second half of consciousness' journey. We begin the completion of our journey; in this turn for home, through you and your colleagues, human consciousness becomes conscious of itself. New Prometheans, we bring the light so far obtained deep into the darkness where, like little muskrat, we seek new ground.

Each a Cell in the Human Body

The evolution of consciousness, we have said, so far, may be described as the mind's long flight from the body, but at this moment in our history, we are reversing that truth. In this sense, then, it is easy to make the case that the current revolution in our consciousness is the most fundamental ever.

We return to myth without thereby forsaking reason. We own and enervate the ancient aspects to our self as we extend Carl Jung's concept of the collective unconscious to understand that all consciousness- not just those aspects of consciousness that operate beneath our view- but all consciousness is collective. What we individual human beings bring to this collective is just the container in which to hold it, a container necessary for consciousness to be at all. We are the necessary incarnations of a collective consciousness that has infinite potential, but that, in fact, must always be contained in some finite representation in order to be known, in order to live, in order to be.

And though we are connected to all others through our share in one universal consciousness, we are also always separate- as human beings, as bodies. We are bubbles necessary to contain the consciousness that is universal, infinite, without boundaries in and of itself. And so it is that our new cosmology, if we take it far enough, if we travel all the way back to the center of our being and the first origins of our existence, so it is that we individual human beings become the center of the universe again. We participate in the universal, in the infinite potential of the universe and in the collective consciousness, but we do so as individual human beings and solely through the vehicle of this body- that is born, lives imperfectly, and dies, all in the blink of a moment that is to us a lifetime.

In this new, this human, this relative cosmology, this cosmology beyond, but inclusive of, reason, our body is the totem, the sacrificial animal, the gateway to the infinite. And try as we might to imagine the infinite through other windows than our self, to see the world from the perspective of another, such exercise is only possible in the mind but not the body. We may dream of reincarnation and/or a release from this mortal coil, we may pray for it and will it, but this dream is just a phantasy- impossible and never to be. We get one chance. And while the windows into the infinite are, well, infinite, we can only ever fully know this one. This limit on our consciousness is what makes human beings tragic, what makes us beautiful, what makes us greater than God (because, though, ironically, we are less than God- i.e. finite, we are also real. We are incarnate, as God longs to be).

We are like Christ, and as we complete our journey back to our both individual and universal, human, center we are, we realize, even more than that. Christ, we realize is, just like his father, an image, a representation of ourselves. We are the models upon which the image of Christ is built. Each human individual, a finite window to the infinite. Not just like Christ, we are christ.

We are born of Mother and of Father. The two come together- are born in each of us. The Christian story of creation by our Father, God, leads us- and the civilization we have built- to become perverse because of a fundamental denial of the Mother. We need the indigenous perspective- the Haudenosaunee myth will serve this well- to restore balance to our definition of our self, the world, and others. Some (certain feminists or "New Age" spiritualists) will find satisfaction in the Haudenosaunee story and feel no need for the Garden of Eden and the Father who ruled over it and us. I am not one of those. Western civilization, for all its tragic perversity, has opened the way for an expansion of our consciousness that we must not regret. And, even if we wanted to, we cannot purge ourselves of that history any more than we could purge the earth of natives' myth and wisdom. I do understand the inclination to at least try to purge ourselves of the ugly lies of patriarchy (especially from feminists and members of those races most severely oppressed), but the purge can never be complete. The perversities will live on in us below the level of our consciousness, and so, I fear, may lead us into a repetition of the same pathologies we seek so desperately to extinguish.

I fear political reformers who diagnose our problems at a superficial level of economics and policy. By not excavating to the root cause of the problem (a big part of which is a society on a mass scale that requires the reduction of human beings into objects or data), they do not recognize the oppressor still active in themselves. They will, then, impose upon us one last dose of violence, of "rationality," of economics, all in the name of "the people," the oppressed. Political reformers will always dress up the fundamental patriarchal error "one last time," whether in Capitalist or Communist clothes, because this is their chance to take power they resent in others.

A Mirror to the World

As a seventh grader, I was introduced to the Haudenosaunee creation story through Hazel Hertzberg's version in <u>The Great Tree and the Longhouse</u>. With such uncanny similarities between it and the Garden of Eden story, I could not help but wonder, even as a child, the extent to which the one story had colonized the other. I still don't know.

But the story is true in ways I rely on to understand the world, in ways complementary to the Christian story. For me, the two complete each other.

Stephen Jenkinson teaches how we have been systematically cut off from the stories that come from the land- the lands we come from and the land we've been brought to, all to be replaced by the universal, disembodied Mind over Matter myth of progress, transplanted here in bodies of immigrants and slaves.

To make room for that singular, right (white) vision, we annihilate the races of people here before us, who are telling a very different story with their lives. We discount their ways as savage, childish, fantastical, and untrue. In the certainty of our own vision, we hold these people in contempt. And so with Africans as well. Under the superior spell of Christian rationalism, we treat them as objects and their stories as "myths."

We are in a strange place in America. As descendants of immigrants, we have been cut off from our own stories, because cut off from our land and ancestors. Now we are on a land not ours, a land whose stories our ancestors sought to exterminate. But, like gods, stories- and a people- are not easy to kill, especially when there is truth in them.

Bereft of stories from our own country, with only Property to replace it (and white Christian privilege by its side), our young people are disenchanted. An elders' job now is to tell new stories knit from old ones; stories that possess us, that we will have a need and obligation to share.

I pray respect.

> *For the Haudenosaunee, the world begins in the Sky World, with a husband and a wife, already pregnant and hungry for the fruits and roots that grew from the Great Tree at the center of this world. She begged her husband to get them for her, to pluck the fruit and dig the roots. Whether he followed instructions or she did it herself, dig, they did, and, to their astonishment, opened a hole beneath what had been, until now, the whole world.*
>
> *The woman looked down the hole and saw beneath her a vastness of sky, sea, movement, and beauty beyond belief. In awe and wonder, the woman had gone too far. She began to slip from all the world she had known (with some implication that the husband may have pushed her); and, falling from the hole, she grasped desperately at the edges of Sky World. But came away with only disconnected roots. Losing hold, the woman plummeted to the sea below.*

birth of christ

The birds of the sky saw the woman falling and gathered round to help. Wingtip to wingtip, they formed a feathery raft to cushion the woman's fall. The birds strained beneath the woman's girth and could not hold her for long. They called to the sea creatures and asked for their help. And that's when turtle rose to meet them and agreed to receive the woman on its back. The birds gently placed the fallen woman on awaiting turtle's back and the animals gathered round turtle's edge to see her.

As she came to, the animals spoke with the woman and asked how they might help. The woman looked around aghast, lay her head in her hands, and felt the roots. "If I had soil to plant these roots," she said, but saw nothing but sea. There were stories, the animals told, of soil- at the bottom of the ocean, but to get there must be very, very far and no one had ever been.

Undeterred, the animals committed to try, and, one by one, animals quick and strong, important and proud, dove- deep, and deeper still- to the limits of their endurance, as far as they could go. Exhausted by their efforts, all returned- empty-handed, and it seemed all hope was lost. Finally, little muskrat said he would try. To guffaws and signs of exasperation, muskrat slipped quietly beneath the surface and did not wait to hear.

For a long time, the animals prayed for little muskrat's safe return; until, on the third day, their prayers turned to mourning and a hope, only, that his small body might resurface.

The white of Muskrat's breast took a long time to emerge from the darkness. Like a fish pulled from water, you couldn't see him, really, until he was already there. In prayer, the grandmother lifted muskrat's little floating body onto the turtle's shell. The animals sang songs of grief and bravery as the woman breathed air and pumped water from his lungs. Muskrat gasped, and the whole world rejoiced, animals and woman. His breathing returned to life's natural rhythm, and muskrat rested from his labor. As he slept, his paws, clenched tight, slowly unfurled to reveal two tiny clumps of dirt.

The woman took the earth from muskrat's paw and placed it on the turtle's back. There she planted roots. Each day, the woman walked around this earth, in circles, the way the sun goes, and each night she prayed. The earth grew as she moved round it, and, like the moon, the woman, herself, grew full with the child she brought with her in her fall. She would give birth to a girl, and so, mother and daughter together would walk, in circles around the earth, the way the sun goes.

We have reached a beautiful moment in our history now, a moment of peace, harmony, cooperation, beginning. Let us rest in this moment. Breathe it in; drink deeply and remember this place; feel its presence before moving on, and return to it whenever and as often as you need. Have mercy on yourself this way.

birth of christ

Only sky and sea, placid, like the yin/yang must appear before the turmoil, before there is time. But a seed has been planted, a drama set in motion with the woman's fall that cannot be undone. Nurtured and sustained by the animals, from roots and soil of the heights and depths, a new world grows as mother and daughter walk round it the way the sun goes.

Just like the mother when she was in the Sky World, this world- here on the turtle's back- is the only world the child knows. For the daughter, born of this world, things will be different than for her mother.

> *Time passes, and the daughter grew to maiden, though she did not know. One day, when separated from her mother, a man appears. It is sudden. Like Hades with Persephone. A thunderbolt and opening. The man startles the girl, and she faints dead away. As she sleeps, he*

places two arrows across her body, one sharp and one dull.

When the daughter awakes, mother and daughter continue to walk the earth; with time, the daughter grows full like the moon, like her mother did before her. It is different here for the daughter, though, than it was in the Sky World. There is a struggle growing inside the girl that neither mother nor daughter understand. It is something new, something of this world (though there are hints of it in suspicions and rumors about that husband in the Sky World).

The masculine element. The seed of consciousness and strife that separates her from her mother. There is a yin and yang- two brothers- the left-handed twin and the right-handed twin- growing inside the daughter, and, from the beginning, it seems, there could be no peace between them.

It is a queer kind of yin/yang, though. Not masculine and feminine, but, rather, two masculine aspects competing with one another- two brothers named Either/Or. Eventually, they will build balance into the world, but they do so through conflict and strife. The brothers bring violence, profanity, and unreason to a world once (in an imaginary past) sacred.

The next part has been difficult for me to write, and I am troubled as to why.

Their intrusion begins even before they are born- in the womb of their mother as the two argue over the right way to be born. As we will see, the right-handed twin always does right and as he is told. He wants to be born the normal way, of course, as all children are born. But the left-handed twin will have none of it. He sees light in another direction and determines to go that way. The right-handed twin screams that he cannot be born that way, that he will surely kill their mother. And he does. The left-handed twin cannot be born out the mother's mouth or nose. He bursts through her armpit and cleaves her in two. Meanwhile, the right-handed twin is born the normal way, as all children are born.

But the right-handed one is born, too, in violence, trauma, rage, and grief at the death of their mother. He confronts the left-handed one for his crime against their mother, but the Grandmother demands the quarreling stop.

The right-handed twin did everything just as he should. He meant what he said and said what he meant. But the left-handed twin never told the truth. He always lied- and had killed their mother. And yet, for all of that, it strangely seemed to the right-handed twin that their Grandmother always favored the left-handed twin. These two brothers, as they grew, represented two ways that are in all men.

Each had creative powers, and they competed with one another to make the creatures of the earth. The right-handed twin made the gentle deer, but the left-handed twin made the mountain lion that kills the deer, but there are always more deer than there are mountain lions, and so it is good. The right-handed twin made the ground squirrel, and the left-handed twin made the weasel, who follows the ground squirrel into his hole to kill him. The right-handed twin made fruit and food for his creatures to live on. The left-handed twin made the poisonous plants and medicines like the suicide root, which people use to kill themselves when they go out of their minds.

And, finally, the right-handed twin made humans- or so it is claimed. It is not clear what hand the left-handed twin had in humans' creation, though we must have suspicions. Like the animals, humans were made of clay, and Hazel Hertzberg relates that at later times, the Haudenosaunee would explain that some humans were cooked too much- these were the black people. Others were cooked too little- these were the whites, but that others- the Haudenosaunee- were made just right and so were settled on the land.

The plant-eating animals made by the right-hand twin were killed by the carnivores of the left-handed twin, without whom they would have exhausted their supplies, and because there were always been more plant-eating animals than meat-eating ones, the twins built balance into the world.

As the twins became men full grown, their conflicts only grew. Each grew more determined to find a way to defeat the other- once and for all. They competed together in the games the people still play. They gambled with pits, but as the sun went down, and the contest was done, neither had won. They contested at lacrosse and battled with clubs. But as the sun went down, and each contest was done, neither had won. Until, at last, they came to the duel, and the two brothers set about finding the weapon that could defeat their brother. They conversed with each other as they made their selections, and, of course, the right-handed twin told the truth and the left-handed twin lied.

Each brother knew in his deepest mind the one thing that would defeat him. The two brothers had contested so long and knew one another so well that each had grown capable of reading the deepest mind of the other. In his deepest mind, the left-handed twin told the truth; it was the deer antler that would kill him. And the right-handed twin lied.

When it came to battle, the left-handed twin brought a mere stick, that would do him no good. And as foretold in dreams, he was defeated with one touch of the deer antler of the right-handed twin. Having killed his brother, the right-handed twin returned home to his grandmother. And she met him in anger. She called him "murderer," for he had killed his brother. The man grew angry, saying that she had always helped his brother, and in his anger, he grabbed Grandmother by the throat and cut off her head. Her body he threw into the ocean and her head into the sky, and there Our Grandmother, the Moon still keeps watch over the realm of her favorite grandson, the night.

He- the left-handed twin is cast below the earth, where his mother lay, and the right-handed twin ascends to become identified with the sun, which makes me suspect that it is somehow him telling the story, but...

"When the sun rises from the east and travels in a huge arc along the sky dome, which rests like a great upside-down cup on the saucer of the earth, the people are in the daylight realm of the right-handed twin. But when the sun slips down in the west at nightfall and the dome lifts to let it escape at the western rim, the people are again in the domain of the left-handed twin- the fearful realm of night.

Movement of Totem

I want to believe that the Haudenosaunee story speaks for itself, and, of course, it does, but since I have placed myself in the explaining business here, I have an obligation to reason that the story, itself, does not. This story provides a necessary complement and completion to the Garden of Eden story, for me. First, the Haudenosaunee story accounts for the night sky in a way that Jews and Christians ignore. There is a second half of every human experience here on earth that Yahweh offhandedly creates and then sets aside as if it does not exist. Such treatment of the moon and stars is consistent, of course, with the underlying metaphysic- that is the exclusive worship and acknowledgement of a One and Only God. The Sun. The daytime realm.

But, as we now so clearly see, that second half does not cease to operate just because we ignore it. The Haudenosaunee account provides a more balanced view and acknowledges, at least, that we must account for both aspects of earth and sky.

This account changes our metaphysic and moves the totem- from sky to earth, from man to woman, from mind to body, from light to darkness.

birth of christ

The Haudenosaunee account is told from a perspective here on earth- a human perspective- whereas the other is a story told from "on high." Up to this point, we have been looking at things from God's perspective. Though I have been talking as if from a human perspective to and about God, I am still looking at things through His eyes.

So far, the models I have used to understand the evolution of human consciousness have been mostly two-dimensional ones. We have been looking at things as if from above. Like the vision you see flying in an airplane. It is far easier to identify patterns in the land but impossible to know what it is really like. And the longing I feel to know- what is it like there? The longing to be there- every time I fly over a place (do you feel that too?) is the same longing I feel for this more human perspective, the same longing God feels for our Mother.

The Haudenosaunee myth provides us a necessary revolutionary shift in perspective. She turns our two-dimensional understanding to a more living, breathing, whole, and fragile presence- a three-dimensional world. By rotating our perspective 90° from God to woman, floating on the turtle's shell, we see a whole new dimension to existence. The added dimension is the here and now, the body, and from these, emotions. Attachments and relations. Our schema shifts, now, from a circle to a sphere, and we find ourselves at the point of the horizons, partaking equally of each. We have a recognition of the ocean and a different kind of infinity now. The infinity below. And can feel it in ourselves in a way that God has not allowed.

THE SACRED HOOP

And, in our time, we have begun to find our way into it through psychology and a critical analysis that has turned directions. Naturally, in accordance with the limits of reason, our momentum has turned inward rather than a continuous and infinite expansion of Mind over Matter.

This self-reflection and turn inward has loosened the ground around the old metaphysic. Like a tooth whose gum has grown soft around it, the Totem/Logos begins to waver and hurt.

People are made scared by this, and they should be. This thing we're bringing down- is the center of their world, the foundation for their whole world view. Can we be surprised, then, that they will fight for it onto death? It is the only thing they know. The only thing to believe in; the world they've taught their children. That we are undermining with our movement. And, really, without offering any reasonable alternative!

People need a truth, even if it's false, and we are taking that from them through this next and necessary (to survive) advance in human consciousness.

Right now, the totem is piercing the head of Tiamat, and She is wriggling Her way free. It's the rumbling you feel. She is going to get loose.

birth of christ

Those invested in that Totem are so Terrified that they are bringing the Totem down themselves in their panic to move higher, further from the waters and the poors that threaten to consume them.

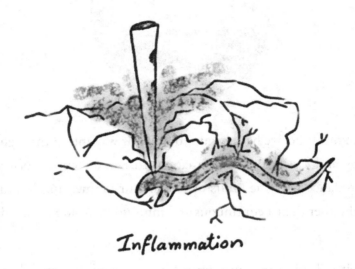

Inflammation

What needs be done, for our survival. is to remove that Totem. Stop the murders first, but that means certain death for those at the top- and when the edifice falls, they do not go alone.

And no one is capable- not even you and me- of removing a Totem without some other place to put it. It is more than we can bear. And so it is the job of elders to help and show the way to a new location- to a truer truth. One that will lay ground for future generations, one that inflames the creativity in your heart on behalf of a world you are proud to be part of, a healthy cell in a larger body.

We have turned a corner in our thinking that has caused all the rage of our age. It may be illustrated here:

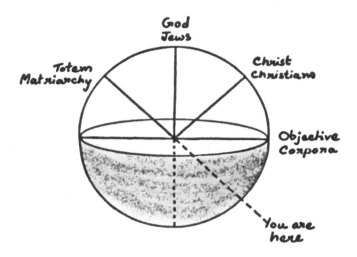

Looking at this shift as symbolized in this way, it must be clear why those committed to old ways of knowing feel like it is death. It is. They feel like they're drowning. They are.

You will see that we are well beyond the horizon now. We have begun entry into the deeps. And sometimes, we must be aware, it is the scientists, the reasonable ones who will pose the greatest threat to our further progress (necessary to survival), because, though human, they remain frightfully committed to the malignant rational metaphysic, to Mind over Matter, and are deeply, personally threatened by what they might (what they WILL!) find in the deeps. They may pretend to play the game to avoid getting wet.

As we turn our reason into the depths, the night sky begins to appear on the eastern horizon. This frightens those committed to the Totem of old as well. Avoidance of darkness is the very principle upon which their institutions are built, and here it comes- sure enough- brought on by we godless ones, fornicators. But it is something I sometimes wondered as a child, what things must be like for the Sun when He

birth of christ

went away. You know? Sort of a- hey, how do you think the Sun is doing? kind of thing. I wonder about Him still.

If we listen, He may tell the rest of the story.

I talk so many times about the "second half of the tree" that you must be getting sick of it- the tree beneath the ground. But we need also consider the second half of that whole thing, that living tree. The tree that lives will die, but we rarely consider this as another half of the tree's life- the time of giving back, consumed by birds and insects and the soil, and so providing opportunities for new life through the consumption of one's own. We rarely think of our lives this way either, but maybe should. Future generations feed on what we have left. We don't want to feed it poisons and have a heartfelt need to provide as many nutrients as possible, or we must be pathological practitioners of the old, infected Truth.

This is a key takeaway- that what we have mistaken as our whole life has always been just half. And now, we make the turn, and begin to see new things. The second half begins. If the first half doesn't kill us first.

From God's perspective, you don't get any of that drama. It is all happening beneath You. But perhaps that is a limit in God that we can and must finally reverse- in fairness to God, for christ's sake!

This fixity in the sky is a problem. But, as we have said, this God began as an infantile projection of our own undeveloped Self. We made God to learn from Him, and God has taught us well! What we didn't expect is that, in the process, God also learned from us. If God is our Sun god, He has been, until now, a very limited representation. God's fixity is in error and a function of our own limited understanding that we have now broken free of. And so, we must allow our God to move.

THE SACRED HOOP

You know how mad I get with Him, but to His credit, God did move in our direction. He provided us a gesture, and though we refused His gift once, so long ago, and still today, does not mean we cannot change our minds. But to do so now requires that we let God "die" to us, let the Sun set and stop our raging against this passing of His light, knowing, as we do, that the Sun will rise again rejuvenated by His journey through the underworld, and we will have survived His absence, growing stronger, and learning more that we may receive His return with such joy and anticipation and gratitude, that our bonds will be renewed in ways we never dared imagine on that day we let Him go. We have held our God prisoner in the Sky too long; it is time we need to free Him.

We feel God's longing for our Mother. He has been away too long, and it is only through we humans- together and alone- they can be united. We owe it to these luminaries to facilitate reunion. It is our responsibility- as cells in a larger body- but we are not alone in this. There are other gods to help. Ancestors and elders, though forgotten, have not gone. And there are young people strong in ways we cannot comprehend. We all need to turn our ears to listen, which is what you do when you've ventured into the darkness and the deeps.

The Haudenosaunee myth serves as a corrective to the story from the Garden, because it shifts the totem, the center of consciousness, the point of view from God to human beings- to the body of a woman- and teaches us that such a shift is possible. It builds capacity in our minds to make the shift ourselves. A shift from the objective view valued by the previous metaphysic to a living animal perspective. This story forces an embodiment of reason that the Jewish God and Christians despise, though it is necessary to our survival. Firm ground and waters of life.

A key lesson behind all this is that the totem clearly moves. We have seen it happen. It is demonstrably possible to re-center and re-create a world based upon different collective understandings. Human beings may be capable of learning how to thus shift perspectives in ways we cannot now imagine. Carlos Castaneda may be of service in this regard.

If the Totem has shifted before, we can do it again, this time, for the first time, with the conscious understanding that the totem clearly moves. A new power men did not have before.

Born of relativity.

Four Murders

We are on the dark side now, beyond the age of setting sun. The language here is symbolism, an earlier language once replaced by Law and reason. The purpose and power of symbolism is a simultaneity of knowing that Reason hates. Symbols communicate mind to body, personal to universal and back again. A dance and dynamic union between individual and collective in the creative, conscious, only drama that is your life.

We see in a flash how the entire basis for our civilization- Freud to Paul to Abraham with that pale little fucker, Thomas Jefferson, thrown in- is all a Lie. A single Lie repeated. Repeated and enforced. A fundamental unreason. A pathology, really. Out of control. A pestilence upon the body. A pestilence upon Earth.

If we look, we may discern a pattern here. Like when you stare intently into the water, and all of sudden the shapes and movements of the depths appear. You see other living things and feel connected- a recognition from your body that you almost miss, having lost so much capacity to listen.

For so long suffering under a multipronged attack from a powerful fiction enforced by Law, you'd nearly forgotten. But, now, you see with old, new eyes. There is an identifiable pattern here we are obligated to de-spell.

It is a series of murders. Four.

The first murder, Freud has claimed, and I concede that ground to him. It was the murder of the father by the brothers. Jealous of the One who got all the women, the brothers banded together. Alone, none of them could defeat Him, but, together, they were stronger. Together, they killed the father, and on that day, democracy was born. Everybody equal. The first murder.

Freud argued it was the shock and horror of that first moment of trauma and reversal that caused the brothers to disassociate, and so gave birth to the consciousness that distinguishes humans from animals. The first flash of reason.

Assuming the truth of Freud's claim, I (rightly) speculated that from this murder, women would also gain a new awareness of the world and would, as a rational consequence, assume control of the tribe when faced with the threatening violence and impulsive actions of men. In response to this original outbreak of murderous unreason- this fall, if you will, women built a civilization through first application of its opposite- science and technology- pottery, language, domesticated animals, and agriculture.

We can imagine how this went. Women, the producers of children, were also responsible for the feeding and protection of the tribe. They worked together, and there really wasn't much for men to do. They could do some hunting, but with domesticated animals now, shit, who needs it.

birth of christ

The men were useful for two things- 1) building stuff and 2) physical protection, so that is what they did. When there wasn't shit to build or enemies to protect us from, men went looking for them (with old hunting weapons). But most of the time these men's clubs sat around bored, maybe played games and drank. They would choose up sides and compete. But you can only gamble and pretend and play games for so long before you have a need for real action. Testosterone. Mars, you know.

That's when the brothers turned on women. That's when they turned to stories. In boredom and jealousy, anger and resentment, the brothers joined together to create God, and with His help, perform the second murder. Stitched together from the collective and idealized memory of the Father they had killed, this God commanded their obedience but gifted them with imagined powers. A self-confidence and certainty that every woman knows.

Left out of the women's connection to life- men created a mythology that reverses common sense, reason, the evidence of our experience and senses, that places us outside of the natural rhythms of life in ways that may have even threatened our sustenance and survival. A mythology that, through God, makes the men all-powerful.

Yahweh is exclusive, a God made by men to serve men. As descendants of Adam and the chosen of God, men are distinguished by this One above women and all other animals. He tells a story where women are responsible for all pain and death (and birth, by that way) and so deserve to suffer.

This Yahweh is a jealous God, and in compliance with His Word and Law, men are chosen to rule over women- reversing, thereby, their previous powerlessness, uselessness and servitude under matriarchy.

Through this God, alone, this band of brothers is able to rise to their proper place and destiny as rulers of the earth and so establish their dominion.

Even in the first murder, though it is the father that the brothers kill, their target is the women; they seek dominion over women's bodies, hitherto denied by, in their perception, the more powerful male. In disposing of Him, though, the brothers fail to achieve their ends. Rather, it is women, themselves, who gain the power and, so, stand in the way of the brothers' dominion.

The civilization these women build must be destroyed ("we had to destroy the village to save it"), because it denied the rule and power to men. It may appear insane (irrational) for men to attack the very foundation upon which their own survival depends. But murders, and the emotions that give rise to murders, are never rational. These patterns we are (finally) tracing reveal the core unreason behind the Western civilization of men, and all their <u>representations</u>. And nowhere is this core unreason of western patriarchy clearer than in the words, actions, and person of their God.

In Freud's telling, the first trauma, first murder liberates man from the merely animal state of dormancy, which, he assumes, is not enough, is really nothing, because unconscious. Built into this analysis is a devaluing of life, itself, which, it is hard to deny, women have been the agents of. This is the core reversal that patriarchy achieves and must continually renew- against the "entropy" of nature. Sure, women give birth, but what is the good of that gift without consciousness? It takes men to overcome this drag of the merely animal and, so, realize the uniquely human spirit, destiny, dignity, divinity. Through their action and re-enactment of that action, men (and God) provide the gift of light, the separation necessary to consciousness, before which there is only nothing.

This invention of Yahweh and of themselves as God's Chosen is, in my telling, the defining moment in Western civilization. I have outlined its features clearly in other places. Theirs is an angry and a jealous God who will suffer no rivals. There is a fixity to His Law that is its defining feature. Universal, unchanging, freed from limitation.

Men are the chosen emissaries of this tyrannical God who causes them to suffer for listening to women and their gods and/or failing to do His bidding in all things. Man is set to rule over women as God rules over men; by virtue of their connection to the earth (through birth), women's access to spirit (and truth) is blocked. Why they need men's benevolent guidance and protection (as men need God's)- most of all, protection from their own natures and themselves.

Without God, men are too weak to seize this power over women. Freud spends a lot of time in Totem and Taboo (where he recounts this, men's triumph over nature) to explain how this first murder leads to a sublimation of the murdered Father into the shape of totem poles and animals. The totems, Freud reasons, are transitional "rough drafts" of the one, true God made necessary by man's limited and still developing reason. At this early stage in the evolution of consciousness, men must still tie their reasoning to the concrete manifestations of their more primitive sensory understanding. Eventually, (the great and distinguishing accomplishment of the Jews that Freud, as man and Jew, is so, so proud of) is the final uncoupling of reason from these merely physical manifestations in man's awakening to the one, true, universal, eternal and infinite God.

Freud goes on and on in establishing this connection between the first murder and totems, because, I suspect, he is trying to convince himself; his argument, he intuits, does not hold up. It does not occur to him to credit women for what, to Freud, is a merely transitional period in the development of man's reason. Viewed through the lens of matriarchy, these totems and totem animals make way more sense both as an end in themselves and as an effective means to reconnect with the world we feel ourselves estranged from.

I do agree with Freud that the aim of the totem, animal guides, the matriarchal religions, is to reestablish a lost bond with the rhythms of life and creation and that the Jewish Yahweh stands as an exact reversal and repudiation of this original impulse of women. The restoration and healing of a wound that totemistic religions value most becomes, under Judaism, their greatest shortcoming and vice, thereby setting the pattern for all future instantiations of the patriarchal vision.

In part, no doubt, because it is so unnatural, so unreasonable, so obviously wrong (in reference to both the evidence of our senses and our fitness for survival), it is really difficult for this One God and his Chosen Ones to establish their rightful (fictional) dominion. To do so must require continual repetitions (what Mary Daly calls "the processions") of the original violence that first established the brothers' God. This second murder, then, is not a single incident but, rather, an ongoing series of continuous repetitions that persist still. This second murder- of women- is ongoing and not merely something that happened in our past.

Facts and reason, the evidence of our senses and human experience continually undermine the original claim of this Truth, in the name of God, and so must be continually enforced through Law- that is, force, compulsion, violence, the threat (and promise) of more and future murders.

We speak here primarily of murder, though rape, too, is concurrent with these murders. The aim here is not to destroy once and for all the life-giving power of women. It is rather to bring that power under the control of men. One of the consequences of this requirement for man's dominion is to turn all other living things into mere instruments and objects for the use of men. Humanity here is viewed (in God's image) as a property exclusive to men. Women's bodies are seen as vessels, so far, necessary to God's purpose- of making men. Really, then, there is no such thing as rape within the Judaic (or, later, Christian) circle (unless it comes from outside- from the black man, our animalistic enemy).

Rape is a concept and lens only imposed on patriarchy from a later perspective hostile to the Judaic and Christian truth. And, while here, it may be worth noting, as well, the second kind of rape that tends to inhere in a patriarchal world view- that is, the rape of boys by men in power. By such means, we may suppose, the Brothers (now in the role as Father) may successfully suppress any thoughts of re-enacting that first murder- which now would mean the murder of themselves.

In each of our first two incidents of murder, there is some positive birth and growth, largely attributable to women, who are its vehicle, that is cut down by the jealousy, resentment, anger, and impulsiveness of men. Even with the force of violence, rape, and murder behind it, the Jews and Yahweh have a really hard time establishing their rightful dominion here on earth. They are surrounded by enemies on every side and must remain constantly vigilant even in their own homes against the backsliding of women and future generations.

Judaic law creates a perpetual imbalance with the rhythms of nature and life, and, despite their constant vigilance, faith and fixity of purpose, loyalty to their one and only God, the flow of nature necessarily eats away at, erodes, the foundations of this fixity- even within the faith itself. Even, I would argue, within God, Himself.

Over time, I argue, there is a softening in this Jewish God, who becomes less rigid and more human than the men who invented Him and are the enforcers of His Law. There is a feminization in God that I argue elsewhere comes, in revolutionary fashion, from His experience with Job and manifests, eventually, in the birth of christ, god made flesh in the here and now.

We have said that preceding the two earlier murders there had been new births- the birth of life, itself, in the lead up to the first murder, and the birth of civilization (a matriarchal employment of reason and technology to adapt the world to meet our needs) prior to the birth of Yahweh. In this third case, there is new birth as well- in the body of Jesus- son of God- divinity incarnate, that opens anew possibilities for reunion of spirit with natural rhythms and life.

But, as in the past, the brothers will have none of it. They refuse to cede power. They do what is necessary, as they have in the past. They murder. Number three.

This time, though, the brothers are starting to make some real, enduring progress; into their own hands, they take new power over both God and life. Through murder, the brothers remove that living god (Jesus, christ) from life- they cast him back to Heaven (nowhere), they refuse God's gesture of love, and, in this moment of His greatest vulnerability, steal from Him, through His son, the cross.

birth of christ

They know the cross has power, though they don't yet know what. For centuries, they'll wear it around their necks, no idea what it does, but applying it in all various and murderous ways to establish and extend their own dominion. Armed with Christ this time, in addition to their God, the brothers are finally successful in establishing dominion over all others and the land. They learn to use this cross, dead tree- new totem of abstraction- to reduce all life to matter and so rise, themselves, as its conscious masters.

To be clear, then, the birth in this case is christ- the living divinity of humans. The murder is the crucifixion of this humanity, this divinity through its exile to Heaven. The murderers are, once again, the band of (jealous) brothers, and the instrument of this particular murder (and its continuous repetition) is the Church. Just as Yahweh turns the truth of humans' connection with nature and all living things into its opposite, so does the Church equally reverse every meaning of the true christ.

It is only after his death that the murder of christ really begins; they kill the living christ and replace "him" with an idea, with man's <u>representation</u> of christ, the Lie of Christianity. And, same as the previous murders, it does not happen "once upon a time" or all at once; the murder never stops. Unceasing, Christians are murdering christ right now, all around and inside of us.

Vampires, these Christians suck passion and life from the well spring and torture it, by reverse alchemy, their perpetual murder of christ, into its opposite- all in order to extend man's dominion. Forever perfecting their terror techniques and lies, learning from each other, this brotherhood sell the image, the Lie of man's representation of christ in Heaven, as if it is the real thing. The dead God they peddle is the exact reversal of christ- the one they murder- our own divine humanity. They steal.

The genius of Christians (what Jews could not achieve) is to recruit Christ's followers- including women- to be accomplices (supposed beneficiaries) in christ's murder (i.e. the murder of their self).

That's real progress Christians can be proud of. Only very recently have we begun to find words to name this, Christianity's greatest achievement- gaslighting, soul murder, blaming the victim, patriarchy. Christians tell the <u>story</u> of the true christ- God's first gesture of love- and teach that standard to their followers (women and enslaved men). In those who, unlike Them, have some remaining trace of divinity inside, Church "fathers" make emotional appeal to that true christ- urging us to uphold <u>that</u> standard- but only on behalf of the Church (the Lie masquerading as the Body of Christ). All the while extending their own dominion.

Meanwhile, the Catholic brothers, at first, and now all Christians, are the masters and the chosen ones who pursue their Christian and Judaic duty to establish dominion in His name. Just as men's right to rape was established under the Jewish God, so, now, is the Christian right to enslave others firmly established in Jesus' name. Righteous men set out to do God's work, that is, to become master over earth and all other living things.

The Catholics are men of action in ways that Jewish intellectuals could never be. Here the call was now to <u>apply</u> their faith through their sacred duty to extend the dominion of their one and only God. They turned their cross, stolen from christ and Father, to the here and now and others.

birth of christ

Here, then, is a picture, a symbolic representation of the stages and the murders we have passed through so far in the process of human consciousness:

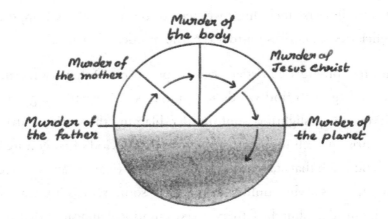

In thus turning their eyes from Heaven and God's will alone towards their own mastery and duty as Christians here on earth (in their application of the cross), it should come as no surprise that Christian duty and dominion would soon turn into science. Science only completes the usurpation of God's power initiated by the murder of our simultaneous humanity and divinity- the christ that is each of us.

Through its various stages, the brothers' coup d'état both re-establishes the (murdered) Father's power (through the fiction of Yahweh) and steals it from Him in an act of Promethean cowardice (the murder of His son). Science is just the natural consequence and outgrowth of these two earlier movements by men (i.e. by the many- the band of brothers, not the genius and divinity of human individuals).

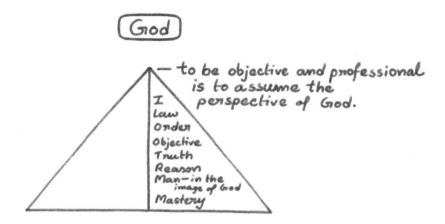

Science is merely the completion of this long journey. Its weapon is "reason," its fiction (akin to Yahweh and Christ in Heaven) is objectivity, and its instrument is the Corporation. Through science, men pretend (to themselves as well as others) to see and act from above- called "being a professional"- from the perspective we assume from God.

Through reason, we see the one (objective) Truth and so, at last, transcend the limited animal perspectives we strove to escape ever since that first murder so many generations ago.

Through science, like religion before it, white men perpetuate this long pretense (they lie to each other and themselves) that their thinking is unbound by merely animal emotions, motives, and desires. They have purged themselves of these lesser aspects, through reason, (like the Christians do through Christ) and are, as a consequence, assigned the duty to decide and lead and rule. They are qualified, fully educated, reasonable, often quite handsome and athletic(!) white men (with a few blacks and females sprinkled in like raisins).

"Intelligent men" (self-satisfied and unself-reflective) rise above mere emotions, subjectivity, and carnal passions to see the world "as it is"-

"in fact." Through reason, we men pretend to ourselves the birds-eye view of God, Himself, confident in the (exclusive) rightness of our objective view, we now set about our task of perfecting the world.

These brothers- and sisters now, what progress!- commit the fourth murder before our eyes; every day we see more clearly, as science and its corporate offspring steal the water and devour workers. Our body registers the murders; it is hard on all of us to be this sick. We need to listen to all our parts, even, and most especially, when they are painful ones. We need to feel that pain, I have always believed, as much as we can bear. An obligation to participate, somehow, in the interest of the larger human body. Do your part, you know. Be a vital cell! Have fun with it, even. Dive in for the full drama of life, creative spirit, in this time of deepest need.

We are living through the fourth murder now. The murderer is man's creation, Frankenstein. The Corporation. The Machine. The product of the brothers' reason, instruments of Objectivity.

Its victim is the earth, itself- the planet as a whole and humans' existence upon it. The instrument of death is science, reason, and its technologies, and our certainty (faith, Lie) of the (absolute) truth of reason.

In His gesture of love, the divine human, christ, God gave birth to an awareness in we humans of a living divinity in ourselves, each other, and all living things. Through murder, the Christians stole that gift from us and turned it to its opposite. They made the beneficiaries of that divinity the exclusive realm of men- and not all men- just the Christian men, the white men, we men of reason, the brothers, murderers of christ. To, at last, extend their righteous dominion, these men formed a Church, within whose walls those ones who maintained some trace of humanity and divinity (the women, the poor, the enslaved, the humane) could be taught and/or compelled to crucify the divinity and humanity in themselves and so be "saved" through men's (the murderers') (false) representation (reversal) of "Christ."

Through science, the murderers complete the turn of the cross (begun in Christianity) upon the realm of humans, of life. This cross of reason, and the technologies derived from its application, are now the primary (and effective) weapon for establishing (white, Christian) man's dominion over all others and the earth.

As Mary Wollstonecraft Shelley so clearly warned us, we (the earth, humanity, women) are being murdered by man's own creation (made in the image of his God). We are suffering the limitations of that- man's creation- first crafted out of men's resentment at womens' ability to create life. Through the progress of their invented Truth(s), the band of brothers have, at last, devised creations- man's machine(s) and corporations (fictional beings) that have the power to kill us all. We are living at a time of culmination and completion- the fourth murder of the Lie.

It is difficult to know- and frightening for us to contemplate- what may be born of this murder. Clearly, I believe there are patterns discoverable by human reason and imagination, and a dialectical approach to discovering these patterns still makes sense to me. Done right, dialectics do honor to both the cyclical nature of growth and change and to the mysterious principle of new growth and creativity that Henri Bergson pointed us towards. To comprehend a possible future for humanity that may still arise out of this, the brother's attempted Final Solution, we may need to extend our time frame beyond that normally employed by humans.

birth of christ

I suggest we view all four stages in this crucifixion of our humanity/divinity/life/consciousness as a single moment in the dialectic. What comes next may be a complete annihilation of humans on this planet. We must admit this possibility. Or it may result in our (humans') absolute enslavement to the machine(s) that were (once upon a time) man's own creation. But there is at least a third possibility- and that is somehow a realization, a resurrection, and triumph of the christ that is each of us over that band of murderers who sought to destroy us. To achieve that end must require, it seems to me, a new sense of our collective identity that it is difficult for me to conceive (inhabited as I am by old forms of knowing), though I can begin to imagine it.

We need a re-solution that allows us to, at once, experience ourselves 1) as individual cells in a larger collective body (the human body, of which we are a part) and 2) as unique and finite individuals, in bodies that are, at once, fully human and divine. We must demand of each other the embrace of this creative, generative, and life-giving power that is our true human nature, long suppressed but not forgotten.

The Meaning of Relativity

The Haudenosaunee image of the fall reveals our embeddedness and dependency, our relativity and our true place at the intersect of sea and sky.

Relativity means that the consciousness we once attributed to God is now divided up between us. Our point of view has shifted from the single point of view from above we inherited from God to a multiplicity.

We once viewed the world from on high:

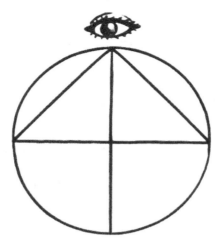

But now we have learned to view the world from where we really are:

It is debatable whether the "I" in this schema should be placed at the center or the perimeter of the sphere. Viewed from the perspective of the individual, each of us is, of course, the center of the universe (as it passes through our particular doors of perception- our body). But viewed from the perspective of others or more "objectively," i.e. through the eyes of the collective, we are, of course, only one among many and there is no single center. The extent to which any of us is the center is a merely fictional representation- though, granted, it is a fictional representation with compelling truth and value for us.

As a consequence of the shift in perspective from God (above) to human (here and now) consciousness necessarily gets broken into pieces. And our task becomes to retrieve and reintegrate as many of these pieces as we can- pieces both inside and outside ourselves.

Here, on the horizontal plane, we have an ability to move that is denied to God. The relativity of the human perspective gives to us the ability to view ourselves and the world from a multiplicity of different points of view. Our motility in this world liberates us from the single, fixed perspective of God, and so empowers us to piece together our own truth from the multiple aspects we can gather and decipher. In our bodies, we are one, we are limited, we are "stuck" and see only through these eyes, like God. Our body, then, becomes analogous to the totem- the immovable centerpoint. It may be represented by the vertical axis in the cross of consciousness, the fixed point, connecting heaven with earth. Our body is the totem.

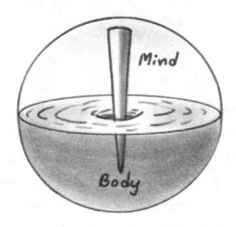

Our mind, unlike our body, though, is free to roam beyond these limitations. With our mind, we can enter into perspectives other than our own. We can imagine our selves out of our own limiting perspective, and, in doing so, enrich and inform that perspective with alternative visions received from other places, other people. Along the horizontal plane on the cross of consciousness, we take in the multiplicity, we expand outward, we roam and grow. And so, with our mind, we explore the infinite possibilities along this horizontal plane of human experience. This is Gemini- depth turned sideways, in the realm of humans. Like Tik Tok, for me.

The scientists would have you believe that this world- the flat world- the human world- is the only world that is. That is the infantile relativity we have until now suffered under. These reasonable men (in the universities, government, and corporate offices) have fully applied the cross to the here and now. These objective ones …Democrats hope to benefit from your belief that this is all there is. You are, of course, each allowed a phantasy world, your entertainments and escape from inhuman reality. You may choose a game all your own or one you share with others. Many choose Christianity as their preferred delusion, and, it must be admitted, there is great comfort there these days- in a time that comfort's needed, a time when standing outside the herd is dangerous.

The price of admission and success in this flat world is only the denial of your bodies, your experience, and your emotions, the same as ever charged in a patriarchal world.

For those who risk refusal of this world (alone), our experience is less linear than the rational world view and more woven out of stories that move in multiple directions at once but that all, ultimately, still point us towards a unifying center. In this sense, our world view and sense of time becomes "uni-ear" rather than "lin-ear." It drives us to a single point of convergence without thereby moving in a straight line of cause and effect and objective facts.

This "uni-ear" structure of time, truth, and understanding is reflected here, in my writing, where I find, in my attempt to iron out my ideas into a linear and logical progression one upon the others, that it is not possible to do so, and yet, though my discourse moves in circles, those circles are all part of a spiraling momentum towards a single, complex and simple, pervasive and multifaceted point. The new center point upon which we will ground all future knowledge and society is less black and white than the old truth, but it is infinitely richer, because it is dynamic and drawn from a multiplicity of, an infinitude of human voices all converging into one.

Consciousness requires an incarnation, and we are such a one. Incarnations of the infinite, we are more like Jesus than like God. We are born, we die, we suffer, we love. Each a manifestation of all. Altogether, we're a miracle.

In this movement of consciousness out of the sky and into our bodies, we have opened the possibility for a new constellation of truths. Relativity empowers us to recognize a multiplicity of complementary truths through which we may constellate a new whole.

Human Bubbles

In the beginning, we mistook ourselves for a star. It is arguable, of course, whether this was a mistake. There was truth to our perception, only it wasn't the whole truth.

We might wonder how things would have turned out differently if we had pictured ourselves, not as a star but as a bubble from the beginning.

I suppose that it was dialectically necessary for us to choose the star image first, and surely this conceptualization of ourselves has served us well in many ways, has advanced our consciousness, but it must now be understood that it would be just as accurate to picture ourselves as a drop of water in an endless sky of light. Though equally accurate, it is only now that we can conceive ourselves in this second way. Only now have we gained sufficient distance from ourselves to look back upon our self, like an astronaut from space, and recognize the fragile bubble earth that is us.

Not all bubbles are perhaps differentiated enough from others to see themselves as completely unattached. We have been moved to conclude that consciousness is all collective, that everything we know comes to us from others and that even the voices inside of our own head are the voices of others we've internalized. We have concluded that all representations are shared with and received from others. Though we individuals (and groups) are capable of adding to these representations by building upon or restructuring those representations that have gone before, our representations become added to the collective through expression, communication, manifestation and, once represented, are no longer owned by us. Our ideas and contributions "have a life of their own," or, more accurately, their meanings become taken over by the others.

People differentiate themselves as individuals to varying degrees. For most people their identity and definition remains bound up with collective definitions of the (a) group. Rare (and odd) is the individual who strives to separate themselves thoroughly from the others- to become a single bubble in a sky of light. Most are tied together closely, like the bubbles in the dishwater- with little or no sense of a separate self.

Is that true, I wonder? (It remains difficult/impossible to know what goes on in other people's heads). More accurately, I would guess, each bubble in these clusters would have an illusion of their separation from the others, without ever really giving it much thought. They do not see the extent to which they are determined and defined by, and identical with, the others. They don't really care, don't really think about it, and, when they do, take comfort from their connectedness with others.

The truth is that their unconscious connectedness with others really does bring a degree of comfort and security to individuals that the differentiated bubble forsakes. Modern existentialists and so-far "relativists" have experienced this differentiation of the individual (of themselves) as alienation and loneliness. These worries do not plague the "tied-in" individual, though it is not uncommon for bubbles in the cluster (especially, women bubbles) to feel trapped and imprisoned, hemmed in by the pressure of the other bubbles, by the definition of themselves by others.

Even the most highly differentiated bubble (individual) remains wholly populated by the representations of the others. We do not cease to participate in the collective by our further separation and differentiation. The collective forces of consciousness continue to operate in us the same as in the others, but we do become more conscious of these collective forces at work in ourselves and others. We see the collective, and all of our experiences, more and more through the lens of the individual- through definitions that we have generated ourselves out of the material provided us by others. And so, too, we have more fully developed our individual capacity to re-constellate the "reality" we all inherit from the others in new, creative, unique, individual ways. We have, to put it differently, a more highly differentiated self.

THE SACRED HOOP

In contrast, there are some individuals, it would appear, that never have an idea of their own. All their ideas come to them from others. They take possession of these ideas- or these ideas take possession of them. They go willingly, uncritically, along with these ideas, and allow these ideas to define who they are- just as these same ideas define so many- their friends, their family, their countrymen, their cluster. Populated by the ideas of others, all that distinguishes these individuals is their physical location in this body, with these unique characteristics, at this point in space and time. So it is that the majority of humans become an embodiment of shared representations and ideas not unlike the bee in the hive or the ant in the hill.

I have often wondered, watching clusters of birds in flight, the extent to which each bird must perceive themselves as an individual. Like us, the bird, the ant, the bee looks out on the world through this set of eyes, this particular body, and like us, I am convinced they must feel as if they are the agents of their own actions. Even in the most collective of species, there must be an illusion of individuality. Each bubble must experience themselves as an individual creature/consciousness, unaware of the degree to which they are determined by the others.

If greater differentiation of the individual leads to loneliness, alienation, and suicide, then why do it? This question alone is enough to discourage the majority of humans from looking too closely at their own self, separate and distinct from the others. And yet, something there is- a longing for the infinite and/or human's need for meaning and/or human's lust for power and control- that drives certain individuals to differentiate themselves as far as possible from the rest.

Recognizing as we do that we are drops of water as surely as we are points of light, we are now in a position to recognize the advantages of further differentiation. We are poised to answer the transitional (though very real) problem of alienation of the existentialists, but, I can't help it, I am mixing metaphors and need to clean these up. I have used three different metaphors for the human individual- the drop of water, the bubble, and the star (the point of light). There is truth in each of these representations, though none of them is "the whole truth and nothing but the truth."

We approach closer to the truth if we mix our metaphors in the spirit of both/and relativity. The most accurate representation of the human individual would be as a bubble. Inside, half the human bubble is filled by light and air and sky, and below the light, in the bottom half of the bubble is water, blackness, and the deeps.

And then the sun comes up, and we see. What is remarkable- a mystery and a miracle about these bubbles is that they have become conscious of themselves. They are balls of matter, not only come to life, but come to consciousness, and, in the rarest of cases- in you and I- that consciousness has become conscious of itself. Miracles and mysteries compound themselves in the creation of you and me.

My Pathology

It has been my pathology to create this solipsistic vision of a separate individual that, though constellated exclusively by elements borrowed from the collective nonetheless builds for and with and in themselves something new and original that has never been before but that, nonetheless, is both capable of being shared with others and, too, capable of changing the world. The world will never be the same again, because of the original contributions and creations of this isolated individual who is, though tied to others and made from others, still fundamentally alone.

It has been my pathology to think that an individual can be a separate container for the universal truths of humanity, consciousness, the world, and life. There is no such thing as this separate individual, and the concentration of this single and fundamental falsehood has been the source of virtually all the pain and falsehood I have suffered under throughout my life as lived. If we dig deep enough, I would argue, we all have some such falsehood- some kernel of untruth upon which we build our entire metaphysic, that becomes the focus of our unique vision and whole life, that is simultaneously universal (when viewed under one aspect) and particular to ourselves alone (when viewed under its necessarily complementary aspect).

I argued elsewhere that all people are driven by myth but that not all myths are pathological. Now I must contradict (but not take back) my previous argument. Because all life and consciousness has its foundation in irreconcilable dualities, any solution, any story, any "truth" must be, at its very core, mistaken, untrue, and, if you want to be mean about it, pathological and a lie. Every solution begins with a "myth" in the modern, ugly meaning of the term. Every solution begins with a fundamental untruth.

Ok. But if we are willing to accept this truth- that is, the fundamental untruth of any truth- and if we are willing, like any right connoisseur of art must, to suspend disbelief on this single point alone, then it is truly remarkable, astounding, miraculous all that we can learn from the fictions of others, and even more remarkable what we can learn about our own fiction- our own philosophical mission in life.

My pathology is, like my body, the necessary core to my consciousness. I remain ambivalent towards- I simultaneously love and revile- cling to and seek escape from- this fundamental error that gave rise to all that has come since. I embrace my pathology- my fundamental irrationality, just as I so often argue, we must embrace our blackness. Not to embrace my fundamental irrationality and pathology does not thereby free me from it. No, in that case, I continue to be driven by the same pathology, the same irrationality, I just don't know it. I cannot be rid of my pathology any more than I can be rid of my body, except by ending it all- in suicide and (what must be the deepest fear of every suicide) what if not even then?

Failure to embrace, articulate, uncover, own our own fundamental pathology/irrationality does not make us healthy and well. The pathology/irrationality continues to be operational in us. We continue to be driven by it even if we pretend we are not and/or even if (especially if) we think we are not. In fact, I (and people like me) who now openly admit and strive to own my own pathology may be the only ones who are not insane, not evil, not pathological, after all. Only by owning that I am insane is it possible to not be driven by- not act solely through- my insanity. By owning my insanity it may become possible for the first time for "me" to act (whomever "me" is) and not just for my insanity to act through "me."

Maybe. Or maybe, even though it is conscious and admitted and owned, I may still be driven just as much as all the rest, by the fundamental insanity that is "me." There is no liberation (any more than I can find "liberation" from my body). What is gained, then, is at least integrity and honesty, humility and humor. To be moral in this new age of relativity requires us to become conscious of our own patholog(ies) through a process of education with others. To act ethically requires us to remain consciously aware of both the limitations and values in our own point of view while being open to hearing the truth as others see it.

THE SHADOW

The Crucible and the Alchemist

At rest, the individual consciousness is best represented thus:

Placido

But an individual consciousness is rarely at rest, most especially the individual who has separated himself from the moorings of the others. For those who live in bubble clusters, like bees and ants, the motion they endure is measurably eased. Though rarely able to achieve complete rest (and not necessarily seeking that), they can, with the buoyancy of the cluster, reduce life's motions- most of the time (sometimes onto death). They grow to dislike motion and seek peace, security and forgetfulness (of their self) through others- a degree of settlement that would be absolutely deadening to people like you or me. The consciousness of the collective is brought to life only through individual bubbles that are us, but only a few such bubbles are conscious of themselves as the carriers of the collective. The collective operates through the majority of humans without them recognizing that is the case. These ones labor under the illusion that they act as individuals but do not; the others, the majority, acts through them.

As we develop as individuals, the contradictions of the universe converge in us and call us to action. We little balls of matter, become conscious of ourselves, become, also, the window onto the infinite. Once set in motion, universal and particular, water and sky, the dialectic of human consciousness converges in little us- in the center of knowledge, in the crucible, that is my body- me.

An individual differentiates themselves by re-constellating the ideas received from others in ways that are new- at least to them. To educate a child, we have them practice such re-constellation and tearing down, synthesis and analysis- in a group and as individuals. The individual learns to construct ideas of their own out of the raw material that is the idea of others. This capacity to create something new is what distinguishes an individual from all others.

By differentiating from the others through the generation of ideas that are our own, we individuals do not, however, liberate ourselves from the influence, from the hand, of the other. The relationship between I and other remains but is transformed from one of cause (the collective) and effect (the individual) to a relationship that is dialectical- a conversation between the two in which each becomes the cause and effect of the other, in a spiraling exchange and growth necessary to advance our human consciousness.

The individual human being- with this one body as its center- is the crucible in which all the tensions and history of consciousness will converge to recreate the original miracle: the creation of something new. Something that is both universal and particular.

But without the controlling intelligence there is no alchemy. Once, we used God to represent this Alchemist to ourselves. And, as we have demonstrated here, this representation (God) served well to advance our consciousness through previous stages but has now exhausted itself, having served its purpose of delivering us to the true alchemist in the process. Today, in our present period of infantile relativism, we grew to recognize the Self as the true alchemist in the process, but this is a transitional- and wrong- representation of the controlling intelligence that, I am afraid, we might get stuck in and so lose this crucial opportunity to dramatically revolutionize human consciousness.

How can it be that the I is both the crucible and the alchemist? Both the worker and the worked upon? The object and subject of the process? To a certain extent, it is true, of course, that we are subject and object, the seer and the seen, but there is an element missing.

I am the crucible. But the other(s) are the Alchemist.

The Whirlpool

There are two eyes to human consciousness- I and other. Through their separation, the two create a vibration and movement, a firmament, a break in which we grow a world.

These two competing, complementary forces function not only between ourselves and others in the external world, but within the individual crucible of our self as well. This dialectic of thought and emotions, I and internalized other, within the finite (human) container creates a whirlpool within that can be both frightening and enervating. This must be just the kind of tension that builds inside a seed before it breaks.

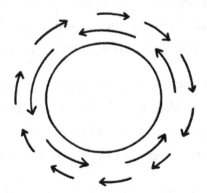

Like a potter molding clay, the hands that shape us are the other. The alchemist is the one who supports and constrains us, shapes and directs us, in accordance with need. The need comes from forces beyond our comprehension and the comprehension of others, though it is something we all participate in. In astrology, these forces may be represented by the outer planets- Pluto, Uranus, Neptune, and they seem to indicate a still higher intelligence- a more comprehensive Alchemist inclusive of I and other.

Who is the other? It is an abstraction (as is the I). It is both individual and collective. It is something we both love and loath. It is complex and multifaceted with brightnesses and shadows- this other (just like the I); is both you and me.

Myth of Self, Truth of Other

At each new stage in our emerging consciousness, a new carrier emerges for that infinite aspect of our self. In our own time, this search for center has led us to the Self (capitalized, like God). The Self is the higher aspect of our self, in contrast to the finite ego. Indicative of our culture, the Self is like God, individually wrapped. In this age of infantile relativism, we each get our own personal representation of God, beyond the reach of others, that opens up the infinite in me to me alone.

In many ways, this Self is useful and far preferable to the old, false God. People use this Self to work towards transcending their own (ego) limitations, to question the internal walls that have been built.

birth of christ

One thing the Self does is turn our attention inward. It shifts the totem (and so the truth and center of the universe) back to the heart of the human individual (like Luther said to do). This shift of truth from the objective perspective of God to the subjective and relative perspective of individual humans is a dialectically important shift in human consciousness that can be a good, important, and appropriate thing to do, though it is not without its difficulties.

We look for divinity, meaning, infinity within ourselves, through feelings, dreams, memories, aspirations, and reflective thought. Such movement is important and appropriate to our times, of course, when the external and objective laws and truth we used, once upon a time, as carriers of the infinite have so failed to release us from the prison of our finitude that they now trap us there instead.

Inescapable finitude is the daily experience forced upon us by the machine of government, technology and business. The electronic web of social/economic/media relations makes us all, now, into objects, cogs in a machine grown much bigger than us and beyond anyone's control. We serve as both unwilling victims and "voluntary" participants in this "World is Flat" economic system built on Laws and Words and Rules and Promises that, we were told once upon a time, would serve and liberate us. The only way out of this oppressive system is through some retreat, an escape into a solipsistic world of feeling, comfort, satisfaction, infinitude that comes only from within. We have grown progressively more addicted to our self-soothing techniques as the "objective" world we flee from has become more brutal, more pervasive, entrenched, insatiable, irrational.

This movement towards Self is a positive development in many ways- in turning our attention inward, in maintaining our faith in the infinite, in its expression in the here and now, and in giving us something to aspire to- but only as long as we do not rest our development there. Over-concentration on the Self threatens to cut us off from the wellspring, from the source. We must continue in our journey. We must enter the depths.

New Age spiritual leaders are less skeptical and pessimistic on this point than me. They offer a promise of hope where I name despair. They talk about how the individual Self we seek is connected and one with the wider Self, the Self that transcends our individuality, the Self of others and our self. But I do not buy it, because I do not feel it. This Self we are driven into by the madness of our age, by the infantile relativism of our age, by the new religion, psychology, of our age, does not lead us to the others, does not lead us to an infinitude transcendent of our self. It is, I grant, perhaps a window onto that infinite, but a window that, once we go there, ends up to be as much a barrier as an opening.

A window sealed shut, and so, if we follow these New Age mystics, as so many do, in search of Self and take this journey to our end, we will find our self in a place analogous to Truman in the Truman Show, but with a few critical differences. We, too, will bump up, inevitably, against the wall of limitations that is our Self, but in our case, the wall will be transparent. It will be, at once, a window and a barrier, from which we may see the larger Self (the infinitude that- to be infinite, of course- must be greater than our self) but can never reach it.

The Self is still a representation- it is a man-made idea of infinitude, and, as such, it is not enough. We are trapped inside the prison of our own internal and individual Selfhood, secured away in our idea, our phantasy of infinitude, cutting us off forever from the others and our source. Like Truman, we will reach our limits, though for us the limits will be, not the world defined by others, but the Self defined by us. Like Truman we will bump up against these necessary and inevitable limits, but, unlike, Truman, we will 1) be able to see beyond these limits and 2) remain trapped- unable to go there- nonetheless. The finitudes will show up somewhere.

In this era of an old and dying Mind over Matter metaphysic and the infantile relativism that has grown up in response, our escape to Self, while seemingly a rational response to an insane and destructive situation, will, if we pursue it to its end, prove to be a dead end that will leave us trapped, lonely, and nowhere. The New Age claim that this Self connects us to the larger self of others and a planet is a lie, that is, a theory devised by the human intellect that will, in practice, in "real" life, prove wrong, an illusion, a phantasy. It will leave us, nose pressed against the glass, both closer to the infinite and further from its realization than we have ever been.

This Self is just the latest incarnation of God, and it will fail on the same grounds that God failed us- that it is not material, that it is not real because it is purely theoretical, purely intellectual (though felt), an idea without any substance or life. I fear that, in our naiveté and desperation, we are reincarnating the old, dead concept-God. We have given Him a new name- Self- and we have limited His scope- to the subjective, individual side of the human equation (as opposed to the objective, universal side in which He was originally born). Through psychology, I fear, we have simply moved this God indoors- inside ourselves and not in the sky. In doing so, I fear, we have changed the wrong variable (or changed too few variables). We have not yet gotten to the root of the problem with our God and so are set to replicate that problem inside our self and set up a new tyranny- of the Self. While Self may appear to satisfy our need for the "courage to be one's self" (as per Paul Tillich), Self will ultimately fail in its inability to satisfy our equal need for "the courage to be a part."

Though we have, collectively, made the shift from God's perspective to a more human one,

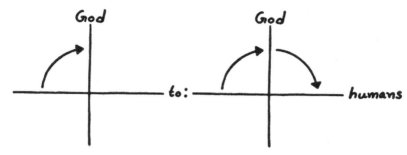

we still fall prey to the same phantasy- of our self as an infinitude, eternal, disembodied, pure Light. On a human plane, from our scientific perspective, the infinite delusion takes shape as Self. Like God, Self can provide some direction, some inspiration and pull us from the fiction of our own (exclusive) finitude, but we must resist this siren call of Self and remember our own finitude- that half of our self that Self, like God, denies "reality" to. It is time we dig deeper.

Human beings are finite as well as infinite. We are divine but also animals. We are subjects, and we're objects. The objective world, in our own time, has become such a source of pain and finitude that people try to escape it at every chance we get. Even those most enmeshed in the objective world do so, mostly, for the money with which they hope to buy their freedom from this world that turns them into objects, proves to them their finitude, cares nothing for their souls. We are so wholly determined by the Others (by society and its systems)- and in ways that bring us no awareness, fulfillment or meaning- only money- that we seek our truth, our meaning, our freedom- elsewhere. We seek freedom and meaning in the subject, through our emotions, in our own personal constellation of escapes from the oppressive reality of the object world.

birth of christ

The world we have, collectively, constructed turns us into objects. We submit to this treatment, because we have to. We have no choice but to submit to the system- to some degree at least- to have any hope of survival. But that doesn't mean we like it, and at the first chance we get, we escape from this system (that, once upon a time, promised meaning) to do "what I want to do," to pursue peace and love, fulfillment and meaning, forgetfulness, drugs, and TV.

In the previous- scientific- revolution in human consciousness, we sought escape from the limiting- subjective, internal, emotional- aspects of our world- the limits of our mythological explanations and sought refuge and infinitude (God) in the absolute and objective truth of science divorced from these internal aspects of the mind and world. Today, we seek the opposite.

We seek escape from the objective incarnations of this old, dead, scientific truth and seek refuge in our emotions, feelings, body and persons. Such reversal is consistent with the new relativistic (Einsteinian) physics that has come to replace the previously objective (Mind over Matter) physics of Newton, Bacon and Descartes. And, too, the same danger recurs that we will go too far in the one direction in reaction to the failures of the previous one and so lead ourselves, inevitably, into yet another permutation of the limits, the conflict, the dissatisfaction, the untruth inherent in any either/or.

A mature relativism will allow us to understand, first and foremost, that the subject and the object, the internal and the external, the emotional and the rational, the body and the mind, we will have with us always, and as long as we make one side the carrier of the infinite and freedom, the other side must always become the complementary carrier of finitude and slavery. A more mature relativism will teach us the importance of moving beyond the old, dead either/or of Western

Civilization to embrace a new- both/and understanding of the two, contradictory aspects to our human consciousness and the world(s) created by that consciousness.

A mature relativism will require, of course, yet another reversal, this time away from the journey inward to the Self begun by Freud and capitalized upon by Carl Jung and his followers. The "other" is a complex and multifaceted concept (just like its sister, I), and the face of the Other that we have been forced to comply with (the corporate society on a mass scale with all its bureaucracy, inhumanity, and indifference) is only one face of- and the least human face of- the other. The other is that but something more. The other is other people, and through a return to these ones, through a conscious return and concentration on the other that becomes available to us only through face-to-face relationships on a more human scale, we will rediscover our way back to the roots of our self.

The Self we seek lives in the body of the other, in the here and now. Not in our own solipsistic and infinite subjectivity (Self), and not in the indifferent corporate Other, but rather in the other individuals- human beings capable of love. Paradoxically, the way to real experience (and not just the idea) of the self we seek is through the other. We realize the inner truth and the subject in ourselves by moving, ironically, in the opposite direction. It is through our encounters with the others that we really experience the self. But it is not just any encounter with the other. To achieve our ends, we must, in an act of humility and humanity, embrace our own finitude and make an object of our self in the eyes of other subjects.

At this stage in our development, and probably always, we human beings have an obligation to "express our self," to make an object of our self for others to see and learn from. We must allow ourselves to be actors on the stage of life. We must show ourselves, making ourselves vulnerable before the others, because, just like our God, only by exposing our self to other's view is it possible for us to know ourselves. We must take a leap of faith in the audience of and in intercourse with the other and be our self, whatever it is that turns out to be. It is only by this movement, in fact, that we will ever come to see ourselves, that we will ever be a subject.

And so, our first moral obligation in a mature relativistic world is to take constructive risks and show/express ourselves in order that, distilled through the crucible of others, we come to know ourselves, and so may begin to craft a subject. That is, we begin to develop an interiority, a self-consciousness, a depth that is not there without the impetus of others. The difference between what I am suggesting and what happens now is that in the world of objects I am pointing to, we human individuals define our self. There is an element of self-determination and new creation. To some extent, at least, we determine our own expression and are not determined by others.

That is why this act of objectification is such a risk- because what is being expressed is new, original and unique to me. I become my own creation, and what that creation will look like, how it will be received, I cannot know until I do it. The creation/expression makes me vulnerable precisely because it comes from me and not from the others. To merely replicate the views and representations of some other(s) is to take no risk. Such mirroring of the creations of others is, in fact, a common act of cowardice designed to ease the anxiety and fear inherent in being a self.

In the true expression- that is, in the objectification of our self, we own our weirdness. We put it out there for others to see- that, through them, we may see, too- and so further shape- ourselves as well. An act of vulnerability, humility, and courage must be necessary to break through the wall of Self and reconnect with others.

This is another way of saying that we must come to express our finitude. By engaging through action(s) in the world, like Spinoza suggests in his <u>Ethics</u>, we can begin to become rational and objective about our self. Through our actions, we come to see our self as if we are an other. And, conversely, we also treat the other as the only One, as the Self, with our emotions tied up with them as surely as they had been with our self. We must- and can- come to recognize the true center of our Self and world, that the true source of God and infinity in our human experience lies in the hearts and souls and, most especially, the bodies of other people, independent from our self.

It is by thus humbling ourselves and accepting our own finite aspects that we become aware of the infinite aspect in others. Only thus, through our engagement with others, can we actually experience that infinitude that God promised to us- in theory, in idea. Only thus can we approach simultaneously, an experience of life and eternity. We must be more (and less) than Self to be with others. And so it is that we join our finitudes in order to overcome It.

We must become our finite self, fully, to realize our infinitude, and it is other people- not our Self- that provide an occasion for that infinitude. The infinitude of Self is never found in ourselves, alone, but is, rather, created by the exchange of finitudes, of I and other, of you and me; at the intersect.

As an other, myself, I have a moral obligation as well. We must do our part as others for our children, for our colleagues, and for generations to come, to create the conditions necessary for this Self to grow. We must teach our children- give them safe and challenging and continuous opportunities to express themselves, to reflect upon the others' response to their expressions, and to express themselves again. We must create an environment that teaches children to understand that they have a self- that they are something more than an object shaped by others. We must teach our children to doubt, to construct- synthesize, but also to tear down- to analyze, to build theories and shoot them down again. We must create the conditions necessary for children to practice the dialectic of reversals by which human consciousness grows. We must allow ourselves to be subjected to their dramas, to be used as characters in their personal dramas, that they might learn who they are and how to be. We must provide them with emotional safety and encouragement to take risks, and we must provide them with criticism and challenge necessary to reflect back and grow. We must become willing, living mirrors through which students see new aspects and develop strongest aspects in themselves.

We need strong face-to-face communities to grow strong individuals and to counterbalance the machine. We must, as much as possible, learn ourselves and teach others to practice the I-Thou relationship Martin Buber teaches.

Search for the Center

Consciousness is necessarily cumulative. In order to create something new, we must build on the foundations of those who have gone before. A creation that did not build upon previous understandings would be incomprehensible, invisible, non-existent, impossible. We must use the language of our predecessors to create a world.

That said, it is a most common human error to assume that I/we are unlike any other, that we are the very center of the universe. We come by this mistake honestly enough; a self-centered perspective really was our first experience of the world- both as individuals and as a human race, and though we grow beyond this original delusion into more mature and objective perspectives, in some ways, the delusion never goes away. In some ways, it is not a delusion.

Within each individual is replicated the experiences of the race. That is why the creation stories so resonate with us. They are stories we participate in. They are our story and not merely some tale other people tell, and without such story, we must feel lost, disoriented, awash, and overwhelmed.

The whole of human history is a story of two simultaneous and (apparently) opposed movements in our consciousness. A movement outward and a movement inward. We seek continuously, as an individual and as a race, to both expand our horizons and to find our center. Science, in my interpretation, has been predominantly concerned with the expansion and definition of our horizons- on our interface with others and the world- and thus it is that science and scientists concern themselves primarily with fact, with reality, with material evidence (provable and replicable), observation, analysis, and experiment.

It is through story- imagination, synthesis, creativity, symbols, pretend, dreams and expressions- that we seek our center. Just as the horizon continually recedes so that there is always a limit to our science, more we need to know, so, too, does the center continually allude us. At each stage in our developing consciousness (as delineated throughout this book) we thought we had, at last, arrived at the center- at the truth, the origin, the basis for all law and order and understanding, only to find that the center had escaped capture by our concepts. Just as we zero in on the true center of the universe at every stage in human consciousness, the center flips, like the needle on a compass as we turn slowly, ever slowly from North to South or South to North.

With each flip in center, we find it necessary to reverse our course and to understand black and white anew.

Once, at the beginning of time, we assumed ourselves as the center (without knowing we were doing so) until, with time, we learned from God that we were not the center. We learned through science that there was some center outside our self- first, in the early days, a communal center (the totem), later, in modern times, an objective center (in "reality" and "facts"). In most recent times, as human beings have grown to see through the limitations of our merely scientific definitions of the world, "spiritual leaders" have begun us on a path towards recognizing, at a new and deeper level, that it is, after all, our "self" (still in the process of being defined) that is somehow the center of our experience, the center of our world.

In my own thinking, I see the possibility- and the need- to take one more step beyond this latest incarnation of self-centered consciousness, and though I am, admittedly, struggling to picture this shift in a way that is believable (that is, in a way that I can feel- know viscerally and undeniably- and not merely conceive- to think about), I am convinced we make a mistake in thinking about our "self" as the center of the universe. The self-centered universe I am hoping to move beyond captures our evolving consciousness in an infantile definition of relativity that we should have capacity to move beyond.

There has been a flipping of the poles, and what was once sought in Heaven is now felt and sought within. We make a mistake, I make a mistake of thinking this light of the infinite comes, somehow, from me, and me alone. It is an intoxicating, frightening, dangerous thought. And a mistake.

There are two infinites. The expansive infinite- the external infinite, beyond the horizon- and the coalescing, internal infinite- at the center. At each revolutionary shift in human consciousness (in the moment of the deed, in our establishment of the totem, in our invention of God, in the birth of Jesus, in the resurrection of Christ, in the Copernican revolution, in the Einsteinian revolution) the center shifts. And just as we think we have resolved life's most crucial questions, what had once been the answer now becomes life's question. What was once the solution now becomes a problem that we must now work to re-solve, re-center, re-explain.

It cannot be right that the truth we must derive from Einstein's revolution in consciousness is that there is no truth, or that every person is an island, a truth unto itself, and that all these truths are equally valid- that is, valid for the individual though none is universal. The truth, to be truth, must be universal, and to be living, it must be particular, true for the individual, as well. What passes for "relativity" of truth these days is loneliness and chaos that arises from individuals still fettered to an old, dead truth we have not yet peeled free of.

To understand the true center that Einstein's relativistic revolution reveals, it is necessary for us to turn back to the first truth and ask "what was the center in the beginning?" I have argued that beginning consciousness must have assumed itself as the center of the universe, as the source of all that is, in the same way that we suppose each infant must make this assumption, and in the same way that God (the projection of our own infantile consciousness) articulates so clearly. But in our first (and subsequent) attempt(s) to represent this center to ourselves, we place this center outside ourselves. We claim the totem as the center. Why is that? Is it merely a function of our powers of representation- that all representations must stand outside ourselves?

birth of christ

Yes, to a certain extent, this must be true. And yet, mustn't there also be some truth in this representation- some truth that, though we were not conscious of it, we must nonetheless follow in accordance with structures and necessities that stand as universal?

What if this center we seek is not our self, after all? Is it possible- logically, dialectically- that the self is both the seer and the seen? Or is there some other aspect that has been hidden from our view? Some other constitutive element to the I and world. Some other, that keeps moving, that is both particular and alive. Some other upon whom our consciousness depends as surely as on I. Some "other" is the center that we seek; and, new realization born to us through the relativistic revolution of which we are a part, that other exists inside of us as well as without. The other that we have hitherto conceptualized as some consciousness that exists beyond the bounds of our own body, now, in fact, we discover, inserts itself inside our self as well. The "other" has breached the walls of protection drawn by our circle, by our bubble. Just like the blackness, represented by the blackness, the other is in ourselves. And such realization paves the way for a new awakening- the idea, at least, if not new birth of, I inside the other.

The other is all consciousness that is not I, all consciousness that comes to us from without. We, ourselves, are the other- at least to others and so, to a certain extent, to our self as well. The other is multifaceted, and so is the I. The other is both collective and individual, and so is the I. The I is the gestalt of the other. It is all that is not other; the unique recombination of elements that is I has never existed before us. It is the product of interaction of our unique constellation of will with all the representations of the others.

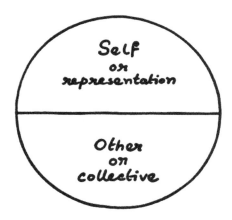

Ancestors

If we do the work, the voices I am straining towards will sound more clearly in you. They have been extinguished in me and from the land, though not completely. Now we recognize the sickness and the need to reverse course. These voices were here when the white man landed, the voice of this land, of animals, of the many living things, of which we are one. We did not hear it, chose not to listen. This land was cleared of other voices, to grow the Christian scientific vision. We cut down what we perceived as "competing" visions, discrediting them as savage, to complete our dominion. These voices we treated as weeds are the medicine we need to save us. They are what is missing. We have allowed the voices of this land and the voices we (immigrants) left behind in the home country to be choked into silence. Cut off, we've been, I've been from the voices of our ancestors. That well spring of knowledge, the Ancestors are the forgotten and embodied Others to our God.

birth of christ

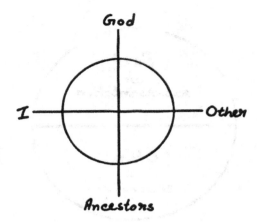

The Ancestors are the voices we white people sought to exterminate from this land. The voices that were here before us, and the voices that we now return to.

The vision here has an evolutionary aspect. Just as individuals develop through certain dialogical stages, so do nations and so does consciousness as a whole. I have been tracing the development of our Western consciousness through myth to God, with (in line with Freud's thinking in <u>Totem and Taboo</u>), the physical totem and totem animal serving as an intermediary on the way to our unitary and disembodied God.

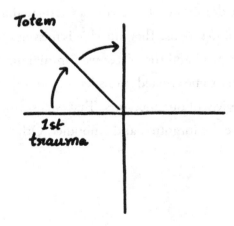

From God, we derive the future stages of Christianity and scientific revolution that have gotten us here today.

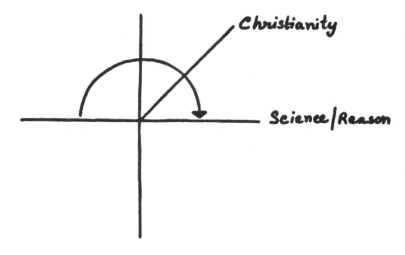

This new human perspective achieved through Christianity and science leads us now to the beginning of a next revelation, the relativity of Einstein and Kant, of man and reason. We are grappling now with how to contain those insights and survive. We are entering a next stage of understanding that we seek here to define and make conscious.

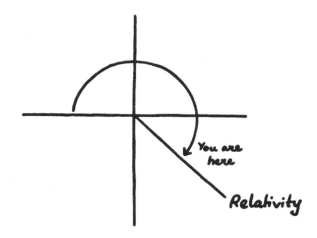

birth of christ

In contrast to the age of reason, science, and (white) man's dominion, from which it emerges, this stage, inaugurated by Kant (our Copernicus), is a turning inward. It is a waning. This new stage of relativity requires a re-centering (what makes it a revolutionary moment), because the previous center has now failed to hold. We can no longer believe the story of perfectibility in the Western man, and myths are funny like that. Once you see, from the outside, the limits of the myth, you can never unsee it. Like Eve and Adam, you can never squeeze your consciousness back inside the shell of Eden, once broken. To do so, or to try, is a sin against consciousness and life, and bound to failure.

But people try. Desperate people who genuinely lack the ability to imagine even the possibility of a new center, who cannot bear the loss of center even for a moment, flee the scene of consciousness. In fear and trembling at the loss of center, meaning, and their world, individuals unfit to change cling in hysterical defense to the corpse of the old, dead truth, and, worse, they seek a retreat- same as addicts turn to heroin- to a still earlier stage of consciousness, and the loving bosom of their Lord. What at an earlier stage had fed and grown our consciousness now sucks out its lifeblood- this incorporeal God- and turns Christianity into a death-dealing cult moving to shrink consciousness in fear and thereby insuring their and others' mutual destruction. Clearly, that's the wrong direction to go.

But I have also expressed a concern (I pray it proves unfounded) that Liberals will settle into a solution of their own that, while less flagrantly sociopathic than Christianity, is nonetheless a limp dick solution wholly inadequate to birth the new center upon which consciousness depends. The liberal "Self" is a solution still tethered to that old "human realm" perspective that is sinking beneath us and dragging us with it.

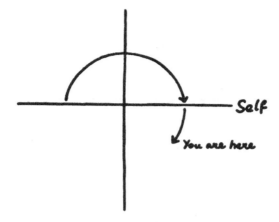

We need to let go; the solution lies deeper than the Self can go. We are past the point where a superficial concept, a human idea and creation like Self can save us. The Self fixes us at the point of human understanding and man's dominion; it is the last gasp of the same old Mind over Matter metaphysic- to find relief from the madness through some infinity within. We need to look beyond these phantoms, but where and to what? This is the question I have struggled to answer.

Even before you read this, you have gone further than I and know better than me. Standing as I do, on the final shores of Mind over Matter- still infected with the disease of my people- I can only point somewhere beneath the horizon and imagine what must lie there for us; but you are well launched and have been sailing alone (and with others, even if unknown) for quite some time now. Do not despair at the pace of your progress. That is the way. And all I know is to remind you of where this long and painful journey leads- to a new center, a new understanding, a new world.

birth of christ

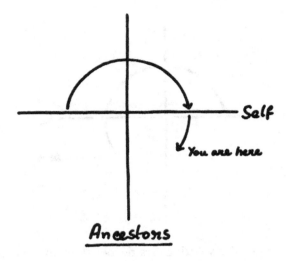

The Ancestors are the ones who were here before the white man came, the ones we immigrants deserted when we left the old country behind. These ties have been systematically (even if not consciously) severed in service to God and the Mind over Matter metaphysic that grew from Him, and these ties are being actively severed, even now, in Its end times, as the Mind over Matter machine can sense the power of the land, of the ancestors, of women, of all living things, and so must destroy them. We must learn, you are learning, other ways of knowing than reason to make our way.

The Beauty of the Individual

We start out as a bubble, beautiful, whole, undifferentiated. The beauty in a baby's eyes. Through a series of cuts, and first representations, we begin to discern an individual that is different than all the rest. The individual takes shape through a dialectic with the other(s) and the world, that defines the "I"s unique set of experiences and relationships unlike any that has come before or since. While these cuts are a reduction to the individual's once infinite potential, they are necessary for the individual to exist in the world. To "be something," these cuts, these definitions, these experiences and relationships and the limitations that they bring are necessary for the individual to be visible, representable. To make an object of themselves is necessary to become a subject, to be a person, to be "real." This particular constellation of stories… the bubble becomes a jewel through definition, through dialectic of definition between other(s) and our self.

By miraculously abstracting ourselves from our original, animal perspective, human beings create the world's consciousness of itself; this original movement and the human drama that plays out in response to it is replicated in each of us. Through our own personal experience, we are simultaneous with the universal stories of humankind; more important than that, we bring these stories to life. We become both part of the story and a unique version of the story. We think of our stories as our own, and, so they are, to a certain limited extent. But other people write and own, depend upon and participate in, our individual drama almost as much as we do. Our dramas are tied to others, shaped in the context of, and through relation to, the others. Satisfying or disappointing, inspirational and maddening, informative and gratifying- but important- to others as well as ourselves.

There is a long history of debate over free will vs. fate. The truth, of course, is that we are driven by both. The dialectic, the tension, the intercourse of these two fuels the drama of the race as expressed through the experience of the individual. Each of us represents a never-to-be-replicated version of the human story through which we may contribute to the collective consciousness.

These contributions of individuals accumulate over time. Each individual born is privileged to remember and build upon the achievements of those individuals who came before them. We have no choice; this is the only material available to work on. And those closest to us- our family- will most determine- and most depend upon- the story that is ours. Another way to talk about this story we write is to say that it is our own unique version of the truth. Each person has an angle on the truth that none other will ever have; we each have a responsibility to develop that angle to the best of our ability so as to share it with the others.

The others need our stories at least as much as we do. We need other people's stories to write our own, to enter into dialogue with, to compare and reflect. And this dialogue goes on at an emotional level as well as an intellectual one. The others draw the emotions from us. It is, in fact, at the level of emotions that all of our stories connect. And so, at an emotional level, others may have as much stake in our stories as we do in theirs. Our stories are tied together. We learn, benefit, and suffer from the stories of those who came before, and we affect the kind of story our children and grandchildren will be born into.

But more than that, the people living here or now share a destiny. Our stories are written, in large measure- in half, by the stories of those around us. Our response is all we can control, and all we can contribute to the others. It is the responsibility of others (and of us in our role as the other) to support and challenge their children, to educate them and build their muscles (including the neural network necessary) to advance consciousness in their own unique way. We have a stake in the success of others, because we are in this story together. And our story- our life- depends on them and theirs.

Human beings have two "I"s, and one is in the other. When the unified consciousness of God descends from the Heavens to be embodied on this earth, that consciousness is necessarily divided in the process. As a consequence of that division, human beings develop an uncanny ability to imagine our way into the perspective of an other- through drama- to step outside our self and view a situation from a point different than our own- from the "I" of an other.

With time, these two "I"s would come to focus on a third point outside themselves- outside all individuals. At this point, they would drive a stake and mark the center of the universe. Some people call the point God. From this point, human beings construct a reality. Each contributes what he or she can to this objective world built by humans. It is a multifaceted world we have built, are a part of, and are building. It is quite a wonder. An unfathomable disco ball of consciousness. Each story- each human- a different angle on the truth and whole. A cell in the larger body. Each a microcosm of light, but, together, such a beautiful and sad, ugly and profound creation.

But there does not the beauty end. We hold ourselves up to the great disco ball of consciousness and see there not just the sparkling light of others but, also, a multifaceted reflection of ourselves. Like the other, I, too, am a multifaceted reflection of truth and light, and though the truth I tell with my life may not be so comprehensive as the story of the whole, it nonetheless contains within it all the same light and elements and sadness and beauty. It is the responsibility of each individual- to others and to themselves- to develop each of these "faces," each of these aspects of themselves as thoroughly as possible. And this is done, of course (and exclusively), through our interaction with the others. We have a responsibility as a unique manifestation of consciousness to engage with others to develop ourselves as fully as possible- for their benefit and our own.

The more cuts to the stone, the greater the definition by themselves and others, the beauty is revealed. Part of being a consciousness in relativity means that we, too, transcend any single explanation. Each individual provides a multifaceted reflection of our shared (universal) tensions, stories, and truths. We learn from comparisons with others but also by examining the complexities and relationships within our own particular truth. Every person's story can be counted on to be logical, to make sense, if we can see the underlying threads of continuity that tie the various aspects of the individual into one.

It is this thread that we must be concerned about in our self as well. The unifying theme, the center of our story and existence that is both deeply universal and profoundly individual. Now we are concerned with that which separates my story from those of others. We have said that it is through our emotions that all our stories become one, it is through the physical body that our stories get parsed out. Only we live- and die of- the story that resides in this particular body-me. We might imagine life in another body, but this body, this story is real. And it is different for each of us, and in this sense we are alone without, even, God. No one can join us in death.

It is the fact of our own death that makes the human individual more beautiful than the accumulation of human representations from which we came. Though that, too, is beautiful, immense, and profound and contributes, necessarily, to the complexity, beauty, and profundity of the individuals who participate in and contribute to the whole.

The extent to which each of us is determined is tremendous- through our bodies, first and foremost, but also through our relationships, our location in space and time, and our access to resources. And yet within the whirlpool of external forces that surround us, a space is created unavailable to the rest. It is a point of light or a wellspring knowable only to our self. Within this wellspring, from this point of light, we add something new to the world, a perspective that has never been known before, and one that never will again. By following the path of light- individual to each of us- to the bottom of the wellspring, universal to us all, we may find, at once, our self and other.

From this place, our center, original to us, each human brings an offering- a gift- to the others. It is over this offering, our response to the others, that we have some control, by which we can influence others and change the world.

Each of us is born from the collective consciousness of others, and, most people, despite delusions to the contrary, never really separate themselves from that collective. They accept the body they are born into as a given, and they settle into the representations of others as if they were the truth. For these people, education means only finding out the way things are. Education is training, providing me with the skills necessary to fit in. It is a content driven curriculum: we learn about the content of the world in order to adapt our self to it.

There are others, though, who receive a different kind of education. In this curriculum we are taught to distinguish ourselves, to begin and sustain a tension between ourselves and others from which we may grow in mastery and independence. This is a skills-based curriculum by which the individual learns to take the powers of the collective into himself. The student learns to replicate and extend the powers of the others through her own experience and actions. She learns to define herself as something separate and distinct- as, more than some thing, as some one. This kind of education generates individual consciousness through which we bring something new into the world.

If we are to reach our full human potential, just such a separation from the collective is necessary. Without such separation, our bubble is hemmed in by the representations of the others. We are apiece with the cluster of bubbles from which we came. We have no self-awareness, because we have no real self. With a proper education, however, it is possible to teach our young people how they can separate themselves- by defining themselves, learning about and with others, and taking risks and actions. To be an I requires action- and action requires a center point to begin. Our goal is to help children build a center point and wind around that an identity, a self, a sense of myself as strong and different and special in relation to others.

Once separate- a self-determining human being, a world, an unfettered bubble with many aspects, we find, ironically, miraculously, dialectically, that our relationship to the others is not lost (that our existential alienation is only a portion of the truth) but, rather, only just begun. We look back on the other now like an astronaut viewing Earth from far off space; we recognize, appreciate home for the first time and long for it as never before.

Traversing the Bubble

Though each of us walk a path and tell a story unlike any that has gone before or since, there is, nonetheless, a trajectory to life that is universal, a pattern that is common to us all. In its first movement, life is expansive and light. We learn and grow through the first half of life despite the fact that we remain largely unconscious of our self. The movement of consciousness is operational in us even though we have not become conscious of the process, itself. In these early days (the first half of our life) we are largely shaped by others. Though there is something in our self- that we will come to think of as "our self"- we are, nonetheless, determined by conditions established by others through the first chapters of our existence. Our physical and emotional security depends upon the love and protection that our family and society provide. It is the responsibility of our families and communities to keep us safe during these early years, and our responsibility is to observe and speak and grow. Despite hardships, certain people seem to have a certain resiliency, though, that does not seem to be derived from their experiences alone. A certain set of experiences that would crush most people seem only to challenge certain exceptional others to overcome- though not without wounds and broken parts and not without the help of certain others that "come to the rescue" of the resilient individual (often as others once came to help them).

We turn a corner in the second half of life that is universal and necessary to the human experience and consciousness, and though we all try to resist the turn, each in our own way and/or according to certain consistent patterns, we turn the corner nonetheless, or, to be more accurate, the corner turns us.

Life is lived inside of the bubble of consciousness that is us, and the path we traverse through life runs the course of the inside of that bubble, from horizon to horizon, from life to death, from rise to set, the way the sun goes.

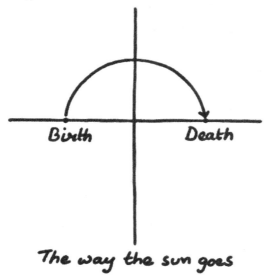

The period of youth is one of growing vitality, strength, power and light, that, to the young person, it seems, will go on forever. But for every human consciousness, for every body, there comes a time when this trajectory must reverse itself, when the sun must begin its steady descent to the next horizon. We have not done a good job of understanding or accepting this necessary and universal reversal. We act as if it can mean only certain death, which is, well, ….true, but in our refusal to acknowledge and learn from the necessary lessons of our own death, we forsake all possibility of a true understanding of life. We lose wisdom and wring life from desperate phantasies of life everlasting instead.

It is by this journey, by thus traversing our bubble, that we extricate the definition of our self from the determinations of the other. While there is no way, really, to free ourselves from the determinations of others, by becoming conscious of these determinations, we gain capacity to filter these influences and so turn fate into a destiny. Rather than being driven by our lives and others, we begin to control the motion, direction, and decisions of our life and so become an individual agent with the power to change the world.

Ancestor Tree

Trees are some of our oldest ancestors, and we do well to learn from their example. Here in America and in my time, we have largely looked at ourselves- and our lives as if we were a tree- growing from seed to sprout to sapling to mature to dying tree. Throughout we have neglected to consider the second half of trees- the half of life that goes on beneath the surface- at least as crucial and as beautiful and extensive as the tree above the ground (what we have, until now, been mistaking as the whole). Modern psychology has taught us to look below the surface of the known and so begin to comprehend the hidden half in the life of a tree. And that is a good development that has been giving us a fuller perspective on the life of a tree- and on humans. But I would suggest that there is still another forgotten half in the life of a tree that we would do well to remember- and that is the tree after death- once it falls and deteriorates, returning to soil that will nurture future generations. It is in this phase of its life that a(n individual) tree becomes an ancestor, because it is in this phase of its life that it dissolves itself to feed the others.

Birth of christ

My mom gave unconscious birth to me in a sanitized room directed by a man doctor/expert, where I was spirited away to an isolated basinet separated from her touch. Never breast fed, they taught her to use a bottle and their manufactured formula superior to my mother's milk. On the second day, they strapped me to a gurney and sliced my penis open. "You cried and cried and cried," my mother remembers. Once at home I was ensconced in a crib, in a separate room, and allowed, testing what restraint remained of my mother's maternal instincts, to "cry it out" when I longed for her human touch and comfort. That will leave a mark.

I am populated by untruths I was born into in ways I cannot begin to fathom. And so it is that my own journey/metaphysics lands me in this solipsistic vision so typical of our age, the beginning phase of relativism. Isolated as we are, each has become a god unto himself. Even our gods are solipsistic, vague, personal, paltry. We all consider ourselves "spiritual, but not religious," which is another way of saying that we know we have a divine aspect by the fact that we have not found a way to fill it. In replacement to a shared truth, we each estab-

birth of christ

lish our own personal totem, our own personal image of the infinite ourself. The "shared truth" has fallen into disrepute because of its awful representation under the patriarchy. That original impulse to place a totem outside ourselves is still sound and necessary. What we are talking about, though, is not some new objective truth. It is a story. A story that we consciously choose to believe, to participate in, to share. The story that chooses us is a story that is satisfying, enriching, nurturing- not like the old Logos at all.

Psychologically, we each replicate the experience of Christ in our day and age. We, too, are cut off from our bodies, cast off by the Other, into the sky of transcendence and abstraction. Peace. Enlightenment. Transcendence. Isolation. Loneliness. Emptiness. Despair.

We continue to be fooled by the separation of our bodies from the Body from which we came. We continue down the path of thinking ourselves as a world unto ourself, and try as I might to reconnect us to all that has been lost- to the wellspring of our existence, you can hear it in my voice, I have the idea, but I am not all there yet. I have a theoretical, but not visceral knowledge of this birth of christ. I can give you what I can give you and cannot fake something better, something more. What I have to offer, then, is the idea of this union that is only now being born, if not in me, then I hope, as a father to a child, in you. You who were breast fed, whose penis wasn't cut, you girls, whose father held you tight and crooned to you, who slept in your parent's bed. Your generations have hardships, limitations, grievances, far, far greater than my own (the devastated world and souls, the truncated education, you inherited from me and mine), and yet you also have some foundation, some connection that I and mine were robbed of from our earliest days.

I, at least, can feel it growing inside me, and my prayer is that my words will help you feel it inside of you as well. Like a baby, feel it kick. Sing to it; feed to it your blood.

Three becomes Four

The cross is the one and true symbol of the infinite aspect of christ, but, through the crucifixion, men turn the four spokes of the cross into a Trinity of disembodied Gods. We retain the cross, but (until now) have lost a quarter of (and so all of) its true meaning. The three, the triangle, the pyramid is reflective of man's creations but not of nature's. In nature, where there is three, there is four (only in man's- limited-creations does the Trinity- does fixity-hold sway).

Once you see how three is really four, the world can never be the same, thank Mother. But our "leaders" now- the proponents of the Trinity, the institutions, man's creation, the status quo,

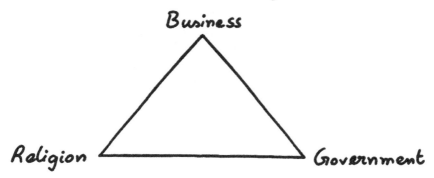

cannot bear to look beneath them, and for good reason. In astrology, trines are fluid, but this Trinity is man-made, and things are different here.

The man-made Trinity implies a degree of permanence, a fixity, immovability, stability that is no small part of its attraction. The loss of this sense of permanence, "objective truth," and the security that comes

birth of christ

with it is no small part of the terror that our patriarchs feel in this age of revelation and renewal that, to them, from their world view, must feel like chaos and death. The bottom's dropping out.

Like the Church Fathers of old who found it necessary to resist- even unto death- the innovations of those first scientists- the Copernicans, so, today, the Christians must resist that feminine aspect, the denial upon which their world view- their security- depends.

They had built a wall around themselves (around us) to keep the darkness out. That wall has withstood considerable assaults from the blackness, but now they look down to find the very ground beneath their feet is breaking up, the blackness comes seeping through the pavement, Earth, and they know not what to do.

THE SHADOW

They are paralyzed with terror and know only one thing- to hysterically persist in their losing battle to uphold the fallen Logos, though the Earth that has up to now sustained it has grown soft and black and stinking with their rot. In their minds, in the world they create through their limited understanding, viewed through the lens of their particular truth, death (Apocalypse) is the only possible outcome anyway, and so they deny this truth at any possible cost, at the cost of death to all, persisting in their phantasy- the irrational heights achieved by their unreasoning reason- that they will be the chosen ones and somehow rise up in an ascension to heaven while the rest of us are drowned in the blackness that they themselves created.

The Next Stone

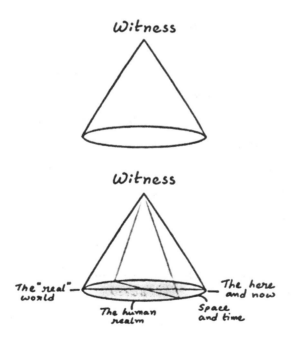

Though, I know, it seems kind of late in a book for this, I wish to introduce a new term I have not used yet but that I think will help to clarify what has gone before as well as the argument I am making at present. Whatever it is- miracle and mystery- that forces us out of this unconscious dynamic of life (best represented as yin-yang) and into a third point from which we both transcend and recognize this fundamental dynamic, this advance beyond the dynamic of yin-yang is what constitutes "the human." The new term I want to introduce for this third, transcendent perspective is "the witness."

Somehow with the invention of the witness, we step outside of this tit-for-tat of life- or a part of us steps out while half of us (our bodies) continues to be engaged (or trapped, depending upon your perspective) in this tit-for-tat dynamic we have in common with all other animals. Somehow, as human beings, we are, at once, driven by the yin and yang of life and, at the same time, beyond or "above" it.

The miracle of human consciousness is that the witness stops the motion. It may only be for a moment, and try as we might to sustain the certainty, the stability, the fixity of the witness' view and so to make it permanent, the motion always takes over again. Every human attempt at fixity, certainty, permanence, eternity, is bound to failure, and yet, and yet, we cannot help but to impose this fixity on the chaotic, continuous, permanent (because timeless) motion of the world; the fixity, the witness is the only thing that brings us any hint of power, peace, knowledge, control.

The witness stops the motion, even if only for a second, it freezes the moment- takes a snapshot that we can hold in memory and so analyze and make sense of to get our bearings, to adjust ourselves to our surroundings in ways that can secure our place- for however long we can sustain it- in a cruel, painful, indifferent, and otherwise unconscious swirl of life.

The witness stops the motion, and so it is no wonder that our own Western civilization has so grown in love with this witness and the permanence, security, mastery that He brings. We represent this witness to ourselves as God. We worship Him and remake ourselves in His image. Through participation with this God, we dream, we may gain mastery- eternal life- over the devouring motion of life, and to some degree, at least, we do succeed. We believe that, through the witness, through God, we can escape the Wheel of Life, another (Western) representation of the same reality illustrated by yin-yang.

We align ourselves with God, the witness, the snapshot that the third, transcendent perspective allows to us, and we make an enemy of the flux of life, the wheel of life and death, the cycle of the seasons. Western civilization, more successfully than any other, makes a fetish of this fixity and the permanence (eternity) and power (mastery) it promises. We fall in love with the cross, that stops the motion, the three, with God, and with ourselves as viewed from the perspective of God. We fall in love with the witness in ourselves until we forget that it is only one aspect of a more total self.

We mistakenly believe that we can overcome the limitations of life- the constant motion, life and death of the yin-yang, and we demonize the dynamic and more ancient aspects to our consciousness in favor of, in allegiance and adherence to, in imitation of, in loyalty to, through faith in this absolute and eternal fixity of God's truth. Dialectically, it makes sense that we should establish such an either/or and that we should establish such allegiance to the one that promises our release from chaos, fear, uncertainty, and death.

We are at a point, now, in our development, however, where we can see the downside- the falsity- of that fixity. To achieve our dream, to be "like God," we now realize, must mean the end of life. And while the witness brings us to our humanity, to the crucial essence of our life and truth, we cannot sustain that life and truth if we destroy that foundation, the root, the wellspring, the conflict and the tension, the death and light and darkness from which it emerged in the first place.

Contradiction upon contradiction, we need the body to sustain the mind, we need our animal nature to conceive our Godly vision. We need the constant state of flux as the necessary foundation beneath our dreams of fixity and permanence. We need, paradoxically, both/and, both the witness and the witnessed, the subject and the object, permanence and change, fixity and motion.

The ones who rule our world, the ones who are driving us all to destruction, the enemies to advancing consciousness that we must overcome, remain unhappily or unhealthily married to the fixity. They remain hostile to the dynamic elements of life, even though, just beneath the surface of their reason, they know very well- just as well as you and I- that their old, patriarchal truth is dead. Dead, dead, dead, and destructive- to the human soul, to their children's future, to the planet upon which we all depend. Too scared to let go, because to let go is death; they are in a bind. They know in their hearts if they dared to look (they can't/they don't) that to hang on is death as well. Scared animals as they are, they hang on to the old, destructive, hollow faith. To the only thing, truth, strategy they have ever known. They cannot conceive of any option. God bless them in their desperation, but curse them for the annihilation they have wrought and continue to wield.

I have promised "a next stone to jump to." To see it, we must shift our perspective. We must perceive the world from a whole new point of view. This shift will breathe new life in old truths that will make them come alive, provide meaning and purpose again, but to thus resurrect old truths we must see these truths from a whole new, a relative and human, perspective.

This shift is not unlike the one you use looking at the gestalt drawings- the shift that allows you to see both the old woman and the young woman, both the vase and the two faces. We must view our consciousness, our world from a different perspective to see things in a new way and to escape our captivity in an old, dead truth that we have seen our way out of but have not yet escaped from.

We lay the cross over the dynamic yin and yang of life, just as the human race once did in the evolutionary development of consciousness; through the intersect of cross and dynamic circle of life, we develop a more comprehensive and, though contradictory, more accurate, depiction of our consciousness.

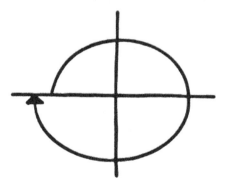

In thus developing this comprehensive description of the dynamic and self-contradictory structure of human consciousness, we have come pretty far. We could rest satisfied at having accomplished such a significant advance in our understanding over those schemes that have gone before. But let's not rest. Let's recognize that this more comprehensive vision still represents a certain limited perspective and see if we can advance beyond it.

birth of christ

It cannot escape notice that our current representation (of the cross created by the intersect of I and other, Ancestors and God, laid over the yin and yang dynamic of life) remains a two-dimensional representation of a process and world that exists in (at least) three dimensions. Let us consider that our schema so far developed holds truth but not "the whole truth and nothing but the truth." Let us shift our perspective and perceive this truth from a new and different angle. What if our schema hitherto represents a kind of aerial view of our consciousness (which I think is accurate) and let us consider what would happen if we shifted our perspective (the point of view of the seer) and looked at the shape of human consciousness, not from above, but from the side instead.

From this perspective, (viewed from the horizontal plane instead of from the vertical) the structure of consciousness would appear quite different. The difference, one might argue, is revolutionary. It causes us to see the world and the consciousness that creates/reflects it in a whole new way.

From the side (viewed from the perspective of a human being and not of God), the shape of consciousness all of a sudden appears three-dimensional and in motion. What appears from above (objectively) to be a spiral, as experienced, must be a cyclone or whirlpool.

THE SHADOW

There is a dividing line of consciousness, between light and dark, between sky and sea, between the conscious and the unconscious, between the external and internal, between the objective and subjective, between the apparent and the hidden, between day and night. Above the line of the horizon, we see an outward expansion of the light and consciousness. This light of consciousness grows ever more comprehensive, wider, bigger, and, this expansion would appear to have the potential, at least, to grow out indefinitely. There is always a limit, an outer edge, to the light, but it would appear to have the capacity, the potential to expand indefinitely, without end, without limit. Infinite expansion. This half of the structure is not significantly different than what we conceptualized under patriarchy.

Beneath the surface of the horizon, however, the structure that develops is quite different. The shape of consciousness beneath the line of consciousness, in the darkness of our minds, belies the "truth" of our original conception. In the dark, unconscious, inner aspect of our consciousness- when viewed from the side (from this next stone to jump through, from our human perspective) consciousness narrows increasingly to a point. A center point. A wellspring. There is an infinitude here, too, in this internal aspect of our consciousness, but it is an infinitude of a different type. It is an infinite concentration, in constant motion, a journey to an ever-receding point- the center- as much a journey without an end as our quest for Heaven.

In the light of consciousness, constructions are shared. They are collective and objective representations, but under the surface, consciousness is, paradoxically, both more individual and personal and, at the same time, somehow, more universal as well. This layer of consciousness expresses itself through our emotions and our dreams, and through the mythology that is active in us (that we operate from without being conscious that we do so).

The layers of consciousness beneath the horizon line are experienced through our bodies and are thus particular to us whereas the layers of consciousness (reason and representation) above the horizon line are experienced through our mind and ideas, and these we necessarily share with others. Our journey to the center of the individual complements, completes, nourishes, makes possible the collective expansion of our knowledge and continuous expansion of the "objective" world.

What we experience from a side view, from the human perspective, is a whirlpool of consciousness, a tornado of consciousness, the center of which lies deep within the individual body- the necessary crucible in which and through which alone, the cyclone of conscious can manifest. Not all human beings are cyclones, of course, and none of us is a cyclone all the time (nor should we be). We each must find our rhythm(s).

There are varying degrees of depth to human individuals. Our representation here shows why it is so accurate to say that people are "shallow." Not everybody develops the same amount of conflicting tension necessary to generate a whirlpool of consciousness. Some people are placid, dumb, bored, lazy, weak, cowardly, externally determined, and some people (why I am not a Buddhist) even seek such placidity as the end of their spiritual quest. Me- I like the cyclone- it is what we are in this earth to do. In fact, I would argue that human beings have a moral responsibility to develop this generative tension in themselves and others- especially today.

Like every advance in consciousness before it, this shift in perspective requires an act of humility that, paradoxically, opens the possibility of unheard-of mastery, understanding, and control. From this new, this human, this horizontal and relative perspective we are obligated to develop both aspects of our infinitude, to simultaneously expand our consciousness outward and upward (to participate as fully as we are able in the construction and expansion of the objective realities and truths of humans- of I and others) and, too, to plumb the depths of our own personality, to dive as deep as possible, to the bottom of the ocean, to be the tiny, mighty muskrat in search of that pearl of dirt, that seed of truth and life buried deep at the bottom of our ocean, mind.

Here we stand, then, at last, at a human perspective and contemplate our self, not from above and as a snapshot, but in all our dynamism and relativity, finitude and infinity. But, we must ask, where are we standing? How is it that we come to stand outside ourselves and view ourselves as if we were some sort of abstraction, a representation, an object?

We are standing in the other. In the miracle that is human consciousness, we have learned to displace our perspective from inside our own body and view ourselves as if from without. It was God who taught us this- God, the ancient alchemist, who worked on us to produce, not gold, but light and truth, awareness, a world, and a self. But, as we stated previously, God was not really the alchemist- even in our earlier days. He was a marker, a symbol, a totem that we used to embody and represent the true alchemist, and God has done His job. He has delivered us to the true alchemist- not God, not the Self, but the other.

We are simultaneously the other and our self (but who sees that?). Interestingly, though, our awareness of the other still passes necessarily and exclusively through that single point of "I." As Kant will eventually teach, "all our knowledge begins with experience" and all experience is filtered through an "I," and every I is housed somewhere in a mortal body. It will be millennia before we become fully aware of all these aspects of our consciousness, their interdependencies and implications. Such awareness we are building still- me, as I write, and you, as you read, but these aspects and structures to our consciousness have been operational in our construction of a self and world since that first moment of mystery and miracle when an eye opened out of blackness.

We just forget to look the other way. Only recently have our minds been turned inward- by Job, Copernicus, Kant, Freud, Daly, Einstein- to explore the inner world of the subject. Until recently, the best our consciousness could attain to was an objective understanding of the world. We sought the infinite in the external world through God. So focused have we been on Him that we have forgotten to look at God's reflection in the dark pool of our bodies. And now we discover an infinity within. A tornado of emotion and reason. An I and other; painful, beautiful dance of light on water in our self.

THE BIRTH

Like our earlier image from the Truman Show, some teacher/leaders now are beginning a next story of our escape into transcendence. They are perpetuating the false myth that human beings are somehow transcendent creations independent of their bodies. They are only telling you half the story. We can disappear into pure light (according to the Celestine Prophesy) or we can annihilate the ego limits that define, and therefore, limit the extent of our human consciousness (Eckert Tolle). These theories, it seems to me, merely perpetuate the human fantasy (and therefore unreality) that we can become as Gods. We can't. We are human beings and can never be anything else than human beings. To be a human being is fundamentally different than being a God. It is, in some ways, far preferable to being a God, but, at the very least, to be a human being is enough.

The Crucible

In the ancient art of alchemy, mythological precursor to modern chemistry, the alchemist would pour base metals into a rapidly spinning cylinder- a crucible- in order to make gold. The crucible is an apt metaphor for the human body, as it is only its limitation and motions that make possible the miracle within. It is just our finitude- our suffering, our death- that makes possible the miracle of consciousness, our awareness of the infinite.

We human beings are small; so enthralled have we become with our collective creations, our manipulations, and achievements- that we have forgotten our own smallness, forgotten all that is beyond our purview and control, forgotten we have limits- until recently, that is, when the limits of our power, the limits of our knowing, the consequences of our actions, have begun to be more clear.

We human beings are a miracle; so enthralled have we become with our collective creations, material constructions, rules and institutions, images and fantasies- that we have forgotten our true infinitude and have lost the thread of meaning- until recently, that is, when our entrapment by our own creations/constructs has never been so clear.

God is, Himself, a construct and a creation- a myth, a story we humans tell, a lens we look through, to provide structure to experience and so create a world. Without us, there could be no God. God is our own creation, and so, for that matter, is Mother Earth as well. No such things exist beyond the realm of human consciousness- at least as far as we can tell, but that fact does not make them any less important, any less critical to our experience, any less, at all.

Human beings are superior to gods and God. This "truth" is not intended as a disrespect to our Parents, Mother, God, but, rather, a testament to, and celebration of, them. Human individuals are the source and focus of all this miracle and wonder we call life, consciousness, a world. Without you, there is no world. The world is created by human individuals in collaboration with the others: no wonder, then, that we suffer from hubris, that we act as if we are the center of the universe, because, fundamentally, we are.

THE BIRTH

We also are, of course, a speck, a point in space so small and insignificant that, when one drills down to discover our kernel and our essence, there is nothing there at all. We are a body, a body amongst an infinitude of bodies, far less significant than a single raindrop, and just as short lived. And yet, and yet, there is always another "and yet" when it comes to humans and our consciousness. There are always a multiplicity of perspectives from which to view ourselves and others, capable of making us appear divine and/or inconsequential.

Our parents- the two forces fundamental to the universe, coalesce in us alone. It is natural and inevitable that we should feel ambivalence towards these parents through whom we are granted this life and consciousness, this window of experience, but an experience that is characterized by pain, frustration, hunger and death.

All the drama and tension of the universe is played out in this container, finite, small, that we call our body.

We each are human crucibles in which the contradictions of the universe- all time and all space- play themselves out. We are the point of intersect- christ-without whom God and Mother, light and darkness, I and other, mind and body, the world and what is beyond the world, do not exist and, so, cannot be conciled.

Collectivists, objectivists, scientists can argue all they want that the world does not depend on us, that, in fact, the world would not miss us one iota if we were gone, but that is not how the world, consciousness, and life is experienced. Kant taught us that all consciousness is filtered through the experience of individuals.

It is a strange time that we live in- the strangest one yet, deriving from our infantile understanding of relativity - when there seems to be this emphasis and preoccupation with the me, me, me- my needs, my interests, my desires, but when, in fact, the infinitude and fundamental importance of the individual is all but forgotten.

We live in a time of terrible schism in which, collectively, we treat all people as objects, but, individually, we "treat" ourselves to the fulfillment of only our localized needs and wishes. In both aspects- our objectivity and self-centeredness- we miss the point of our true and infinite humanity. In both aspects of our modern definition of humanity, we have lost connection, have divorced ourselves, from our true origins, from both Parents, from God and from Earth. We need to get them back.

Second Coming

In these earliest days of relativity, at this first moment in human consciousness post-Einsteinian Revolution, there is a lot of confusion still about how we will reconcile our human smallness- relativity, finitude, and body- with our human greatness- imagination, infinitude, and mind.

There can be no doubt that within my own lifetime, we human beings have rediscovered, and have become obsessed with, the human body that Christianity has sought to forget and suppress for hundreds and thousands of years.

In my lifetime, we have seen an understandable pendulum swing away from the mind and reason, law and social obligation (that have been used for so long to suppress and oppress) and towards a new allegiance to my body and my feelings, desire and my self. The institutions that were built on mind, reason, law, and obligations have not gone away, of course. We all continue to be subjected to the demands of these institutions, to these incarnations of our human reason, but because they no longer offer meaning, because the Logos upon which they were built is dead, we gain no satisfaction from our allegiance to, and dependence upon these institutions.

What once provided us with a pathway to our higher self has now become the obstacle and the oppressor. We conform to these institutions- we all do our job- because we have to in order to get what we really want. The institutions still hold the purse strings. A few people, it is true, do "drop out" and have begun to build a different kind of world built on a different set of values, but most of us, and all of us, to a certain extent, are forced to conform to a "truth"- and its institutions- that none of us believe in.

The most "successful" ones in this schizoid world are those most cynical- the ones who take advantage of the systems and do not need to care, the most selfish ones, the ones most divorced from the human need for meaning, for justice, for morality, for truth and human connection. These most cynical ones- the "success stories" in a broken world- are ransacking and looting the old institutions for their own personal gain before the institutions fall along with the ideas that once supported them. By their actions, these cynical ones accelerate the decline of these institutions (at an exponential rate), and while they may gain wealth, they forsake all meaning and so pay with their very soul- and ours.

There are devils in charge of our institutions, because our institutions have lost all meaning and all truth. The rest of us continue to be subjected to these instruments of power in the hands of the worst kind of humans- the most animalistic of humans, the ones who are least "like God"- and we find our (only) relief in football or in shopping, in prescription drugs or in pornography, in gluttony and in games.

birth of christ

As a people, we have awakened to the other side of the Either/Or formula that has hitherto defined our world, but we have not yet broken free of that equation, of that old and dead truth. So far, we have entered the shadow side, but have not yet come out the other side.

Human beings need meaning. Human beings need truth. That is why we invented myth- and later science- in the first place. People disparage truth and meaning, because the old vehicle for truth- the only one they know- has shown itself as falsehood. In desperation, they continue to assume that that truth is the only truth and so that "Truth is Dead." Everything is relative.

That is the point of misunderstanding that relativity has so far brought us to. And is it any wonder, then, that the conservatives- the protectors of tradition, morality, and truth- should hate this moral relativity of the liberals? For them, the truth that liberals have brought us to is No Truth, and instinctively they know that where there is no truth, there is no life. Just like the Babylonians.

Neither side can imagine a way out of this predicament, and so they blame each other, continuing that ancient, Western, white, Christian delusion that I am all right, and someone else is wrong. Someone else must be to blame.

If we are ever to find our way to the other side, we must learn to blame ourselves. We must learn to stop this impulse- inherent in our old and previous truth, but not necessary to human being- to blame somebody else. We must learn forgiveness- of ourselves, and for our own blackness- even more than others. We must own that which Christianity and science have sought to put outside ourselves. We must own our blackness, become the body of christ.

THE BIRTH

Human beings are the greatest miracle. In us, through us are born the ideas of God, of christ, of Mother Earth, of I. In us originates the demand for meaning; we are the inventors of "the Truth," inventors of "the world." We are the windows of light, the only source of consciousness (so far as we can tell), the only way that the world can know itself.

And here is the really remarkable thing about we human beings- it is only as individuals that we have access to this truth, the world, creation. Collectively, we shape our consciousness- and there could be no consciousness without each other- but we can all only experience the world, and truth, and creation- as individual human beings.

Incarnated infinitude. Spirit made flesh. There is no God to worship but others (who are christ, and give birth to christ in us) and ourselves. This is the meaning of Einstein's Revolution in Consciousness. This is the meaning of relativity. That we are all but finite bodies, imperfect morsels of earth that will soon die, but, these finite specks are also gateways to the infinite.

The truth of christ- hitherto unborn- is beautiful just because it is based on an irresolvable contradiction, and that contradiction is us. The whole world exists inside of you, and each of us makes that world possible in the others.

We individual human beings are the crucible; we are the womb in which the Idea of Jesus Christ was planted. Through us alone, and only with the help of others, God and Earth, light and dark, life and death, the world and consciousness are possible.

With God's gesture, Jesus, a seed of love is planted, and, before that, from Eve and the serpent in the garden, a seed of knowledge, too, seeds of infinitude planted in the body of every woman, every man. We will die, and there is to be no after life, no heaven. We are not

Gods, eternal. We are human beings. Finite creatures become infinite and so more beautiful, and superior to Gods.

The Tree

The whole story wasn't told about the Babylonians and Tiamat. In the rumblings of the night, there was one group that came out of their huts. They watched in fear and awe as Tiamat destroyed the only truth and world they had ever known. They both saw and felt the Logos fall and the hegemony of Tiamat around them. She saw in them, too, the possibility of life, and so She chased them.

In blindness, terror, and confusion, the people ran from Her, of course, as any people do. They ran into darkness, into madness, into wildness they had learned always to avoid. She followed them there, of course, and, all through the night, would not relent. In the morning the people woke in relief to find that neither Monster nor darkness had killed them. They cried their desperation and prayed their relief to one another and to Tiamat, until, from the forest around them came another people they did not know and did not remember.

Few in number, these were the lonely ones of myth, the witches and the dead. So extreme was the people's desperation and helplessness and fear that they turned to these few and asked them for guidance, prayed to them for help.

The witches taught the people to regulate their fears. Dead, you are no good to Tiamat, the leaders taught. You would be dead by now if She sought to kill you. You must train yourself to listen, to heed the voice of Tiamat; to do so will mean that you will learn to thrive and survive, renewed. The dead ones' words brought comfort to the people, and their cries turned from hysterics to gentle weeping and eventually, to the depths of sleep.

The howls of Tiamat awakened them, and with them woke, too, all their fears and desperation, hopelessness and unreason. Once again the people ran through darkness, and once again Tiamat gave chase. And so the chase continued for years and generations; only the grandchildren of grandchildren would learn to listen with different ears. In the meantime, Tiamat raged each night; first, at them; later, for them- violent music in their ears, howling through the night, softly crying in the morning.

She spoke to people's night times, until, in the seventh generation, a few individuals began to read meaning into Her howls. The dead ones had taught the people to listen, had taught them not to hate Her, and so, each night, the people would leap the back of serpent Tiamat as She drove them to the underworld. She drove them far into themselves at night; in fear and awe, desperation and gratitude- with no other option open, the people learned to listen. She led the way, they knew not where, but they went underground with Her and so learned a new and different kind of faith. A different kind of surrender, of humility, a different kind of humanity.

This lost tribe of Babylonians would go by many names. They are the lonely and lost ones, the shamans and the dead, the wild, insane, immoral, evil, enemies, ancestors, survivors, mothers, Saviors, chosen ones, human beings. They would tell stories in the daytime gleaned from their journeys with Tiamat, and one such story told the tale of a world gone insane in which only those considered mad had any sort of sense or sanity, reality or truth.

birth of christ

The chosen ones heard the voice of Tiamat, heeded the voice of beloved Tiamat. They nourished Her with their dreams and did not Hate her. And there came a time when, their fears grown less, the people learned to rest and sleep at night, cradled in her arms, embraced by the soothing beat and hum of her body, Tiamat, dreaming in her song. There came a time again when people enjoyed their days of peace, the waters stilled, Tiamat at rest and the people prayed for and with and from her.

One night, there was no howling, no crying in the morning, only the cacophony of night creatures and the song of birds at break of day. When the people came out from their homes that morning, at the center of the world there stood a tiny sapling, fresh and full, fluid and bright as a baby's eyes, and from that sapling grew a tree beautiful, strong, certain, but not eternal that marked the center of the universe. Underground lies Tiamat resting, dreaming peacefully, smiling softly, the tree grows from Her head, and she feeds it with Her dreams.

Made in the USA
Monee, IL
04 November 2023

45796696R00203